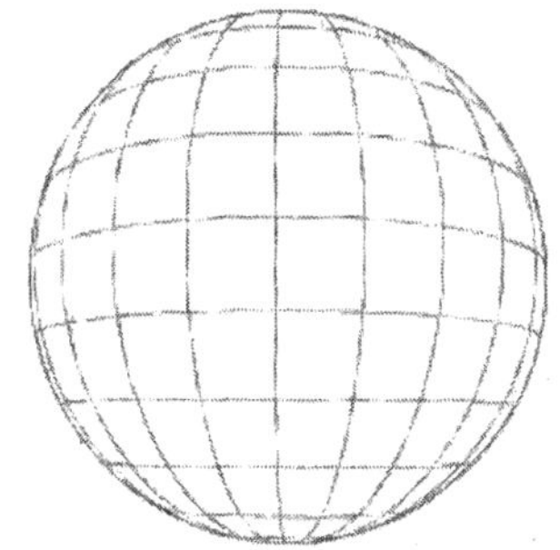

 spssi

2005 Vol. 61, No. 4

Religion as a Meaning System
Issue Editor: Israela Silberman

Jacqueline D. Goodchilds (1974–1978)
Bertram H. Raven (1970–1973)
Joshua A. Fishman (1966–1969)
Leonard Solomon (1963)
Robert Chin (1960–1965)
John Harding (1956–1959)
M. Brewster Smith (1951–1955)
Harold H. Kelley (1949)
Ronald Lippitt (1944–1950)

Journal of Social Issues, Vol. 61, No. 4, 2005, pp. 641–663

Religion as a Meaning System: Implications for the New Millennium

Israela Silberman*

Columbia University

Every human action, ranging from benevolence to inhumane violence has been justified in the name of religion, which has been a pervasive feature of human life throughout history. This article describes religion as a meaning system that is unique in centering on what is perceived as sacred, and in its special ability to address the quest for meaning. The article recommends the meaning system approach for the study of religion, suggesting that this approach can illuminate the resiliency of religion, and its complicated relations with individual and societal well-being. It describes the outline of the volume, and concludes with recommendations for research, education, and policies in the arena of religion that can facilitate well-being in the new millennium.

> *The religious perspective is a particular way of looking at life, a particular manner of construing the world.*
> *Geertz (1973, p. 110)*

> *For the sake of religion men have earnestly affirmed and contradicted almost every idea and form of conduct.*
> *Johnson (1959, p. 47)*

Religion has been a vital and pervasive feature of human life throughout history (Kimball, 2002; Smart, 1989) and in current societies (Fox, 2002), where most people regard themselves as followers of a religious tradition (Beit-Hallahmi & Argyle, 1997; Kimball, 2002). Leading experts from a variety of fields expect

---

*Correspondence concerning this article should be addressed to Israela Silberman, Department of Psychology, 406 Schermerhorn Hall, 1190 Amsterdam Ave., MC 5501, Columbia University, New York, NY 10027 [e-mail: silbermandaytime@yahoo.com or struch@netvision.net.il].

Many thanks to all the authors who participated in this issue, to Benjamin Beit Hallahmi, Chris Ellison, Shalom Schwartz, Carl Thoresen, and to several anonymous reviewers for their very insightful comments. Special thanks to Carol Dweck, Brian Farran, Miriam Frankel, Tory Higgins, Kenneth Pargament, Aviad Shragai, Nechama Silberman, Eliezer Silberman, Itai Sneh, and Naomi Struch for their very helpful feedback and their encouragement throughout the process, and to Irene Frieze for her excellent guidance and support.

religion to continue to be an influential factor in the future (e.g., Gopin, 2000; Huntington, 2003; Pargament, 1997).

The importance of religion in people's lives around the globe has been reported in numerous books (e.g., The Dalai Lama, 1999; Kushner, 1989; Lewis, 2003), insightful documentaries such as "Faith & Doubt at Ground Zero" (Whitney & Rosenbaum, 2002), and in some countries on a regular basis in the daily news (e.g., www.cnn.com., www.arabnews.com, and www.haaretz.com). Religious violence and terrorism (Bergen, 2002; Hoffman, 1993; Juergensmeyer, 2003; Silberman, 2003, 2005b; Stern, 2003), and other clashes between religions or between religious and secular traditions, such as the debate in France over religious symbols in public schools ("France debates head scarf ban," 2004) or the disagreement between the U.N. Committee against Torture and the Saudi representatives over punishments such as amputations for theft and floggings (Martin, this issue), received particularly wide media coverage (at least in the United States). The sex scandal in the Catholic Church (e.g., Farragher, 2002), and the increasing quest for spiritual renewal in the United States (Gunther, 2001) and beyond (Fox, 2002; Gopin, 2000) have also been discussed extensively in the media. Considering the role religion plays in the lives of numerous people around the globe (Beit-Hallahmi & Argyle, 1997; Fox, 2002; Kimball, 2002), it is not surprising that religion has been described as one of the most popular topics of searches on the Internet, with millions of web sites dedicated to religious issues (Jacobson, 1999). It also comes as no surprise that religious figures, such as Osama bin Laden (the founder of the global terrorist organization al-Qaeda), Pope John Paul II (the previous leader of the Catholic Church), and the Dalai Lama (the exiled spiritual leader of Tibet) have been described as some of the world's most influential people (Time, April 26, 2004; Time, April 18, 2005).

On a national level, the importance and cultural meaning of religion seem to vary significantly across nations (e.g., Beit-Hallahmi & Argyle, 1997; Manchin, 2004). While organized religion has declined greatly in many Western nations (Altemeyer, 2004), religion still seems to shape every behavioral aspect of people's lives in religious nations like Iran (Mayer, 1993). Interestingly, even in a leading Western nation like the United States, which has a constitutional separation between religion and state, each dollar bill carries the statement "In God we trust," the pledge of allegiance refers to the United States as "One nation under God" (Gallup & Castelli, 1989), and the voice of religion resonates in major moral and social debates on life and death issues such as abortions, capital punishment, euthanasia, and decisions to wage wars, as well as on issues regarding education, contraception, and same-sex marriages (Silberman, 2005b; Woodward, 2004).

The current importance of religion in people's lives in the United States has been widely recognized. According to the Gallup organization 6 in 10 of U.S. adults say religion "is very important in their lives" and that religion "can answer all or most of today's problems" while only 15% describe religion as "not important at all." Moreover, 6 in 10 adults nationwide say they attend religious services on a semi-regular basis, including 34% who claim they attend services every week. These results have not fluctuated significantly over the past decade of Gallup polling (Carroll, 2004).

The continuous importance and even the resurgence of religion in the lives of numerous people even in the current era, which is characterized by high levels of modernization, scientific discovery, and globalization (Fox, 2002; Marty & Appleby, 1991–1995), seems to contradict to a certain extent (at least in some parts of the world) the secularization thesis, which claims that the importance of religion would decline significantly with modernization (Berger, 1969). This somewhat controversial thesis (Stark, 1999) has been interpreted as predicting either a decrease in the religiosity of individuals or a decline in the impact of religion on social and political institutions (Fox, 2002). The capacity of religions, such as Buddhism, Christianity, and Judaism to survive several thousand years (Smart, 1989) and to be influential during the new millennium (e.g., Gopin, 2000; Kimball, 2002) seems to be particularly remarkable considering the characterization of the twentieth century as the graveyard of major beliefs and ideologies, such as Communism, Fascism (Fukuyama, 1989), Nazism, and Anarchism (Oz-Zaltzburg, 2000).

Throughout history, religion has had both costs and benefits for individual and societal well-being (see Pargament, 2002, and Silberman, 2005a, for reviews). On one hand, exemplary figures and organizations of faith have contributed significantly to social change that aims to correct injustice and to bring about world peace (Appleby, 2000; Gopin, 2000; Silberman, 2005b; Silberman, Higgins, & Dweck, this issue). On the other hand, religion has been a major contributor to hatred and wars all over the world, as can be exemplified in the continuous conflicts between Jews and Muslims in the Middle East, Hindus and Muslims in India, and Catholics and Protestants in Ireland (e.g., Fox, 2002; Huntington, 2003; Silberman, 2005b; Silberman et al., this issue). In this context, the world is still trying to understand the religious hatred that seems to motivate (or is used to justify) numerous worldwide terrorist attacks, for example the September 11, 2001 attacks on the United States, which have been described by Osama bin Laden and his followers as part of a religious war of Islam against infidels (Lewis, 2003). Religious terms such as "Holy War," "Cosmic War," or "crusaders" are often used in analyses of the meaning of these events. These historically loaded concepts have become part of the current academic and nonacademic discourse, as people express their concerns or hopes regarding the world's future (e.g., Bergen, 2002; Carroll, 2001; Juergensmeyer, 2003; Kimball, 2002; Lewis, 2003). These events are consistent with the prediction of Huntington (2003), one of the West's most eminent political scientists, that the revitalization of religion throughout much of the world can reinforce cultural differences and, in turn, may facilitate clashes among civilizations.

Considering the historical and current significant positive and negative impacts of religion on individual and societal well-being around the globe, and the predictions for its continuous future influence (Appleby, 2000; Huntington, 2003; Pargament, 2002), the relative neglect of the study of religion in academia and particularly in psychology is surprising and detrimental (Baumeister, 2002; Emmons et al., 2003; Fox, 2002; Johnstone & Sampson, 1994; Miller & Thoresen, 2003; Wuthnow, 2003). This unjustified neglect of the study of religion in the academia can be corrected by following the steps of major psychologists of the early twentieth century (e.g., James, 1982/1902) in continuing to investigate the positive as well as negative impacts of religion on individuals and on societies at large, and then by utilizing the results of these investigations to increase individual and societal well-being. This volume is presented as a positive step in this direction, one that carries forward the current effort of leading researchers to shed light from a psychological perspective on the complicated and fascinating phenomenon of religion.

The first main goal of this volume is to present the meaning system approach to religion (Durkheim, 1954/1912; Geertz, 1973; James, 1982/1902) in its modern version within social personality psychology and related fields, as a step in the construction of one possible comprehensive theoretical framework for the study of religion. The second main goal is to show how interdisciplinary multimethod research within this frame can shed new light on both the positive and negative impacts that religion as a unique meaning system can have on individuals in terms of their beliefs, goals, emotions, and behaviors, as well as on their interactions on both interpersonal and intergroup (national or international) levels. The volume demonstrates the integrative and unifying power of the meaning system approach by illuminating the important role of religion as a meaning system in a variety of contexts ranging from personal coping with adversity and family relations to human rights, violence, and terrorism on both national and international levels. The volume does not discuss at any point the validity or invalidity of the claims of any particular religious system or religion in general. Rather, the focus is on exploring the impacts of religion when examined from the social sciences point of view. The next paragraphs describe the general concept of psychological meaning systems and how religion can be described as a meaning system that is in certain ways unique.

Religion as a Meaning System

In their everyday lives, individuals operate on the basis of personal beliefs or theories that they have about themselves, about others, about the world of situations they encounter, and their relations to it. These beliefs or theories form idiosyncratic meaning systems that allow individuals to give meaning to the world around them and to their experiences, as well as to set goals, plan activities, and order their behavior (e.g., Bowlby, 1969; Dweck, 1999; Eidelson & Eidelson, 2003; Epstein,

1985; Fox, 2002; Higgins, 2000; Higgins & Silberman, 1998; Janoff-Bulman, 1992; Janoff-Bulman & Frieze, 1983; Kelly, 1955; Lerner, 1980; Silberman, 1999, 2003, 2004; Stark & Bainbridge, 1985).

Meaning systems usually contain descriptive beliefs as well as motivational or prescriptive beliefs. The major descriptive postulates of a meaning system are concerned with the nature of the person (a self theory; e.g., "I am competent"), the nature of the world (a world theory; e.g., "the world is just"), and propositions relating the two (e.g., "I can change the world"). Such postulates may also include contingencies and expectations regarding the world, other people, or the self (e.g., "good people should be awarded" or "the world will improve in the future"). Major motivational or prescriptive postulates are broad generalizations about how to behave in the future in order to obtain what one desires and avoid what one fears (Epstein, 1985; Higgins, 2000). It has been suggested that the construction of such meaning systems is necessary for humans to function in the world. Epstein (1985), for example, explains that meaning systems develop in order to fulfill four basic motives; namely, to maintain (1) the stability and coherence of a personal conceptual system (while assimilating the data of experience); (2) favorable balance of pleasure and pain over the foreseeable future; (3) a favorable balance of self-esteem; and (4) a favorable relationship with significant others.

A growing line of research has supported the idea that people's idiosyncratic meaning systems are very important in everyday life and may be of particular importance in predicting general patterns and individual differences in coping with adversity. Religious and optimistic beliefs, as well as beliefs about a just world, personal vulnerability, and malleability of self and others are some of the beliefs that are important in this context (e.g., Dweck, 1999; Janoff-Bulman, 1992; Janoff-Bulman et al., 1983; Lazarus & Folkman, 1984; Lerner, 1980; McIntosh, 1995; Pargament, 1997; Park et al., 1997; Scheier & Carver, 1985; Silberman, 2003).

The idiosyncratic religious meaning systems of individuals, in similar ways to any other idiosyncratic nonreligious meaning systems (e.g., Higgins, 2000, on basic cognitive processes in social cognition), function as a lens through which reality is perceived and interpreted (McIntosh, 1995). Like other meaning systems (e.g., Epstein, 1985; Higgins, 2000; Janoff-Bulman, 1992), religion can influence the formation of goals for self-regulation, affect emotions, and influence behavior (e.g., Batson, Schoenrade, & Ventis, 1993; Baumeister, 1991; Cohen & Rankin, 2004; Emmons, 1999; Geertz, 1973; George, Ellison, & Larson, 2002; James, 1982/1902; Pargament, 1997; Park et al., 1997; see Silberman 1999, 2003, 2004 for reviews).

The Uniqueness of Religion as a Meaning System

Yet, religion as a meaning system is unique in that it centers on what is perceived to be the sacred (cf. Pargament's definition, 1997, p. 32). The sacred refers to concepts of higher powers, such as the divine, God, or the transcendent, which are considered holy and set apart from the ordinary. As such, they are perceived as worthy of veneration and respect, and can become a unique source of significance in people's lives (Pargament, Magyar, & Murray-Swank, this issue). The connection to the sacred can be fully manifested, as demonstrated below, in each of the components of the meaning system, namely, beliefs, contingencies, expectations, and goals, as well as in prescriptive postulates regarding emotions and actions (Silberman, 2003, 2004).

Self and world beliefs. When religion is incorporated into the meaning system of a person, conceptions of the sacred are connected to beliefs about the nature of people, of the self, of this world, and of whatever may lie beyond it. For example, religious systems may include beliefs about humans as being sinful or pious, and of the world as being evil or holy.

Contingencies and expectations. Religious meaning systems often include beliefs regarding contingencies and outcome expectations. One common contingency is that righteous people should be rewarded for their good deeds, while sinners should be punished for their actions (Kushner, 1989). Other contingencies may describe differential rules for treating in-group versus out-group members, or they may teach the circumstances under which one should treat other groups in compassionate versus hostile ways (Hunsberger & Jackson, this issue; Oman & Thoresen, 2003; Tsang, McCullough, & Hoyt, this issue). Such systems may include self-efficacy expectations regarding the ability of individuals to change themselves and the world around them (The Dalai Lama, 1999; Silberman, 1999, 2004; Silberman et al., this issue; Thurman, 1998). They may also include positive or negative expectations regarding the future of the world, ranging from predictions of utopian redemption to destructive apocalypses (Dan, 2000; Silberman et al., this issue).

Goals. Religious systems basically encourage the ultimate motivation of connecting or adhering to the sacred. However, any goal, ranging from goals of benevolence (Schwartz & Huismars, 1995), forgiveness (Tsang et al., this issue), and altruism (Batson et al., 1993) to goals of destruction and supremacy (e.g., Hunsberger et al., this issue; Martin, this issue), could take on religious value by virtue of connection to the sacred (Silberman et al., this issue).

Actions. On the level of actions, religious systems usually prescribe actions that are considered to be appropriate and proscribe inappropriate actions (Pargament, 1997). While some actions are perceived as prototypical religious or spiritual (e.g., the act of praying), each and every human action including acts of compassion and charity (Oman et al., 2003), as well as acts of violence and terrorism may become connected to the sacred and may receive a special power through a variety of processes, such as the process of sanctification (e.g., Pargament et al., this issue; see Silberman, 2003; Silberman et al., this issue, for reviews).

Emotions. Religions as meaning systems may influence emotions in several ways (see Silberman, 2003, 2005a; Silberman et al., 2001, for reviews). First, they may offer the opportunity to experience a uniquely powerful emotional experience of closeness to a powerful spiritual force (Otto, 1928; Pargament, 1997). Second, they may directly prescribe or discourage certain emotions and emotional levels. For example, religious meaning systems can prescribe emotions such as joy while proscribing other emotions such as sadness or anger (Silberman, 2003). Third, religious meaning systems can encourage certain beliefs, goals, or actions that may impact emotions in either positive or negative ways (e.g., Sethi & Seligman, 1993; Silberman, 2003, 2004). For example, religiously based beliefs about the goodness of the world and about the abilities to change the world and improve the self can mediate the relations between religion and emotional well-being (Silberman et al., 2001), and religious beliefs in a loving-forgiving God or in a revengeful-angry one can determine, in part, whether religion has positive or negative impacts on the emotional well-being of individuals who cope with adversity (Pargament, 1997; Pargament et al., this issue).

The above description suggests that religion has a special power of meaning-making that is exceptional both in terms of its comprehensiveness (i.e., the range of issues to which the system gives meaning), and in its quality (i.e., the type of meaning that the system offers). In terms of comprehensiveness, religion is one of the few meaning systems that can offer meaning to history from the moment of creation until the end of time, as well as to every aspect of human life from birth to death and beyond (Emmons, this issue; Pargament et al., this issue; Silberman et al., this issue). For example, religion as a meaning system can lend significance to time and space (e.g., the Sabbath, mosques, churches), roles (e.g., marriage, parenting, work), cultural products (e.g., literature, music), people (e.g., religious or spiritual leaders), and to material objects (e.g., crucifix, drugs) (Pargament et al., this issue). It can also give unique meaning to any specific situation, that is, religion can influence the appraisals or causal attributions that compose the interpretations given by individuals to any specific event (Park, this issue)

In terms of quality, religion as a source of meaning has been described as qualitatively unique in its ability to propose answers to life's deepest questions (Myers, 2000; Pargament et al., this issue). At times religion provides answers that offer hope and a sense of significance to people. In this context religion has been described as a powerful source of meaning under even the most testing circumstances, such as when stressful events can not be repaired through problem-solving strategies. Religious beliefs seem to prevail in difficult circumstances when other basic personal beliefs, such as the belief in personal invulnerability, the perception of the world as meaningful and comprehensible, and the ability to view ourselves in a positive light may be shattered or at least seriously questioned (Jannoff-Bulman, 1992; Jannoff-Bulman et al., 1983, on the effect of victimization on basic beliefs; Park, this issue; Park et al., 1997; Pargament, 1997; Pargament et al., this issue, on religion and coping). However, at other times, religion answers these questions in ways that can cause unique difficulties and distress (Kushner, 1989; Pargament et al., this issue).

Beyond that, religion as a meaning system that is centered on the sacred is one of the few types of meaning systems that can meet the basic human need for self-transcendence (Sheldon & Kasser, 1995), a striving that has been described as instrumental for accomplishing other strivings and as having especially strong relations with well-being (Emmons, 1999b, this issue). This characteristic is consistent with the view of religion or spirituality as able to give unity to all other concerns (Tillich, 1957), and to serve as an integrating framework that can reduce the overall conflict within a person's goal system and can foster coherence in personality (Emmons, 1999, this issue; Pargament et al., this issue).

The above description of religion as a meaning system is consistent with Geertz's (1973) idea that meaning-making is the most essential function of religion. This unique meaning-making aspect of religion may be one of the main factors that underlie the common perception that beyond offering meaning for one's life and meaning in the world, religion can also facilitate the fulfillment of many other basic human needs, such as needs for comfort, physical health, community, intimacy, a sense of safety and security, and hope for a better world (Pargament, 1997).

Learning, Development, and Change of Religious Meaning Systems

Like other meaning systems, idiosyncratic religious meaning systems can be viewed as malleable systems that can be learned, developed, and changed (e.g., Dweck, 1999; Epstein, 1985; Higgins, 2000; Higgins & Silberman, 1998, on the malleability of psychological meaning systems; Firestone, 1999; Gopin, 2000; Lewis, 2003; Martin, this issue; Park, this issue; Silberman, 2005b; Silberman et al., this issue; Tsang et al., this issue, on the malleability of religious meaning systems). The learning of religious meaning systems involves the learning of the contents of the systems, namely, beliefs, contingencies, expectations and goals, as well as prescriptive postulates regarding emotions and actions. In addition, such learning can involve knowledge about how to connect to the meaning system (Silberman, 2004). For example, connection to a religious meaning system in a quest orientation involves a doubting, flexible approach to religious issues (Batson et al., 1993), while connecting in a fundamentalist way suggests closed-mindedness, and the belief that one has access to absolute truth (Hunsberger et al., this issue).

The basic postulates of religious meaning systems can be learned and modified in several ways (see Silberman, 2004, for a review). First, one can learn beliefs about God or about the nature of the world through explicit oral or written teaching of religious leaders, family members, friends, or other agents. Second, one can learn such postulates through observation of persons serving as exemplars of how to live a spiritually meaningful life (Oman et al., 2003; Silberman, 2003) or, according to some religious frames, through the emulation of God (Silberman, 2003). Finally, meaning systems can change and develop, in a similar way to scientific theories (Kuhn, 1962), by accommodating to observed phenomena that seem to disconfirm the basic, often subconscious, postulates of the system (Silberman, 2003). For example, traumatic events such as criminal victimization or serious accidents can shatter the basic implicit beliefs that constitute the religious meaning systems of individuals, and can encourage people to reevaluate these basic beliefs and to modify them (Park, this issue).

Religions as Collective Meaning Systems

In many contexts it is important to consider not only the idiosyncratic meaning systems of individuals, but also the religious and nonreligious collective world views of the relevant groups (Beck, 1999; Durkheim, 1933; Eidelson et al., 2003; Moscovici, 1988; Silberman, 2005b; Thompson & Fine, 1999; Triandis, 1989). These collective meaning systems compose the "shared reality" of each group (Hardin & Higgins, 1996) and can define the group's very essence (Bar-Tal, 2000). More specifically, these collective meaning systems enable groups and group members to interpret their shared experiences including their historical and recent relations with other groups. They can influence the goals and the behaviors of groups on both national and international levels (Eidelson et al., 2003; Kearney, 1984; Kelman, 1997; Silberman et al., this issue; Staub, 1989; Volkan, 1990, 1997).

In a parallel way to individual meaning systems, collective meaning systems can be viewed as malleable systems (Firestone, 1999; Gopin, 2000; Lewis, 2003; Martin, this issue; Silberman, 2005b; Silberman et al., this issue). They can develop in both conscious and subconscious ways from culturally determined common experiences and through a variety of socialization processes (Bar-Tal, 2000; Ross, 1997; Volkan, 1997). However, like individual meaning systems, and perhaps even more than them, once they are constructed collective meaning systems tend to be viewed within a given group as basic undisputable truths. Accordingly, they are usually held with confidence, and their change or redirection can be very challenging (Bar-Tal, 2000; Lustick, 1993; see Eidelson et al., 2003; Silberman et al., this issue).

In sum, religion as either individual or collective meaning system is similar to other systems in its structure, malleability, and functioning, yet it is unique in centering on what is perceived to be the sacred, and in the comprehensive and special way in which it fulfills the quest for meaning. These characteristics may underlie the potential of religion to serve as a unique source of goals, emotions, and actions, and, in turn, as a unique source of both positive and negative individual and societal well-being.

Reasons for Choosing the Meaning System Approach for the Study of Religion

A good scientific theory has been characterized as being testable, coherent, economical, and generalizable (i.e., as having broad applicability), as well as by being able to explain known findings (Higgins, 2004). According to these criteria the following advantages of the meaning system approach to the study of religion, suggest that this approach can be described as a very promising theoretical framework (Silberman, 2005a).

1. The concept of meaning system refers to cognitive structure, yet goes beyond cognitions to acknowledge explicitly the importance of goals, emotions, and actions. The meaning system frame, as such, supplies the researcher of religion with one language that is comprehensive enough to enable an in-depth psychological analysis of the variety of phenomena that are referred to as religion—yet is parsimonious enough to be efficient as a research tool.

2. The meaning system approach offers a frame for the conceptual study of religion, and yet may also be very fruitful in producing testable hypotheses and in developing organized and coherent research programs. This approach may be facilitated by the application of existing empirical knowledge on the way in which other meaning systems function (e.g., Dweck, 1999; Epstein, 1985; Higgins, 2000; Janoff-Bulman, 1992) to the study of religion.

3. In emphasizing motivational constructs, such as goals, strivings, and values, and in highlighting the role of religion in active processing and interpretation of reality, an analysis of religion as a meaning system facilitates an understanding of the dynamic, process-oriented function of religion in people's lives. Such a process-oriented approach, which has been found to be very fruitful in the study of personality in general (e.g., Dweck, 1999; Emmons, 1999; Epstein, 1985; Higgins, 2000; Pervin, 1989), may be very valuable in the study of religion as well, and could provide a general unifying framework for previous efforts to capture the dynamic aspect of religion (e.g., McIntosh, 1995; Paloutzian et al., 1995; Pargament, 1997; Proudfoot et al., 1975; Spilka, Shaver, & Kirkpatrick, 1985; Weiss, 1997).

4. The meaning system approach may be helpful in the challenging efforts to construct a meaningful typology of the wide range of phenomena that religion encompasses (e.g., Stark, 1965)—a typology that is based on psychological

constructs such as goals, motivations, and well-being. Such a typology may, in turn, facilitate comparisons between religious and nonreligious meaning systems, as well as among different religions and among different types of religious experiences.

5. The meaning system approach illuminates the complexity of major religions that tend to include within themselves a wide variety of messages (e.g., encouragements of both conflicts and their resolutions), and their malleability (i.e., the ability of major religions to develop and change over time). This complexity and malleability, which allow religions to accommodate to different situations, may explain to a certain extent the resiliency of religion throughout history and in the face of modernization and globalization.

6. Viewing religion as a meaning system can contribute significantly to research on the complicated historical and current relations between religion and individual and societal well-being (e.g., Baumeister, 2002; Emmons, 1999; George et al., 2002; Gopin, 2000; Hill & Pargament, 2003; Koenig, McCullough, & Larson, 2000; Miller & Thoresen, 2003; Marty & Appleby, 1991–1995; Pargament, 1997; Silberman, 2005a). For example, the meaning system approach to religion has shed new light on existing data regarding the relations between religion and psychological well-being (Silberman, 2005a). It can also contribute to the identification of additional aspects of religion, spirituality, and well-being, and to the exploration of the relations among them (e.g., Batson et al., 1993; Ciarrocchi & Deneke, 2005; Pargament, 2002; Ventis, 1995). Beyond that, this approach to religion can illuminate the processes through which religion as a unique meaning system influences well-being in both positive and negative ways (e.g., Sethi & Seligman, 1993; Silberman et al., 2001, this issue).

Characteristics of the *JSI* Issue

The articles in this issue demonstrate in the following ways many of the advantages of the meaning system approach to the study of religion:

1. Each of the articles contributes to the understanding of the importance of religion as a meaning system in people's lives, and illuminates the processes by which religion as a source of meaning affects people's lives. The articles show, for example, how religion, as a dynamic meaning system, contributes to the interpretation of reality and how it actively impacts the formation of goals and prescribes behavioral means for the achievement of these goals.

2. The articles contribute to the understanding of the uniqueness of religion as a meaning system in the following ways:

a. By direct comparison of religious and nonreligious meaning systems in general (Emmons, this issue; Pargament et al., this issue; Mahoney, this issue; Park, this issue; Roccas, this issue; Silberman et al., this issue; Tsang et al., this issue) or to other specific systems such as the human rights meaning system (Martin, this issue), the meaning system of scientific psychology, and the social policy meaning system (Maton, Dodgen, Sto. Domingo, & Larson this issue).

b. By illuminating the comprehensiveness and uniqueness of religion as a source of meaning in the everyday lives of individuals (Pargament et al., this issue; Emmons, this issue; Roccas, this issue; Silberman et al., this issue); in times of stress and adversity (Pargament et al., this issue; Park, this issue; Emmons, this issue); in interpersonal relations in general (Hunsberger et al., this issue; Tsang et al., this issue); within the family context (Mahoney, this issue); or in national and international relations (Martin, this issue; Silberman et al., this issue).

3. In each of the articles, whether theoretical, empirical, or policy oriented, the authors refer to the relation of religion with important social issues, which have always been of concern to the *Journal of Social Issues* and its readers. Some of the issues that are discussed are coping (Emmons, this issue; Pargament et al., this issue; Park, this issue), social action (Maton et al., this issue; Pargament et al., this issue; Silberman et al., this issue), forgiveness (Tsang et al., this issue), prejudice (Hunsberger et al., this issue), conflicts and their resolutions (Mahoney, this issue; Pargament et al., this issue; Roccas, this issue; Silberman et al., this issue; Tsang et al., this issue), national and international violence and terrorism (Silberman et al., this issue), human rights and particularly women's rights, tolerance, and pluralism (Martin, this issue), separation between church and state (Roccas, this issue; Maton et al., this issue), modernization and globalization (Pargament et al., this issue), and materialism versus spirituality (Maton et al., this issue).

4. The articles illustrate the usefulness of the meaning system approach for the understanding of the complicated relations between religion and these social issues. For example, they suggest that major religious systems tend to be complex and include within themselves a variety of messages that may seem contradictory, for example, calls for both war and peace. The articles emphasize that the interpretation of religious systems can vary significantly across individuals within each tradition (Hunsberger et al., this issue; Silberman et al., this issue; Tsang et al., this issue), as well as across historical periods, locations, and political conditions (Martin, this issue; Roccas, this issue; Silberman et al., this issue). They suggest, accordingly, that religions can be viewed as malleable meaning systems, and that it is possible to direct them in different paths (e.g., toward conflict and world destruction or toward

conflict resolution and peace) by choosing to selectively emphasize certain religious messages over others (Martin, this issue; Silberman et al., this issue).

This complexity of religious systems suggests that in analyzing the meaning and influence of religion in people's lives one needs to go beyond the general categories of being religious versus nonreligious and beyond labels such as Buddhists, Christian, Jews or Muslims to explore *both* the content of the specific beliefs that individuals endorse as sources of meaning (Martin, this issue; Pargament et al., this issue; Silberman et al., this issue; Tsang et al., this issue) *and* the ways in which individuals relate to their religious meaning system, for example, in a fundamentalist way or as a quest (Hunsberger et al., this issue).

5. Several of the articles (Hunsberger et al., this issue; Silberman et al., this issue; Tsang, et al., this issue) discuss processes of moral justification that can be used by individuals in their efforts to cope with the varied messages and goals of religious meaning systems that can call, for example, for compassion and equality to all, yet encourage their adherents implicitly to develop prejudices and to act in discriminatory and cruel ways toward certain outgroups.

6. Many of the articles refer to historical and recent world events, such as the September 11 terrorist attacks on the United States or the Middle East conflict, where religion as a source of meaning, has been a factor (e.g., Hunsberger et al., this issue; Pargament et al., this issue; Park, this issue; Silberman et al., this issue).

7. While much of the social research on religion has been conducted within a Judeo-Christian context, the articles discuss, whenever possible, the role of religion in cross-cultural and cross-religious contexts (e.g., Hunsberger et al., this issue; Roccas, this issue; Silberman et al., this issue; Tsang et al., this issue).

8. The volume approaches the issue of religion as a meaning system from an interdisciplinary perspective. The participants in the volume are leading researchers from a variety of disciplines ranging from psychology (clinical, social-personality, health, and psychology of religion) to human rights. The articles represent a variety of approaches to the study of religion ranging from theoretical and empirical approaches to policy implications.

9. Most articles highlight the role of religion as a possible causal factor. Yet several of them discuss both directions of causality, suggesting that psychological factors, such as people's motivations (e.g., Tsang et al., this issue), needs and values (Roccas, this issue), and implicit theories (Silberman et al., this issue); or context variables, such as social, political, economic, or historical circumstances (Martin, this issue; Roccas, this issue; Silberman et al., this issue) may influence whether people endorse a religious meaning system to guide their

lives or not, as well as their decision to selectively emphasize certain tenets within a religious system over others.

10. In their description of the uniqueness of religion as a meaning system, the articles suggest explanations for the resiliency of religion despite increased secularization and modernization in terms of psychological and societal needs (Pargament et al., this issue).

11. Through their discussion of the above issues all articles discuss the influence of religion on individual and societal well-being. The articles exemplify the complexity of the concept of *well-being* by discussing different manifestations of both individual and societal well-being, and the relations between them (e.g., Park, this issue). The issue is balanced in terms of discussing both positive and negative potentials of religion for well-being.

12. Finally, the articles suggest ways in which the analysis of religion as a meaning system may contribute to individual and societal well-being in the future through applied research, public and professional education, and public policies.

The Outline of the Issue

The first part of the volume highlights the uniqueness and the varieties of the religious experience, and emphasizes the role and importance of religion as a meaning system that can shape individuals' beliefs, motivations, emotions, and actions. In the first article, Pargament et al. (this issue) describe religion as a rich, multidimensional process that can be viewed as a unique form of motivation, a unique source of significance, coping and distress, and a unique contributor to mortality and health. Next, Mahoney (this issue) describes how religious systems of meaning can substantially facilitate both the manifestation of marital and parental-child conflicts, and their resolutions. Park (this issue) adds to the discussion on meaning by describing how religion influences coping with adversity, especially through meaning-making.

The next three papers highlight the distinctive role of religion as a meaning system of beliefs, within which individuals set personal goals that motivate them and guide their everyday lives. Emmons (this issue) describes spiritual strivings as unique goals with particular importance for physical, psychosocial, and interpersonal well-being, and illustrates the role of such goals in the rehabilitation of persons with disabilities. Roccas (this issue) suggests that religion is correlated positively with giving priority to values that reflect the motivation to avoid uncertainty and change, and negatively with values that express the motivations to follow one's hedonistic desires, or to be independent in thoughts and actions. She discusses variables that may moderate the relationship between religion and values. Silberman et al. (this issue) challenge the traditional view of the relationship between religion and change, as reflected in Roccas' (this issue) review. Instead, they portray religious meaning systems as double-edged swords that can, through a variety of processes, facilitate either the goal of maintaining the status quo or both violent and peaceful activism. They review context and personality variables that may determine whether religious groups support world change and either violent or peaceful activism.

The next three articles call attention to the discrepancy between the global vision of compassion to all endorsed by the major religions and the actual way in which religions may affect their followers. Tsang et al. (this issue) offer both methodological and conceptual reasons for this discrepancy in the context of forgiveness. Hunsberger and Jackson (this issue) shed light on the mechanisms through which religion as a source of several types of meaning is linked to prejudice. Finally, Martin (this issue) illustrates how some religious interpretations may cherish moral standards at variance with accepted human rights principles. However, he suggests that shifts within religion in the context of human rights are possible. The concluding article of the volume by Maton et al. (this issue) compares religion and policy making as two different meaning systems, and describes the potential of religion for public policy development.

Concluding Comments

Allport (1966) in his classic article on religion and prejudice suggested that "there is something about religion that makes for prejudice, and something about it that unmakes prejudice" (p. 447). The theoretical and empirical research that is presented in this volume seems to support Allport's insightful comment about the complicated relations between religion and prejudice (Hunsberger & Jackson, this issue; Martin, this issue; Silberman et al., this issue). Beyond that, the volume suggests that this portrayal of religion as a double-edged sword, which has both positive and negative influences on individual and societal well-being, should be extended to many other facets of life, such as individual and communal coping, family relations, interpersonal relations, and national and international relations. The volume as a whole confirms the insightful comments that "For the sake of religion men have earnestly affirmed and contradicted almost every idea and form of conduct" (Johnson, 1959, p. 47), and that "Over its career religion has probably disturbed men as much as it has cheered them" (Geertz, 1973, p. 103).

The interdisciplinary, cross-cultural and cross-religious research in this volume sheds new light on the issue of the uniqueness of religion (Dittes, 1969), which underlies the debate between the reductionistic approach claiming that religion can be reduced to basic psychological, social, or physiological processes, and the nonreductionistic approach suggesting that the uniqueness of religion needs to be acknowledged on both theoretical and methodological levels (see Pargament et al., this issue, for a review). The *JSI* volume contributes to this basic debate by describing religion as a meaning system that is similar to other systems in its structure, malleability, and functioning, yet is unique in centering on what is perceived to be the sacred, and in the comprehensive and special way in which it can serve to fulfill the quest for meaning. The volume suggests that these characteristics may underlie the potential of religion to serve as a unique source of goals, emotions, and actions, and, in turn, as a unique source of individual and societal well-being.

Implications for the New Millennium

The volume suggests that the unique features of religion as a system of meaning may underlie its resiliency in the face of increasing modernization and globalization and predicts that religion will likely continue to exert profound effects during the new millennium. Considering that, the volume as a whole offers several recommendations for the new millennium.

First, by demonstrating the productivity of the meaning system approach to the study of religion, the volume recommends the use of this approach for future interdisciplinary theoretical and applied research. Such research could contribute to a variety of fields within the psychology of religion and beyond. For example, it could contribute significantly to both research on religious violence and terrorism (e.g., Hoffman, 1993; Juergensmeyer, 2003; Kimball, 2002; Silberman, 2003, 2005b; Stern, 2003) and to general research on processes involved in violent group conflicts and their resolutions (e.g., Deutsch & Coleman, 2000; Moghaddam & Marsella, 2004).

More generally, the meaning system approach to religion could enrich the study of the dynamic, process-oriented structure of personality, which emphasizes motivational constructs, such as goals and values as core concepts of human behavior (e.g., Dweck, 1999; Epstein, 1985; Higgins, 2000; Janoff-Bulman, 1992). It could also contribute significantly to psychological, anthropological, and sociological research on the systematic influence of culture on various aspects of cognition, emotion, and motivation (e.g., Geertz, 1973; Markus & Kitayama, 1991; Norenzayan & Nisbett, 2000; Schwartz & Bilsky, 1990; Triandis, 1989). Furthermore, it could be a source of insights for the field of positive psychology that investigates valued subjective experiences such as well-being, optimism, and happiness, and positive traits such as forgiveness and altruism (Myers, 2000; Seligman & Csikszentmihalyi, 2000; Snyder & Lopez, 2002).

However, that being said, it is necessary to emphasize that religion can impact individual and societal well-being in ways that are not limited to meaning. Furthermore, religion does not function in a vacuum. Accordingly, it would be important for future research to shed more light on the ways in which the role of religion as a source of meaning interacts with other functions that religion may have, for example, as a source of health practices and of communal and social support (Baumeister, 1991; Ciarrocio & Denke, 2005; George et al., 2002; Hill & Pargament, 2003; Silberman, 2003, 2005a). Future research could also further explore how religion interacts with social-political and economic systems (e.g., Roccas, this issue; Martin, this issue; Silberman, 2005a, 2005b; Silberman et al., this issue) in influencing individual and societal well-being.

Second, many people, including researchers, tend to have somewhat over-simplified views of the role of religion in people's lives as being all negative or all positive (see Pargament, 1997, 2002; and Silberman, 2003, 2005a, for reviews). This volume seeks to enhance professional and public awareness of the influence of religion as a unique meaning system with *both* positive *and* negative potentials for individual and societal well-being. It seems to me that this awareness should, in turn, increase the appreciation of both religious freedom and separation between religion and state as facilitators of well-being.

Third, the volume encourages collaboration between social science, policy making, health, and religious communities for the benefit of the larger society. Such collaboration can be productive in supporting those most in need in society (Maton et al., this issue; Pargament et al., this issue) and in efforts to solve ethno-religious conflicts and to prevent religious terrorism on both national and international levels (Gopin, 2000; Lewis, 2003; Silberman et al., this issue). Psychologists endorsing the meaning system approach to religion could contribute significantly to such collaboration as demonstrated below.

Conflict resolution efforts. Psychologists could contribute to efforts to solve ethno-religious conflicts by promoting the valuing of religious diversity and plural-ism (Wuthnow, 2004), and by helping to redirect individual and collective religious meaning systems toward more tolerant and peaceful goals (Gopin, 2000; Lewis, 2003; Martin, this issue; see Silberman, 2005b, and Silberman et al., this issue, for reviews). For example, psychologists could combine existing knowledge of conflict and conflict resolution theories (Deutsch & Coleman, 2000) and of prim-ing/accessibility techniques and motivated cognition techniques (Higgins et al., 1996) with knowledge about religions as malleable meaning systems (Silberman, 2003) to develop conflict resolution theories and strategies that take into account the religious background of the participants (Gopin, 2000; Silberman et al., this issue; Silberman, 2005b). Psychologists could also help evaluate existing national and international interfaith dialogue programs, which have become an increasingly popular response to religious conflicts (Garfinkel, 2004).

Prevention of religious terrorism and fighting against it. Psychologists could contribute to the prevention of terrorism through analyses of the conditions and the processes that facilitate religious terrorism and by suggesting effective ways to influence them (Juergensmeyer, 2003; Silberman, 2005b; Silberman et al., this issue). For example, psychologists could recommend ways to remove social, polit-ical, and economic conditions that provide the contexts for religious violence and terrorism (Silberman et al., this issue). They could also help discourage religious (or nonreligious) ideas and prejudices that may facilitate terrorism, such as the anti-West, and particularly anti-U.S., propaganda that seems to scapegoat the United States, blaming it for all of the difficulties of the Arab world, and portraying it inaccurately as heading a Crusade against Islam (Staub, 2004; Lewis, 2003). Further, they could contribute to the deterrence of religious terrorists by illuminating their religious meaning systems in terms of their decision-making processes (Silberman et al., this issue) and by suggesting creative ways of influencing these processes (Ganor, 2005; Silberman, 2005b). For example, psychologists collaborating with policy makers and with an interfaith team of peace-oriented religious leaders could suggest ways to deter potential suicide (homicide) bombers by changing their perceptions of the cost-benefit ratios that guide them in their actions (Silberman, 2005b).

Coping with the consequences of religious terrorism. Psychologists who endorse the meaning system approach to religious terrorism could contribute to individual and communal efforts to cope with this dangerous phenomenon. For example, they could help increase the awareness of decision makers, security personnel, media representatives, and the public of the nature of religious terrorism as a war that is fundamentally psychological and, particularly, of the psychological manipulations used by terrorists in order to magnify the fears of populations and increase their support of the terrorists' cause. Such awareness could facilitate more responsible and effective reactions by decision makers and by the media, as well as the psychological resiliency of the public (Ganor, 2005; Silberman, 2005b). In this context, psychologists could also be the leaders in discouraging prejudice and discrimination toward innocent individuals who belong to the same religion as certain terrorists, for example, by discouraging anti-Islamic and anti-Middle Eastern hate crime incidents and the attrition of civil liberties in the United States, which has increased after the September 11, 2001 terrorist attacks on the United States (Silberman, 2005b).

References

Allport, G. W. (1966). The religious context of prejudice. *Journal for the Scientific Study of Religion, 5*, 447–457.

Altemeyer, B. (2004). The decline of organized religion in Western civilization. *International Journal for the Psychology of Religion, 14*(2), 77–89.

Appleby, R. S. (2000). *The ambivalence of the sacred: Religion, violence and reconciliation.* Lahman: Rowman & Littlefield Publishers, Inc.

Bar-Tal, D. (2000). *Shared beliefs in society: Social psychological analysis.* Thousand Oaks, CA: Sage.

Beck, A. T. (1999). *Prisoners of hate: The cognitive basis of anger, hostility, and violence.* New York: HarperCollins.

Batson, C. D., Schoenrade, P., & Ventis, W. L. (1993). *Religion and the individual: A social psychological perspective.* New York: Oxford University Press.

Baumeister, R. F. (1991). *Meanings in life.* New York: The Guilford Press.

Baumeister, R. F. (2002). Religion and psychology: Introduction to the special issue. *Psychological Inquiry, 13*(3), 165–167.

Bowlby, J. (1969). *Attachment and loss* (Vol. 1). Attachment. London: Hogarth.

Beit-Hallahmi, B., & Argyle, M. (1997). *The psychology of religious behavior, belief and experience.* London and New York: Routledge.

Bergen, P. L. (2002). *Holy war Inc.: Inside the secret world of Osama bin Laden.* New York: A Touchstone Book Published by Simon & Schuster.

Berger, P. L. (1969). *The sacred canopy.* New York: Anchor Books: Doubleday & Company, Inc.

Carroll, J. (2001). *Constantine's sword: The Church and the Jews—A history.* Boston and New York: Houghton Mifflin Company.

Carroll, J. (2004). *Religion is "very important" to 6 in 10 Americans.* Retrieved September 26, 2004, from http://www.gallup.com/poll/content/print.aspx?ci=12115

Ciarrocchi, J. W., & Deneke, E. (2005). Happiness and the varieties of religious experience: Religious support, practices, and spirituality as predictors of well-being. *Research in the Social Scientific Study of Religion, 15,* 209–233.

Cohen, A. B., & Rankin, A. (2004). Religion and the morality of positive mentality. *Basic and Applied Social Psychology, 26*(1), 45–57.

Dan, J. (2000). *Apocalypse then and now.* Tel Aviv, Israel: Yediot Aharonot and Sifrei Hemed.

Deutsch, M., & Coleman, P. T. (Eds.). (2000). *The handbook of conflict resolution: Theory and practice* (pp. 428–450). San Francisco: Jossey-Bass Publishers.

Dittes, J. E. (1969). Psychology of religion. In G. Lindzey & E. Aronson (Eds.), *Handbook of social psychology, V* (pp. 602–659). Reading, MA: Addison-Wesley.

Durkheim, E. (1933). *The division of labor in society.* New York: Macmillan.

Durkheim, E. (1954/1912). *Elementary forms of religious life.* (J. W. Swain Trans.). Glencoe, IL: Free Press.

Dweck, C. S. (1999). *Self theories: Their role in motivation, personality and development.* Philadelphia: Psychology Press.

Eidelson, R. J., & Eidelson, J. I. (2003). Dangerous ideas: Five beliefs that propel groups toward conflict. *American Psychologist, 58*(3), 182–192.

Emmons, R. A. (1999). *The psychology of ultimate concerns.* New York: The Guilford Press.

Emmons, R. A. (this issue). Striving for the sacred: Personal goals, life meaning and religion. *Journal of Social Issues.*

Emmons, R. A., & Paloutzian, R. F. (2003). The psychology of religion. *Annual Review of Psychology, 54,* 377–402.

Epstein, S. (1985). The implications of cognitive-experiential self theory for research in social psychology and personality. *Journal of the Theory of Social Behavior, 15*(3), 283–310.

Farragher, T. (2002, February 24). Church cloaked in culture of silence. *Boston Globe,* Section: Metro/Region. p. A1.

Fireston, R. (1999). *Jihad: The origin of holy war in Islam.* New York: Oxford University Press.

Fox, J. (2002). *Ethnoreligious conflict in the late twentieth century: A general theory.* Lanham: Lexington Books.

"*France debates head scarf ban.*" (2004, February, 3). Retrieved April 23, 2004, from http://cnn.worldnews.printthis.clickability.com.

Fukuyama, F. (1989). The end of history? *The National Interest, 16,* 3–18.

Gallup, G., Jr., & Castelli, J. (1989). *The people's religion: American faith in the 90's.* New York: Macmillan.

Ganor, B. (2005). *The counter-terrorism puzzle: A guide for decision makers.* New Brunswick & London: Transaction Publishers.

Garfinkel, R. (2004). What worked? Evaluating interfaith dialogue programs. *Special Report* (Vol. 123, pp. 1–12). Washington, DC: United States Institute of Peace.

Geertz, C. (1973). *The interpretation of culture.* New York: Basic Books, Inc.

George, L. K., Ellison, C. G., & Larson, D. B. (2002). Explaining the relationships between religious involvement and health. *Psychological Inquiry, 13*(3), 190–200.

Gopin, M. (2000). *Between Eden and Armageddon: The future of religion, violence and peacemaking.* New York and London: Oxford University Press.

Gunther, M. (2001, July 9). God & business. *Fortune*, pp. 59–80

Hardin, C., & Higgins, E. T. (1996). Shared reality: How social verification makes the subjective objective. In R. M. Sorrentino & E. T. Higgins (Eds.), *Handbook of motivation and cognition: Vol. 3. The interpersonal context* (pp. 28–84). New York: Guilford Press.

Higgins, E. T. (2000). Social cognition: Learning about what matters in the social world. *European Journal of Social Psychology, 30*, 3–39.

Higgins, E. T. (2004). Making a theory useful. *Personality and Social Psychological Review, 8*(2), 138–145.

Higgins, E. T., & Kruglanski, A. W. (Eds.). (1996). *Social psychology: Handbook of basic principles.* New York: Guilford Press.

Higgins, E. T., & Silberman, I. (1998). Development of regulatory focus: Promotion and prevention as ways of living. In J. Heckhausen & C. S. Dweck (Eds.), *Motivation and self-regulation across the life span* (pp. 78–113). Cambridge: Cambridge University Press.

Hill, P. C., & Pargament, K. I. (2003). Advances in the conceptualization and measurement of religion and spirituality: Implications for physical and mental health research. *American Psychologist, 58*(1), 64–74.

Hoffman, B. (1993). *Holy terror: The implications of terrorism motivated by a religious imperative* (RAND Research Paper P-7834). Santa Monica, CA: RAND.

Huntington, S. P. (2003). *The clash of civilizations and the remaking of the world.* New York: Simon & Schuster.

Hunsberger, B., & Jackson, L. M. (this issue). Religion, meaning, and prejudice. *Journal of Social Issues.*

Jacobson, B. (June 30, 1999). Religion trumps porn in web popularity. Retrieved April 4, 2004, from http://www.cnn.com/TECH/computing/9906/30/religion.idg/index.html.

James, W. (1982/1902). *The varieties of religious experience.* New York: Penguin Books.

Janoff-Bulman, R. (1992). *Shattered assumptions. Toward a new psychology of trauma.* New York: Free Press.

Jannof-Bulman, R., & Frieze, I. H. (Eds.). (1983). Reactions to victimization. *Journal of Social Issues, 39*(2).

Johnson, P. E. (1959). *Psychology of religion.* Nashville: Abingdon Press.

Johnston, D., & Sampson, C. (Eds.). (1994). *Religion, the missing dimension in state craft.* New York: Oxford University Press.

Juergensmeyer, M. (2003). *Terror in the mind of God: The global rise of religious violence.* Berkeley: University of California Press.

Kearney, M. (1984). *World view.* Novato, CA: Chandler & Sharp.

Kelley, G. A. (1955). *The psychology of personal constructs.* New York: Norton.

Kelman, H. C. (1999). The interdependence of Israel and Palestinian national identities: The role of the Other in existential conflicts. *Journal of Social Issues, 55*, 581–600.

Kimball, C. (2002). *When religion becomes evil.* San Francisco: Harper Collins Publishers.

Koenig, H. G., McCullough, M. E., & Larson, D. B. (2000). *Handbook of religion and health.* New York: Oxford University Press.

Kuhn, T. S. (1962). *The structure of scientific revolutions.* Chicago: University of Chicago Press.

Kushner, H. S. (1989). *When bad things happen to good people.* New York: Avon Books.

Lazarus, R. S., & Folkman, S. (1984). *Stress, appraisal, and coping.* New York: Springer Publishing.

Lerner, M. J. (1980). *The belief in a just world: A fundamental delusion.* New York: Plenum Press.

Lewis, B. (2003). *The crisis of Islam: Holy war and unholy terror.* New York: The Modern Library.

Lustick, I. S. (1993). *Unsettled states, disputed lands, Britain and Ireland, France and Algeria, Israel and the West Bank-Gaza.* Ithaca, NY: Cornell University Press.

Mahoney, A. (this issue). Religion and conflict in marital and parent-child relationships. *Journal of Social Issues.*

Manchin, R. (2004). Trust in religious institutions varies across EU map. Retrieved September 26, 2004, from http://www.gallup.com/poll/content/print.aspx?ci=12796.

Markus, H. R., & Kitayama, S. (1991). Culture and the self: Implications for cognition, emotion, and motivation. *Psychological Review, 98*(2), 224–253.

Martin, J. P. (this issue). The three Monotheistic world religions and international human rights. *Journal of Social Issues.*

Marty, M. E., & Appleby, R. S. (Eds.). (1991–1995). *The fundamentalism project.* Chicago: University of Chicago Press.

Maton, K. I., Dodgen, D., Sto. Domingo, M. R., & Larson, D. B. (this issue). Religion as a meaning system: Policy implications for the new millennium. *Journal of Social Issues.*

Mayer, A. E. (1993). The fundamentalist impact on law, politics, and constitutions in Iran, Pakistan, and the Sudan. In M. E. Marty & R. S. Appleby (Eds.), *Fundamentalsims and the state* (pp. 110–151). Chicago: University of Chicago Press.

McIntosh, D. N. (1995). Religion as a schema, with implications for the relation between religion and coping. *International Journal for the Psychology of Religion, 5,* 1–16.

Miller, W. R., & Thoresen, C. E. (2003). Spirituality, religion and health: An emerging research field. *American Psychologists, 58*(1), 24–35.

Moghaddam, F. M., & Marsella, A. J. (Eds.). (2004). *Understanding terrorism: Psychological roots, consequences, and interventions* (pp. 151–168). Washington, DC: American Psychological Association.

Moscovici, S. (1988). Notes toward a description of social representations. *European Journal of Social Psychology, 18,* 211–250.

Myers, D. G. (2000). The funds, friends, and faith of happy people. *American Psychologist, 55*(1), 56–67.

Norenzayan, A., & Nisbett, R. E. (2000). Culture and causal cognition. *Current Directions in Psychological Science, 9*(4), 132–135.

Oman, D., & Thoresen, C. E. (2003). Spiritual modeling: A key to spiritual and religious growth? *The International Journal for the Psychology of Religion, 13*(3), 149–165.

Otto, R. (1928). *The idea of the holy: An inquiry into the non-rational factor in the idea of the divine and its relation to the rational.* London: Oxford University Press.

Oz-Zaltzburg, P. (2000). Gan melavlev b'gai Haharega. *Panim, 12,* 3–8. (In Hebrew).

Paloutzian, R. F., & Kirkpatrick, L. A. (Eds.). (1995). Religious influences on personal and societal well-being. *Journal of Social Issues, 51*(2).

Pargament, K. I. (1997). *The psychology of religion and coping.* New York: The Guilford Press.

Pargament, K. I. (2002). The bitter and the sweet: An evaluation of the costs and benefits of religiousness. *Psychological Inquiry, 13*(3), 168–181.

Pargament, K. I., Magyar, G. M., & Murray-Swank, N. (this issue). The Sacred and the search for significance: Religion as a unique process. *Journal of Social Issues.*

Park, C. L. (this issue). Religion as a meaning-making framework in coping with life stress. *Journal of Social Issues.*

Park, C. L., & Folkman, S. (1997). Meaning in the context of stress and coping. *Review of General Psychology, 1*(2), 115–144.

Pervin, L. A. (Ed.). (1989). *Goal concepts in personality and social psychology.* Hillsdale, NJ: Erlbaum.

Proudfoot, W., & Shaver, P. R. (1975). Attribution theory and the psychology of religion. *Journal for the Scientific Study of Religion, 14,* 317–330.

Roccas, S. (this issue). Religion and value systems. *Journal of Social Issues.*

Ross, J. I. (1997). The relevance of culture for the study of political psychology and ethnic conflict. *Political Psychology, 18,* 299–326.

Scheier, M. F., & Carver, S. C. (1985). Optimism, coping, and health: Assessment and implications of generalized outcome expectancies. *Health Psychology, 4*(3), 219–247.

Schwartz, S. H., & Bilski, W. (1990). Toward a theory of the universal content and structure of values: Extensions and cross-cultural replications. *Journal of Personality and Social Psychology, 58,* 878–891.

Schwartz, S. H., & Huismars, S. (1995). Value priorities and religiosity in four Western religions. *Social Psychology Quarterly, 58,* 88–107.

Seligman, M. E. P., & Csikszentmihalyi, M. (2000). Positive psychology: An introduction. *American Psychologist, 55*(1), 5–14.

Sethi, S., & Seligman, M. E. P. (1993). Optimism and fundamentalism. *Psychological Science, 4*(4), 256–259.

Sheldon, K. M., & Kasser, T. (1995). Coherence and congruence: Two aspects of personality integration. *Journal of Personality and Social Psychology, 68*, 531–543.

Silberman, I. (1999). *Religiosity as a call for world change: Contradiction in terms or Messianism?* Unpublished Dissertation. Columbia University.

Silberman, I. (2003). Spiritual role modeling: The teaching of meaning systems. *The International Journal for the Psychology of Religion, 13*(3), 175–195.

Silberman, I. (2004). Religion as a meaning system: Implications for pastoral care and guidance. In D. Herl & M. L. Berman (Eds.), *Building bridges over troubled waters: Enhancing pastoral care and guidance*. Lima, Ohio: Wyndham Hall Press.

Silberman, I. (2005a). Religion as a meaning-system: Implications for individual and societal well-being. *Psychology of Religion Newsletter: American Psychological Association Division 36, 30*(2), 1–9.

Silberman, I. (2005b). Religious violence, terrorism and peace: A meaning system analysis. In R. F. Paloutzian & C. L. Park (Eds.), *Handbook of the psychology of religion and spirituality* (pp. 524–549). New York: The Guilford Press.

Silberman, I., Higgins, E. T., & Dweck, C. S. (this issue). Religion and world change: Violence and terrorism versus peace. *Journal of Social Issues*.

Silberman, I., Higgins, E. T., & Dweck, C. S. (2001). *Religion and well-being: World beliefs as mediators*. Paper presented at the 109th Annual Convention of the American Psychological Association. San Francisco, CA.

Smart, N. (1989). *The world's religions*. Cambridge: Cambridge University Press.

Snyder, C. R., & Lopez, S. J. (Eds.). (2002). *Handbook of positive psychology*. Oxford, UK: Oxford University Press.

Spilka, B., Shaver, P. R., & Kirkpatrick, L. A. (1985). A general attribution theory for the psychology of religion. *Journal for the Scientific Study of Religion, 24*, 1–20.

Stark, R. (1965). A taxonomy of religious experience. *Journal for the Scientific Study of Religion, 5*, 97–116.

Stark, R. (1999). Secularization, R. I. P. *Sociology of Religion, 60*(3), 249–273.

Stark, R., & Bainbridge, W. (1985). *The future of religion: Secularization, revival and cult formation*. Berkley: University of California Press.

Staub, E. (1989). *The roots of evil: The origins of genocide and other group violence*. Cambridge, England: Cambridge University Press.

Staub, E. (2004). Understanding and responding to group violence: Genocide, mass killing and terrorism. In F. M. Moghaddam & A. J. Marsella (Eds.), *Understanding terrorism: Psychological roots, consequences, and interventions* (pp. 151–168). Washington, DC: American Psychological Association.

Stern, J. (2003). *Terror in the name of God: Why religious militants kill*. New York: HarperCollins Publishers.

The Dalai Lama. (1999). *Ethics for the new millennium*. New York: Riverhead Books—A member of Penguin Putnam Inc.

Thompson, L., & Fine, G. A. (1999). Socially shared cognition, affect, and behavior: A review and integration. *Personality and Social Psychology Review, 3*, 278–302.

Thurman, R. (1998). *Inner revolution: Life, liberty, and the pursuit of real happiness*. New York: Riverhead Books (A member of Penguin Putnam Inc).

Tillich, P. (1957). *Dynamics of faith*. New York: Harper and Row.

Triandis, H. C. (1989). The self and social behavior in differing cultural contexts. *Psychological Review, 96*, 506–520.

Tsang, J., McCullough, M. E., & Hoyt, W. T. (this issue). Psychometric and rationalization accounts of the religion-forgiveness discrepancy. *Journal of Social Issues*.

Ventis, W. L. (1995). The relationships between religion and mental health. *Journal of Social Issues, 51*(2), 33–48.

Volkan, V. D. (1990). An overview of psychological concepts pertinent to interethnic and/or international relationships. In V. D. Volkan, D. A. Julius, & J. V. Montville (Eds.), *The psychodynamics of international relationships* (pp. 31–46). Lexington, MA: Lexington Books.

Volkan, V. (1997). *Bloodlines: From ethnic pride to ethnic terrorism.* New York: Farrar, Strauss & Giroux.
Weiss, O. (1997). In the eye of the beholder: A social-cognitive model of religious belief. In B. Spilka & D. N. McIntosh (Eds.), *Psychology of religion: Theoretical approaches* (pp. 194–203). Colorado: Westview Press, A Division of HarperCollins Publishers, Inc.
Whitney, H., & Rosenbaum, R. (2002). *Faith and doubt at Ground Zero.* Retrieved December 9, 2003, from http://www.pbs.org/wgbh.pages/frontline/shows/faith/etc/script.html.
Woodward, K. L. (2004, May 28). A political sacrament. *The New York Times*, p. A21.
Wuthnow, R. (2003). Is there a place for 'scientific' studies of religion? *The Chronicle of Higher Education, 49*(20), B10–B11.
Wuthnow, R. (2004). Presidential Address 2003: The challenge of diversity. *Journal for the Scientific Study of Religion, 43*(2), 159–170.

ISRAELA SILBERMAN received her BA from the Hebrew University of Jerusalem in psychology and philosophy and her PhD (with distinction) in social-personality psychology in 1999 from Columbia University. She is currently Associate Research Scientist at the Psychology Department of Columbia University. Dr. Silberman has written extensively on the relations between religion and individual and societal well-being, in general, and on the role of religion in recent world events, in particular. Her theoretical and applied research illuminates the importance of religion as a powerful system of meaning that can affect the lives of individuals in terms of their beliefs, motivations, emotions, and behaviors, and can influence their interactions on both interpersonal and intergroup levels. Dr. Silberman received the Richard Christie Award for Research on Social Issues (1996), awards from the Memorial Foundation for Jewish Culture (1999, 2000) to support her research on the psychological worlds of American Jewry, a teaching grant from the Columbia University Center for the Study of Science and Religion (2002) for her seminar on the psychology of religion, and the Margaret Gorman Early Career Award (2004) from the American Psychological Association (Div. 36) for her research on the psychology of religion.

Journal of Social Issues, Vol. 61, No. 4, 2005, pp. 665–687

The Sacred and the Search for Significance: Religion as a Unique Process

Kenneth I. Pargament*
Bowling Green State University

Gina M. Magyar-Russell
Johns Hopkins University School of Medicine

Nichole A. Murray-Swank
Loyola College in Maryland

Although many social scientists have assumed that religion can be reduced to more basic processes, there may be something unique about religion. By definition, religion has a distinctively meaningful point of reference, the sacred. Empirically, studies also suggest that religion may be a unique: form of motivation; source of value and significance; contributor to mortality and health; source of coping; and source of distress. These findings point to the need for: theory and research on the sacred; attention to the pluralization of religious beliefs and practices; evaluation of individual and social interventions that address spiritual problems and apply spiritual resources to their resolution; and collaboration between psychological and religious groups that draws on their unique identities and strengths.

"How unique is religion?" This is the question Dittes (1969) posed to begin his landmark 1969 review of the psychology of religion for the *Handbook of Social Psychology*. Dittes was not the first psychologist to raise this question. In 1933, one of the early figures in the psychology of religion, Leuba, asked: "Is there a religious instinct? Is there at least a specific religious purpose? Is there a religious emotion?" (pp. 17–19). Today, psychologists of religion continue to grapple with the question

---

*Correspondence concerning this article should be addressed to Kenneth I. Pargament, Department of Psychology, Bowling Green State University, Bowling Green, OH 43403 [e-mail: kpargam@bgnet.bgsu.edu].

We are grateful to the Fetzer Foundation, Retirement Research Foundation, and Templeton Foundation for their support of research cited in this article.*

665

of the uniqueness of religion. Why the fuss? The answer to the question has important theoretical and applied implications for the ways that psychologists study, understand, and approach religion.

On the one hand, many social scientists hold that there is nothing particularly unique about religion. Like other human phenomena, religion can be examined and ultimately understood through basic psychological methods and theory. Religion, from this perspective, is reducible to fundamental psychological, social, or physiological processes. For example, Leuba (1933) found nothing unique about religion when he turned his attention to mystical experience. Ultimately, he believed, mystical experience could be explained in purely physiological terms. Similarly, Freud (1927, 1961) argued that religious beliefs were examples of illusions, psychological mechanisms designed to allay deep-seated anxieties and satisfy child-like wishes. Durkheim (1915) saw religion as an expression of basic social needs. "The idea of society," he said, "is the soul of religion" (p. 433). Like other institutions, Durkheim believed, religion provides its members with a representation of society and unites its adherents within that worldview. Each of these theorists was able to integrate and explain religious phenomena within his general psychological or sociological framework. None saw the need for special concepts, theories, or methods tailored to religious life.

Others, however, have taken issue with reductionistic approaches to religion. For example, Richards and Bergin (1997) introduce their book on religion and psychotherapy by making clear their underlying belief: "We assume that spiritual is its own unique domain and cannot be subsumed by other domains such as cognitions, emotions, social systems, and so on" (p. 13). Alone among human concerns, the nonreductionists argue, religion has as its point of reference some concept of a higher power, be it God, ultimacy, transcendence, or Being. Johnson (1959) put it succinctly: "It is the ultimate Thou whom the religious person seeks most of all" (p. 70). This "ultimate Thou" cannot be reduced to purportedly more basic processes without distorting the character of religion and, indeed, life itself. "A world without God," Kushner (1989) wrote, "would be a flat, monochromatic world, a world without color or texture, a world in which all days would be the same" (p. 206). From this perspective, a psychology of religion that fails to take seriously "the idea of God" is crippled from the start. As a unique meaning-making phenomenon, the religious realm calls for special concepts, theories, and methods.

It is important to recognize that different responses to the question of the uniqueness of religion can, at times, reflect deeper ontological assumptions about the reality of religious experience. However, psychologists have little to contribute to debates about the existence of God or the reality of religious beliefs. We have no instruments capable of detecting the presence or absence of God. Neither can we test the ultimate truth of religious claims. However, we can consider the question of the uniqueness of religion on a different set of grounds, the empirical. For example, we can consider whether religious indices add something special to the prediction of important dimensions of personal and social functioning above and beyond the effects of general secular indices. We can examine whether psychological and social variables explain the links that have been observed between religiousness and other criteria, such as mortality, physical health, and mental health. We can determine whether people treat and respond to objects that hold sacred meaning differently from other objects in their lives. In short, a review of the empirical evidence can shed some important light on the question of the uniqueness of religion. In this article, initial empirical evidence will be presented to suggest that religion is, at least in some respects, a unique phenomenon. The implications of this conclusion will be considered for the ways psychologists study, understand, and work with religious processes. We begin with a definition of religion.

A Definition of Religion

Social scientists have tended to keep their distance from religion. Systematic reviews of the empirical literature indicate that religion is a relatively neglected topic (Larson, Pattison, Blazer, Omran, & Kaplan, 1986). When religion is studied, it is often measured by global indices, such as frequency of prayer, frequency of church attendance, or self-rated religiousness (see review by Hill & Hood, 1999). Like other objects, religion appears to be undifferentiated and uniform when viewed from afar. Those who have taken a closer look at religious experience, however, have reached different conclusions. Gordon Allport (1950) saw exceptional diversity and complexity in religiousness. "The subjective religious attitude of every individual," he wrote, "is in both its essential and nonessential features, unlike that of any other individual. The roots of religion are so numerous, the weight of their influence in individual lives so varied, and the forms of rational interpretation so endless, that uniformity of product is impossible" (p. 26). Recent research has also underscored the rich, multidimensional nature of religious experience (e.g., Batson, Schoenrade, & Ventis, 1993; Hood, Spilka, Hunsberger, & Gorsuch, 1996; Koenig, Pargament, & Nielsen, 1998; Paloutzian, 1996).

Complexity is apparent even in the meaning of the term religion. Scientists and the general public define religion in diverse ways (Clark, 1958; Pargament, Sullivan, Balzer, Van Haitsma, & Raymark, 1995). The multiplicity of these definitions may be an accurate reflection of the multifaceted nature of religious life. However, some definition is needed to organize and orient any discussion on this topic. Religion will be defined in this article as "a search for significance in ways related to the sacred" (Pargament, 1997, p. 32). There are three key terms in this definition: "significance," "search," and "sacred." It is assumed here that people seek whatever they hold to be of value or significance in life (Pargament, 1997). This definition of religion also rests on the assumption that people are proactive and goal-directed beings (see Ford, 1987), *searching* for significance. Searching is a dynamic process that involves discovering significance, conserving or holding on to significance once it has been found, and transforming significance when it becomes necessary (Pargament, 1997; Pargament & Mahoney, 2002). There are many kinds of searches and not all of them are religious. What makes religion distinctive is the involvement of the sacred in the search for significance. According to the *Oxford English Dictionary* (1989), the sacred refers to things that are holy, "set apart" from the ordinary, and worthy of veneration and respect. The sacred includes concepts of higher powers, such as the divine, God, and the transcendent, but, as Durkheim (1915) noted, "by sacred things one must not understand simply those personal beings which are called gods or spirits" (p. 52). The sacred also includes objects that are sanctified or take on a sacred status through their association with, or representation of the divine (Mahoney et al., 1999; Pargament, 1999). Theorists have noted that several classes of objects can be viewed or experienced as sacred (LaMothe, 1998; Paden, 1992; Pargament & Mahoney, 2002). These include: material objects (crucifix, drugs), time and space (the Sabbath, churches, mosques), events and transitions (birth, coming of age, death), cultural products (literature, music), people (saints, monks, cult leaders), psychological attributes (meaning, self-actualization), social attributes (caste, patriotism), and roles (marriage, parenting, work). Even seemingly secular objects (e.g., golf, war, sexual intercourse) can take on sacred value when they are linked to the divine.

Pargament (1997, 1999) has described the religious search for significance in terms of both the pathways that people take to reach their goals and the destinations or goals themselves. More specifically, he notes, the sacred can be a part of the pathways people follow in life and/or the destinations they seek. As defined here, religion encompasses a wide range of pathways and destinations: the charismatic Christian struggling with cancer who seeks a final healing through spiritual surrender; the abused woman who has never seen herself as religious yet suspects that God is punishing her for her transgressions; the Native American who experiences a sense of the sacred in the mountains, the woods, and the rivers; the Jew who finds no greater pleasure in life than studying Torah; the foster care parents of eight who see their work as a "higher calling"; the student of Zen who meditates on the koan "Who am I" for 2 years to gain enlightenment; the alcoholic in detox who experiences a profound spiritual conversion; the zealous believer who is convinced of the righteousness of like-minded individuals and the sinfulness of others. Thus, religion appears in many forms, traditional and nontraditional, functional and dysfunctional.

What is the common denominator underlying these myriad religious expressions? What distinguishes religious pathways and destinations from others? The sacred is the answer to this question, according to many theorists (Durkheim, 1915; Eliade, 1957; Paden, 1992; Pargament, 1997, 1999). They assert that, to the religiously minded, the sacred is not illusory. It is not a means to achieve psychological and social ends devoid of spiritual value. It is not merely one part of living. It is the core of life. Eliade (1957) is eloquent in his description: "The sacred is equivalent to a power and, in the last analysis, to reality. The sacred is saturated with being. Sacred power means reality and at the same time enduringness and efficacity" (p. 13). The religious individual, Eliade goes on to note, desires to participate in that reality, remaining as long as possible in a sacred universe.

Religion then is, by our definition, unique, for no other human process organizes itself around the sacred. Going beyond definitions, there is also a growing body of empirical literature that speaks to the question of the uniqueness of religion and suggests that there is indeed something special about religion and the meaning it provides. We turn now to that literature.

Religion as a Unique Form of Motivation and Dimension of Personality

One line of fruitful study on the uniqueness of religion comes from personality and motivational psychology. Perhaps the first psychologist who spoke of religion as a motive in and of itself was Gordon Allport. Allport's (1961) understanding of religious motivation grew out of his earlier work on motivational theory. He believed that motivations could become separate or "functionally autonomous" from their original association with basic drives and motives. With respect to the religious realm, although specific religious beliefs and practices could be initially motivated by the desire to gain approval from parents, to gain rewards, or to avoid self-punishment or stigma, religion could move beyond these initial roots and become a motive in and of itself.

Allport later coined the terms "intrinsic" and "extrinsic" to describe the two poles of individual religious motivation. An extrinsically motivated individual, he said, "uses his religion, whereas the intrinsically motivated lives his" (Allport & Ross, 1967, p. 434). Those individuals who use their religion do so in order to gain other interests such as security, comfort, sociability, or status. In contrast, Allport and Ross (1967) wrote: "Persons with [an intrinsic] orientation find their master motive in religion. Other needs, strong as they may be, are regarded as of less ultimate significance" (p. 434). Thus, Allport posited that religion is, for some individuals, an end in itself, a primary motivating force that cannot be reduced to other motives.

Empirical support for the distinctiveness of religious motivation comes from the work of Emmons (1999). Emmons examined the topic of spiritual motivation in the context of his research on personal strivings. He defined a personal striving as "what a person is characteristically trying to do" in his/her daily life (Emmons, 1986, p. 1059). Strivings are enduring and idiographic, and they lend coherence to the goals that people pursue. In his research, Emmons had participants generate lists of strivings. He found that spiritual strivings, or strivings of "ultimate concern," appeared regularly in people's lists of life goals. Spiritual strivings are those "pertaining to the transcendent realm of experience, most notably those making reference to God or some conception of the Divine [e.g., 'Discern and follow God's will for my life,' 'Be aware of the spiritual meaningfulness of my life' (Emmons, 1999, pp. 89–91)]." They are "centered on the search for the sacred" (p. 95). The proportion of spontaneously generated spiritual strivings ranged from 7% in a college student sample to 28% in two samples of community adults (Emmons, 1999; Emmons, Cheung, & Tehrani, 1998).

Like Allport, Emmons (1999) maintained that there is something unique about spiritual motivation. He acknowledged that religious and spiritual goals are similar to other types of goals in form. Like other goals, religious and spiritual strivings are internal mental representations of desired states for a person. In both content and function, however, spiritual goals differ from other types of strivings. Unlike other goals, the contents of spiritual strivings are uniquely tied to the sacred. Functionally, Emmons argued, spiritual strivings are unique in that they supersede all others; they are "literally at the end of the striving line." As such, these spiritual goals "should assume a level of primacy within a person's overall goal hierarchy" (Emmons, 1999, p. 96).

In support of this argument, Emmons et al. (1998) found that the correlations between measures of well-being and spiritual strivings were stronger than the correlations for other types of strivings. More specifically, an increased proportion of spiritual strivings was associated with higher satisfaction with life, lower depression, and increased marital satisfaction. In addition, these associations maintained their strength after controlling for intimacy strivings (strivings that expressed a desire for close, reciprocal relationships; e.g., "Help my friends and let them know I care"). Thus, spiritual strivings could not be explained by purportedly more basic desires for intimacy or closeness with others. Finally, spiritual strivings were uniquely associated with less conflict in a person's goal system (the degree to which each striving facilitates or impedes other strivings). Therefore, there was a greater degree of overall "goal integration," presumably one aspect of personality coherence. In summary, Emmons' research points to a unique role for spiritual motivation for personality and individual well-being.

Piedmont has also examined spirituality as a "motivational trait," one he described as an intrinsic, stable dimension of personality. Working with undergraduates, Piedmont (1999) constructed the Spiritual Transcendence Scale (STS) that assessed prayer fulfillment (e.g., "I have experienced deep fulfillment and bliss through my prayers or meditations"), universality (e.g., "I believe there is a larger meaning to life"), and connectedness (e.g., "It is important for me to give something back to my community"). Piedmont demonstrated that the STS uniquely predicted psychological outcomes (e.g., social support, interpersonal style, stress experience) above the effects of personality (the five-factor model of personality). In another study, Piedmont (2001) conducted joint factor analyses of the STS and the five factor personality qualities (i.e., neuroticism, extraversion, openness, agreeableness, and conscientiousness). The STS emerged as a factor independent from the five personality dimensions. Furthermore, the STS predicted unique variance in psychosocial functioning, including observer ratings of well-being, life satisfaction, pro-social behavior, purpose in life, and self-actualization. Across diverse samples, including cross-cultural samples, Piedmont's work also suggests that spiritual motivation may play a distinctive role in personality.

It should be noted that, whereas Allport considered religious motivation as a unidimensional construct, others have suggested that there may be a variety of religious and spiritual motivations. In a factor analytic study of college students, Gorlow and Schroeder (1968) identified seven distinct motivational types: Humble Servants, Self-Improvers, Family-Guidance Seekers, Moralists, God Seekers, Socially Oriented Servants, and Intellectuals. Welch and Barrish (1982) found that these seven motivations were related in distinctive ways to various aspects of religious commitment and behavior, such as church attendance, contributions made, organizational membership, and orthodox religious beliefs.

Religion as a Unique Source of Significance

A related line of research on sanctification also suggests that there is something uniquely meaningful about religion. As noted earlier, virtually any object can be perceived as sacred. Through the process of sanctification, various roles, attributes, and objects are imbued with sacred qualities or perceived as a manifestation of the divine (Pargament & Mahoney, 2002). Theorists assert that once an aspect of life is invested with sacred status, it becomes something very different from the profane. For example, Eliade (1957) wrote that sacred stones or trees are worshipped not because they are stones or trees, but "because they show something that is no longer stone or tree but the sacred" (p. 12). Pargament and Mahoney (2002) have gone on to hypothesize that people will treat sacred objects differently than those that are not perceived as sacred; that is, they are more likely to attempt to preserve and protect objects that have been sanctified. Furthermore, they are more likely to use these objects as sources of support, strength, satisfaction, and significance in their lives. A series of studies covering diverse areas of human functioning (e.g., strivings, parenting, marriage, nature, and sexual intercourse) provides some support for these hypotheses and the important role of sanctification as a meaning-making process (see Mahoney, Pargament, Murray-Swank, & Murray-Swank, 2003; Pargament & Mahoney, 2005).

As discussed previously, Emmons (1999) demonstrated that people strive for a variety of goals in their daily lives, including spiritual goals. Mahoney (2005) and her colleagues conducted a study that examined what happens when people sanctify or attribute spiritual significance to their personal strivings. Working with a representative sample of 150 adults, they found that those who attributed spiritual significance to their strivings reported greater importance of the striving, derived greater meaning from pursuit of the striving, endorsed stronger commitment to the striving, felt more supported by others, and derived more satisfaction from the pursuit of the sacred striving. Asked to indicate how they were spending their time and energy over five different days, the participants also indicated that they had devoted more time to pursuits that were more highly sanctified.

In a study on marriage, 97 couples from a Midwestern community completed measures of individual religiousness, joint religious activities, marital adjustment, marital conflict, and problem-solving strategies (Mahoney et al., 1999). In addition, they completed two scales designed to assess two ways that an object can become sanctified (nontheistically and theistically). The nontheistic measure assessed the degree to which the couples perceived their relationship as having qualities often associated with divine or transcendent phenomena (e.g., "Holy," "Blessed"). The theistic measure assessed the degree to which the couple perceived their marriage as a manifestation of their experience of God and their religious faith (e.g., "God is present in my marriage," "My marriage reflects my image of what God wants for me"). The results demonstrated that couples who viewed their marriage as sacred treated their relationships differently. They were less verbally aggressive and more collaborative in problem solving, reported more investment in their marriages, and derived more satisfaction from their marriages.

Tarakeshwar, Swank, Pargament, and Mahoney (2001) considered the implications of the sanctification of nature. In a large national, randomly selected sample of participants affiliated with the Presbyterian Church, U.S.A. (i.e., members, leaders, elders), they found that the sanctification of nature (e.g., "Nature is sacred because it was created by God," "Human beings should respect nature because it was created by God") was associated with greater pro-environmental beliefs, a greater willingness to invest in protecting the environment, and somewhat more environmentally friendly behaviors.

Researchers have found that sexual intercourse can also take on sacred qualities. In a sample of 150 college students, Murray-Swank, Pargament, and Mahoney (2005) found that when college students perceived sex as sacred, they engaged in it more frequently and derived more satisfaction from it.

This body of research is still in its early stage of development. It could be argued that perceiving objects as sacred is merely a case of caring for an object a great deal, viewing it as important, or seeing it positively. However, in unpublished analyses from the sanctification of marriage study, Mahoney et al. (1999) compared couples who viewed their marriages as sacred with couples who saw their marriages as very important but not sacred. In comparison to the "very important but not sacred" group, couples who perceived their marriages as sacred reported significantly greater marital satisfaction, more investment in their marriages, and better marital problem solving strategies. In addition, in the sanctification of sexual intercourse study, sanctification predicted unique variance in sexual functioning above and beyond the effects of positive and negative attitudes toward sex (Murray-Swank et al., 2005). These initial findings suggest that perceptions of objects as sacred are more than perceptions of importance. Nevertheless, further research should address the questions of whether sacred objects do indeed hold extraordinary significance in people's lives, and whether sanctification is indeed a special religious meaning-making process.

Religion as a Unique Contributor to Mortality and Health

A growing body of literature points to significant relationships between various aspects of religion and various aspects of health (see George, Ellison, & Larson, 2002; Koenig, McCullough, & Larson, 2001, for extensive reviews). A number of researchers have tried to identify mediating variables that may explain these relationships. Social support and health practices, in particular, have received considerable attention for their potential mediating role in the association between religion and health. Religion, it is asserted, may exert its effects on health indirectly by enhancing social support and health practices that are, in turn, directly related to better health. Thus far, these studies have not been able to fully account for the religion/health connection.

McCullough, Hoyt, Larson, Koenig, and Thoresen (2000) conducted a meta-analytic review of 42 independent effect sizes of the association between religious involvement and all-cause mortality. Most of these studies used frequency of attendance at services and/or self-rated religiousness as the measure of religious involvement. In general, highly religious individuals had 29% higher odds of survival than less religious individuals. Moreover, McCullough et al. (2000) examined whether potential mediating and confounding variables could explain the relationship between religiousness and mortality. They considered the effects of health status, health behaviors (e.g., smoking, alcohol, body mass), social support, and socio-demographic variables. Studies that controlled for these variables demonstrated a smaller, but still substantial, association between religious involvement and mortality.

For example, Hummer, Rogers, Nam, and Ellison (1999) collected survey data from a nationally representative sample of noninstitutionalized adults. They examined the association between attendance at services and mortality over a 9-year period (1987–1995). The results indicated that more frequent attendance was predictive of less risk of mortality, after controlling for a variety of social and psychological variables. Although health status, social ties, and health behaviors partially mediated the association, religion remained predictive of mortality after all controls. More specifically, after controlling for age, gender, race, education, income, physical activity, health status, health behaviors (e.g., weight, smoking, drinking), and social ties (e.g., marital status, friends, social activity), those who never attended services exhibited a 50% higher risk of mortality than those who attended most frequently. This relationship was generally consistent among all causes of mortality. As yet then, the relationship between religiousness and mortality cannot be fully explained by mediating factors such as health practices, social support, physical health status, or socio-demographic variables.

Other researchers have attempted to identify the factors that may mediate the connection between religiousness and measures of physical and mental health. George et al. (2002), reviewed an extensive body of research on the links between religious involvement and health. They found only mixed effects for the mediating effects of health practices, social support, psychosocial resources, and belief structures on health. They concluded, "It seems likely...that these four factors will prove to be insufficient to explain fully the pathways by which religious involvement promotes health and longevity" (p. 197). Along these lines, Koenig, McCullough, and Larson (2001) cite a 7-year longitudinal study of 8,866 randomly sampled, largely Christian Americans, conducted by Musick and Strulowitz. The results indicated that involvement in religious activities at baseline predicted fewer depressive symptoms at follow-up, after controlling for demographic variables, baseline levels of depressive symptoms, physical health, and social support.

Koenig, George, and Peterson (1998) examined the association between religious involvement and depression in a medically ill elderly sample. These researchers found that intrinsic religiosity was related to remission of depression, after controlling for the effects of covariates (e.g., quality of life, social support, medical diagnoses, change in functional status).

In summary, sophisticated research endeavors have begun to untangle the complexities of the relationship between religion and health. And what is the result? It appears that, empirically, religion cannot be easily boiled down to other processes. Although some of the associations between religiousness and health may be reduced to more basic social processes (e.g., social support), there appears to be something left, something unique about religion after other explanations have been examined. The most parsimonious explanation for the relationship between religion and health might be that religiousness is a significant dimension in and of itself. Yet, it is also possible that there are other potential mediators that have not yet been measured. It remains to be determined whether more accurate measurement of potential mediators of the religion and health connection may erase the association.

Religion as a Unique Form of Coping

Considerable research has been conducted on one form of religiousness in particular—religious coping. It could be argued that there is little special or distinctive about religious coping methods. Perhaps religious coping is simply a subset of general coping methods. For example, positive religious appraisal of situations could be explained in terms of the more basic propensity to see situations positively. Spiritual support could be understood in terms of the more basic concept of social support. There is some research that speaks to this issue.

First, it is important to note that religious coping can take a number of forms across different faith traditions, denominations, cultures, and situations. Religious coping methods include intercessory prayer in times of suffering, songs of worship and praise during special occasions (e.g., weddings, holy/feast days), religious forgiveness following transgressions, purification rituals after committing a sin, and rites of passage, such as the Bar/Bat Mitzvah in Jewish ritual and the Sacrament of Confirmation in Roman Catholic practice. Another example of religious coping is demonstrated in the doctrine of karma in the Hindu religion. "Karma embodies a causal explanation for events which defy human understanding and provides a method of gaining control over the future by focusing on present actions" (Pargament, Poloma, & Tarakeshwar, 2001, p. 268). These are just a few examples of the many ways religion can be involved in the search for significance in stressful situations across different religious traditions.

Do various forms of religious coping contribute uniquely to physical and mental health? Mickley, Pargament, Brant, and Hipp (1998) conducted a study in which both religious and nonreligious appraisals of caregivers were assessed. Broadly defined, appraisals refer to people's efforts to make meaning of their circumstances. Nonreligious appraisals included: (a) benevolent reframing of the situation; (b) blaming the doctors for the situation; (c) blaming loved ones; and (d) seeing the world as unfair. Examples of religious appraisals included redefining a stressor through religion as (a) a potentially beneficial and benevolent act from God, (b) a punishment from God, (c) the work of the Devil, and (d) demonstrating God's power, or lack of power (Pargament, Koenig, & Perez, 1998). In a sample of 92 hospice caregivers to terminally ill spouses, relatives, or friends, religious appraisals of the meaning of the situation made a significant and unique contribution to the prediction of all psychological variables assessed in the study. Specifically, after controlling for the effects of nonreligious reframing of the situation, appraisals of the situation as having benevolent religious meaning were significant predictors of: (1) greater satisfaction with how participants felt they handled the event, what they learned from the event, and the growth they experienced from the event; (2) stronger feelings of closeness to God and one's church, and perceptions of greater personal spiritual growth; (3) reduced anxiety and depression; and (4) greater meaning, or purpose in life. This study demonstrated that positive religious reframing of stressful and disconcerting situations can add a unique, significant, and beneficial dimension to coping.

In a study of family members waiting in the hospital for loved ones undergoing coronary artery bypass surgery, Pargament et al. (1999) found additional evidence that religious coping methods can uniquely predict outcomes beyond the effects of nonreligious coping and traditional measures of religiousness (church attendance, frequency of prayer, self-rated religiousness). Five control-oriented subscales (planning, suppression, instrumental social support, focus on and venting of emotion, and mental disengagement) were used from the COPE inventory

(Carver, Scheier, & Weintraub, 1989) to assess nonreligious coping. Four control-oriented religious coping methods were assessed: sharing control with God (collaborative), relinquishing control to God (deferring), exerting control with God (self-directing), and seeking control from God (pleading). These methods of religious coping accounted for unique amounts of variance in the prediction of coping outcomes, religious outcomes, and symptoms of anxiety and depression above and beyond the effects of nonreligious coping strategies and traditional measures of religiousness. Collaborative religious coping methods were especially linked to positive religious outcomes and greater coping efficacy.

A study by Tix and Frazier (1998) also points to the distinctiveness of religious coping. Working longitudinally with patients and significant others coping with the stress of kidney transplant surgery, the researchers considered whether the relationships between religious coping and adjustment at 3 and 12 months after transplantation could be explained by more general psychological variables, including cognitive restructuring, internal control, and social support. They found that religious coping was not only predictive of life satisfaction when entered into a regression equation alone, but continued to predict life satisfaction after measures of cognitive restructuring and internal control (for patients) and cognitive restructuring and social support (for significant others) were entered into the model. Thus, the effects of religious coping on adjustment to the kidney transplants could not be explained by nonreligious variables traditionally thought to mediate the relationship between religion and outcomes. Tix and Frazier (1998) concluded: "the results of [psychological] research suggest that religious coping adds a unique component to the prediction of adjustment to stressful life events that cannot be accounted for by other established predictors" (p. 420). Religious coping, it appears, cannot be easily reduced to a nonreligious form of coping. Methods of religious coping seem to contribute something special to the prediction of adjustment to critical life events.

What makes these methods of coping distinctive? The inclusion of the sacred in the coping process may hold the key. In the eyes of many individuals, religion may be more successful than secular systems in offering "a response to the problem of human insufficiency" (Pargament, 1997, p. 310). The language of religion—faith, hope, transcendence, surrender, forbearance, meaning—speaks to the limits of human powers. When life appears out of control, and there seems to be no rational explanation for events—beliefs and practices oriented to the sacred seem to have a special ability to provide ultimate meaning, order, and safety in place of human questions, chaos, and fear.

Religion as a Unique Source of Distress

While the results from such studies as those reviewed above have led many researchers and practitioners to view religion in a positive and constructive light (e.g., Koenig, McCullough, & Larson, 2002; Richards & Bergin, 1997), we believe that certain forms of religiousness may also be sources of problems or distress. In fact, religion may be uniquely tied to costs as well as benefits in living. What could make religion especially risky? Again, the answer may lie in the sacred; in the ultimate and definitive power and meaning associated with the Divine and related objects. For instance, perceived punishment or abandonment from God could imply an ultimate culpability, unacceptability, and unforgiveability of the individual. Similarly, viewing God as angry, vengeful, or powerless against evil could lead to fundamental fear, disillusionment, and distrust that shatters and reshapes one's view of God, people, and the world. Thus, negative forms of religiousness may be exceptionally distressful and problematic because they can be perceived as implying harsh truths about the human condition that are ultimate, immutable, and eternal.

Certain forms of religious coping may be especially problematic for people facing difficult life experiences (Pargament et al., 1998a). For instance, Koenig, Pargament, and Nielsen (1998) studied hospitalized elderly patients and found that those who made more use of negative religious coping strategies (see Table 1 for examples) were more likely to experience unfavorable physical and psychological outcomes, such as greater physical impairment in daily activities, lower cognitive functioning, more symptoms of depressed mood, and lower quality of life. These findings were stronger than those found between nonreligious coping behaviors and physical and psychological outcomes. While this study did not directly consider the unique effects of negative religious coping, it is one of several studies that point to the problems arising from negative religious coping in response to stressful life events (Exline, Yali, & Lobel, 1999; Pargament et al., 1998, Pargament, Smith, Koenig, & Perez, 1998b; Pargament, Koenig, Tarakeshwar, & Hahn, 2004).

Unique adverse effects have been found to result from negative religious coping. Working longitudinally over a 2 year period with a sample of 595 medical hospital inpatients age 55 and older, Pargament, Koenig, Tarakeshwar, and Hahn (2001) found that the use of negative religious coping methods, such as questioning God's love for the individual, perceiving God as punishing, appraising a situation as an act of the devil, and feeling abandoned by God, was significantly predictive of mortality. Even after controlling for possible confounding or mediating variables, including demographics, physical health, and mental health variables, negative religious coping was tied to a 22–33% greater risk of dying over a 2-year period.

Moving beyond religious coping, other forms of religious and spiritual expression may also have serious and distinctive implications for individual health and welfare. For instance, Trenholm, Trent, and Compton (1998) investigated the role of religious conflict in individuals with panic disorder. Working with a sample of 60 adult women divided into three groups (panic disorder without therapy, panic disorder in therapy, and therapy patients without panic disorder), Trenholm et al. (1998) found that religious conflict was a unique predictor of panic disorder, even after taking into account state anxiety, hypochondriacal beliefs and abnormal illness behavior, and irrational thinking. Specifically, people who felt more religious guilt and were more unable to meet religious expectations and cope with religious fears tended to suffer more from panic disorders. These findings offer insights into the etiology of panic disorder that go beyond conventional models (e.g., panic disorder results from the catastrophization of bodily sensations).

Although the sanctification of important life domains has been linked to well-being, there is a potential downside to imbuing objects and relationships with sacred meaning. At some point in life, people are likely to encounter the loss or violation of the sacred. Because sacred objects are likely to be appraised and treated differently than secular objects (Mahoney et al., 1999; Murray-Swank et al., 2005; Swank et al., 1999; Tarakeshwar et al., 2001), the loss or violation of these objects may have particularly potent and destructive implications for coping and well-being.

Consider the conflict between Israelis and Palestinians in the Middle East. Political, economic, and cultural factors, as well as psychological factors, such as trauma and suffering, certainly play key roles in this seemingly intractable conflict. Yet, an in-depth understanding of the Middle East conflict also requires an analysis of the role religion plays in it, in general, and particularly the role it plays in prescribing what is sacred and what should be considered as a violation of the sacred. As Gopin (2000) and Juergensmeyer (2000) note in their astute analyses of this conflict, the disagreements between Israelis and Palestinians are not simply about individuals, buildings, and ground. They are about people of God, sacred sites, and the holy land. The violence there is imbued with an especially powerful meaning; to both parties it signifies a violation of the sacred, one that holds terrible implications. Perceiving that sacred rights, space, and values have been desecrated, both groups feel compelled to retaliate. And ironically, both groups frame the bloodshed that follows as an effort to preserve and protect sacred things from further desecration.

Or consider the September 11th terrorist attacks on the World Trade Center and Pentagon. For both the terrorists who proclaimed a Jihad ("Holy War") and the Americans who were devastated by the attacks, the destruction took on a sacred meaning. The terrorists ascribed sacred meaning to their actions, justifying the violence as a fitting response to the behavior of a morally corrupt nation that had desecrated the soil of holy lands during the Gulf War. In one speech, Osama bin Laden, spoke of the September 11th attacks as "a sword that comes down on America" which has "abused the blood, honor, and sanctuaries of Muslims" (USA Today, 2001). The suicides and destruction of human life that followed were more than acts of vengeance; they were perceived as sacrificial acts that would be ultimately rewarded through the pleasures of the afterlife. Earlier, bin Laden (2001) said: "Those youths know that their rewards in fighting you, the United States, is double than their rewards in fighting some one else not from the people of the book. They have no intention except to enter paradise by killing you. An infidel, and enemy of God like you, cannot be in the same hell with his righteous executioner." By embedding their actions within the language of the sacred and desecration, the terrorists likely increased their level of commitment, morale, and willingness to accept their own personal destruction. In turn, many people in the United States perceived the events of September 11th as more than an attack; it was a violation of values imbued with sacred meaning—life, freedom, and American institutions (Mahoney et al., 2002). For example, 57% of a sample of college students in Ohio and New York City agreed that "This event was both an offense against me and against God" and 64% agreed that "The devil is at work in these people's actions." The perception of desecration led to heightened emotional responses and increased desire for retaliation and justice.

Unfortunately, there is relatively little research on the topic of desecration (see Tetlock, Kristel, Elson, Green, & Lerner, 2000). In one of the few exceptions, Magyar, Pargament, and Mahoney (2000) found that perceptions of sacred violation or desecration uniquely predicted negative health-related outcomes. Working with a sample of college men and women from a mid-sized Midwestern university, Magyar et al. (2000) examined the physical, psychological, and spiritual implications of perceiving that a current or former romantic relationship had been desecrated. Desecration was measured by two scales constructed for this study: a 10-item theistic (God-centered) desecration scale (e.g., something made sacred by God was dishonored), and a 10-item nontheistic desecration scale comprised of a list of descriptive qualities often associated with the divine (e.g., evil, immoral, spiritual violation). Desecration was not an uncommon experience for college students. Over 88% of the sample reported what they perceived as a desecration in a romantic relationship. Desecration had unique adverse effects. Specifically, desecration was associated with more negative affect (e.g., feeling distressed, nervous, scared, irritable, upset), more negative physical health symptoms (e.g., nausea or upset stomach, headaches, loss of appetite), and more symptoms of intrusive and avoidant thoughts and behaviors related to the desecration event(s). Furthermore, the links between desecration and these outcomes were not reduced by controlling for traditional religious variables, the number of offenses committed in the desecration, and the negativity of the impact of the betrayals. These findings were largely replicated in a study of perceptions of desecration and sacred loss within a community sample (Pargament, Magyar, Benore, & Mahoney, 2005). The findings suggest that violations of the sacred have particularly powerful implications for human functioning.

In short, not only do religious sources of meaning have distinctive benefits, the studies reviewed in this section suggest they also have unique costs that cannot be accounted for by other variables, such as negativity or nonreligious forms of coping. Whether positive or negative, experiences tied to the sacred seem to have an exceptionally powerful impact.

Conclusions and Implications

How do we understand religion? Many social scientists have tried to explain religion by reducing it to presumably more basic psychological, social, or physiological processes (see Pargament, 2002). This article has offered a different possibility, that there is something unique about religion in and of itself. Definitionally, we have suggested, religion has a distinctive point of reference, the sacred. The sacred is, as Paden (1992) put it, "the overarching common denominator of all religious life" (p. 71). However, this article has also gone beyond definition and description of religion to examine the question of the uniqueness of religion on empirical grounds. A number of studies suggest that religion may be: (a) a unique form of motivation; (b) a unique source of significance; (c) a unique contributor to mortality and health; (d) a unique form of coping; and (e) a unique source of distress. Admittedly, this area of research is new and still developing. Our review here has been illustrative rather than exhaustive. Better measurement of potential mediators of the links between religion, health, and well-being, and evaluations of novel mediators beyond those currently of interest to researchers may yield different results. On the other hand, they may confirm the conclusion that seems to be emerging from these initial studies: Religion may be a unique aspect of human functioning, one that cannot simply be reduced to or explained away by presumably more basic psychological, social, or physical processes. We conclude by speculating on the implications of this conclusion for theory, research, and practice.

Building Theory

As a unique meaning-making phenomenon, religion deserves special theoretical attention. Conceptual questions about the sacred are particularly important, once they are divorced from efforts to explain the sacred in purely nonreligious terms. Of course, some questions fall outside the purview of psychology. We cannot speak to the ultimate nature or reality of the sacred. Other questions, however, are approachable. How does an individual's concept and experience of the sacred develop and change over the lifespan? What roles does the sacred play in individual, family, community, and cultural life? What accounts for the involvement of the sacred in the full range of behavior, from the noblest to the most nefarious? These are daunting questions. Fortunately, however, there is a rich and relevant body of work by scholars in many disciplines (e.g., history, religious studies, economics, anthropology, medicine, sociology) who treat religion as a distinctive meaning structure (Eliade, 1957; Paden, 1992). Psychologists would do well to draw on this deep body of knowledge as they develop their own theories of the sacred and its roles in human functioning.

Stimulating Research

Studying the sacred poses special challenges for researchers. How do we approach a phenomenon defined by its relationships to the divine? Once again, some questions cannot be answered through scientific methods. Though we have no tools to measure, confirm, or disconfirm the ultimate reality of the sacred, there are a number of ways the meaning associated with the sacred can be studied. We can measure what people perceive to be sacred and the paths that lead to these perceptions. We can study experiences, rituals, relationships, and thoughts associated with the sacred, and we can examine their implications for behavior, personally, socially, and culturally. Furthermore, we can study the sacred as a criterion of human functioning that is significant in its own right.

Especially important will be studies that explore the process through which religious dimensions connect to outcomes of health and well-being. It is possible that more finely differentiated, functionally relevant religious constructs account for the religion-health connection better than secular psychological or social constructs. In this vein, Ellison, Musick, Levin, Taylor, and Chatters (1997) found that the relationship between church attendance and psychological distress was mediated by support from church members rather than by general social support. Sethi and Seligman (1993) found that the link between fundamentalism and greater optimism was fully mediated by higher levels of religious influence in daily life, religious involvement, and religious hope. Working with a sample of Jewish students, Silberman, Higgins, and Dweck (2001) reported that religiousness was associated with optimism, happiness, serenity, and decisiveness; moreover, these associations were partially or (in the case of optimism) fully mediated by three traditional Jewish beliefs: the world is good, the individual can change and improve the world, and the individual can improve himself/herself. Similarly, in the study of desecration by Magyar et al. (2000) cited earlier, the relationship between desecration and several outcomes could be partially explained by both positive and negative forms of religious coping. Negative religious coping mediated the links between desecration and adverse physical health symptoms and negative affect. Positive religious coping mediated the links between desecration and spiritual growth, posttraumatic growth, and positive affect. George, Larson, Koenig, and McCullough (2000) also suggested that "the transcendent sense of being in direct touch with the sacred" may intervene between religion and health (p. 112). Of course, religion may exert its effects on health and well-being through multiple paths, religious and nonreligious. Ultimately, the relationships between religion, health, and well-being may be best explained by a combination of both finely delineated religious and psychosocial mediators (see Murphy et al., 2000).

Respecting Religious Pluralization

In the past 50 years, religious denominations and spiritual groups have proliferated. For example, the United States has been strongly affected by the infusion of Eastern religious practices that focus on the mind-body connection, such as meditation and yoga. Furthermore, as Bibby (1987) has noted, more and more people are constructing individualized religions, picking and choosing from various offerings of established religious traditions to create their own "religions a la carte." Pluralization rather than secularization is the trend that has been taking place in western cultures (Hoge, 1996; Roof & McKinney, 1987). This trend toward diversity in religiousness and spirituality is likely to continue. And we may find that what makes religion distinctive varies from culture to culture. To avoid the dangers of religious ethnocentrism, psychologists need to venture outside their own familiar religious landscapes, entering and exploring new religious worlds. Tolerance for ambiguity, appreciation for puzzles and paradox, and openness to surprises will be prerequisites to work in this area.

Promoting Change

When pushed to the edge of their resources, people may find that religion offers unique ways of finding meaning in and dealing with critical situations. Psychologists may be able to draw on these distinctive resources in their efforts to help people. In the context of psychotherapy, we have found that simply asking people about what they hold sacred provides important insights into their objects of greatest significance. There is some initial evidence that forms of psychotherapy that integrate a spiritual dimension are particularly valuable for at least some groups. For example, in a meta-analysis of 92 studies of the effects of four relaxation and meditation techniques on anxiety, Eppley, Adams, and Shear (1989) found that transcendental meditation, a spiritually based meditation practice, was associated with significantly greater effect sizes than progressive relaxation, others forms of relaxation (e.g., autogenic training), and other forms of meditation.

An appreciation for the sacred may also play a key role in resolving other difficult problems. For example, seemingly intractable marital conflicts may stem from perceptions that a sacred vow has been violated (see Mahoney, this issue). By addressing the underlying spiritual nature of these conflicts and by applying spiritual resources to their resolution, these problems may be more amenable to change. Similarly, at the socio-political level, conflicts between countries or religious groups may rest on fundamentally different views of the sacred as well as failures to respect the views of each other. Long-lasting solutions to these problems are unlikely until the spiritual character of the problems is acknowledged and spiritual resources (e.g., religious leaders, rituals, narratives) from the relevant traditions are brought to bear.

Creating Partnerships with Religious Communities

Social scientists and health professionals should appreciate the unique roles and identities of religious leaders and their communities. Pastors are not quasi-mental health professionals and churches, synagogues, and mosques are not quasi-social service agencies (Rappaport, 1981). Certainly they serve some of these functions, but only because efforts to help others are conceptualized as central to their sacred mission. Collaboration between psychological and religious communities is possible only if both partners recognize their own and each others' unique resources and limitations and only if both partners are willing to share these resources and limitations in efforts to promote their goals (Tyler, Pargament, & Gatz, 1983). Promising starts have been made in this direction (see Kloos & Moore, 2000; Pargament & Maton, 2000), but these are only starts. There are many exciting opportunities for psychologists and religious groups to work together, drawing on their unique identities, worldviews, roles, resources, and languages for the benefit of larger communities.

Of course, questions about the uniqueness of religion could be seen as moot. Many people, particularly those in the academic community, believe that the United States is becoming increasingly secularized. The data, however, do not bear this thesis out (Hoge, 1996). Levels of religious involvement remain high and stable. This should not be too surprising. We continue to struggle with modern-day forms of age-old questions that give rise to the search for religious answers: Why are we here? How do we make meaning out of human suffering? Are there forces that transcend our limited human experience? How should we live our lives? Advances in technology are unlikely to offer answers to these questions; rather, they may generate new questions of their own. Thus, the puzzles will remain, continuing to trigger and sustain that most distinctive of human processes, the search for significance in ways related to the sacred.

References

Allport, G. W. (1950). *The individual and his religion: A psychological interpretation.* New York: MacMillan Publishing Company.

Allport, G. W. (1961). *Pattern and growth in personality.* New York: Holt, Rinhart, and Winston.

Allport, G. W., & Ross, J. M. (1967). Personal religious orientation and prejudice. *Journal of Personality and Social Psychology, 5,* 432–443.

Batson, C. D., Schoenrade, P., & Ventis, W. L. (1993). *Religion and the individual: A social-psychological perspective.* New York: Oxford University Press.

Bibby, R. (1987). *Fragmented gods: The poverty and potential of religion in Canada.* Toronto: Irwin.

bin Laden, O. (2001). *Jihad against Jews and Crusaders.* Washington, DC: Washington Post Company.

Carver, C. S., Scheier, M. F., & Weintraub, J. K. (1989). Assessing coping strategies: A theoretically based approach. *Journal of Personality and Social Psychology, 56,* 267–283.

Clark, W. H. (1958). How do social scientists define religion? *Journal of Social Psychology, 47,* 143–147.

Dittes, J. E. (1969). Psychology of religion. In G. Lindzey & E. Aronson (Eds.), *Handbook of social psychology* (2nd ed., Vol. *V*, pp. 602–659). Reading, MA: Addison-Wesley.

Durkheim, E. (1915). *The elementary forms of the religious life*. New York: Free Press.

Eliade, M. (1957). *The sacred and the profane: The nature of religion*. New York: Harvest Books.

Ellison, C. G., Musick, M., Levin, J., Taylor, R., & Chatters, L. (1997). *The effects of religious attendance, guidance, and support on psychological distress: Longitudinal findings from the National Survey of Black Americans*. Paper presented at the annual meeting of the Society for the Scientific Study of Religion, San Diego.

Emmons, R. A. (1986). Personal strivings: An approach to personality and subjective well-being. *Journal of Personality and Social Psychology, 51*, 1058–1068.

Emmons, R. A. (1999). *The psychology of ultimate concerns: Motivation and spirituality in personality*. New York: The Guilford Press.

Emmons, R. A., Cheung, C., & Therani, K. (1998). Assessing spirituality through personal goals: Implications for research on religion and subjective well-being. *Social Indicators Research, 45*, 391–442.

Eppley, K. R., Abrams, A. I., & Shear, J. (1989). Differential effects of relaxation techniques on trait anxiety: A meta-analysis. *Journal of Clinical Psychology, 45*, 957–974.

Exline, J. J., Yali, A. M., & Lobel, M. (1999). When God disappoints: Difficulty forgiving God and its role in negative emotion. *Journal of Health Psychology, 4*, 364–379.

Ford, D. H. (1987). *Humans as self-constructing living systems: A developmental perspective on behavior and personality*. Hillsdale, NJ: Erlbaum.

Freud, S. (1927/1961). *The future of an illusion*. New York: Norton.

George, L. K., Ellison, C. G., & Larson, D. B. (2002). Exploring the relationship between religious involvement and health. *Psychological Inquiry, 13*, 190–200.

George, L. K., Larson, D. B., Koenig, H. G., & McCullough, M. E. (2000). Spirituality and health: What we know, what we need to know. *Journal of Social and Clinical Psychology, 19*, 102–116.

Gopin, M. (2000). *Between Eden and Armageddon: The future of world religions, violence, and peacemaking*. New York: Oxford.

Gorlow, L., & Schroeder, H. E. (1968). Motives for participating in the religious experience. *Journal for the Scientific Study of Religion, 7*, 241–251.

Hill, P. C., & Hood, R. W., Jr. (Eds.). (1999). *Measures of religiosity*. Birmingham, AL: Religious Education Press.

Hoge, D. R. (1996). Religion in America: The demographics of belief and affiliation. In E. P. Shafranske (Ed.), *Religion and the clinical practice of psychology* (pp. 21–41). Washington, DC: APA Press.

Hood, R. W., Jr., Spilka, B., Hunsberger, B., & Gorsuch, R. (1996). *The psychology of religion: An empirical approach* (2nd ed.). New York: Guilford Press.

Hummer, R. A., Rogers, R. G., Nam, C. B., & Ellison, C. G. (1999). Religious involvement and U.S. adult mortality. *Demography, 36*, 273–285.

Johnson, P. E. (1959). *Psychology of religion*. Nashville, TN: Abingdon Press.

Juergensmeyer, M. (2000). *Terror in the mind of God: The global rise of religious violence*. Berkeley: University of California Press.

Kloos, B., & Moore, T. (2000). The prospect and purpose of locating community research and action in religious settings. *Journal of Community Psychology, 28*, 119–138.

Koenig, H. G. (1998). *Handbook of religion and mental health*. San Diego, CA: Academic Press.

Koenig, H. G., George, L. K., & Peterson, B. L. (1998). Religiosity and remission from depression in medically ill older patients. *American Journal of Psychiatry, 155*, 536–542.

Koenig, H. G., McCullough, M. E., & Larson, D. B. (2001). *Handbook of religion and health*. New York: Oxford University Press.

Koenig, H. G., Pargament, K. I., & Nielsen, J. (1998). Religious coping and health status in medically ill hospitalized older adults. *Journal of Nervous and Mental Disease, 186*, 513–521.

Kushner, H. S. (1989). *Who needs God?* New York: Summit Books.

LaMothe, R. (1998). Sacred objects as vital objects: Transitional objects reconsidered. *Journal of Psychology and Theology, 26*, 159–167.

Larson, D. B., Pattison, E. M., Blazer, D. G., Omran, A. R., & Kaplan, B. H. (1986). Systematic analysis of research on religious variables in four major psychiatric journals, 1978-1982. *American Journal of Psychiatry, 143*, 329–334.

Leuba, J. H. (1933). *God or man? A study of the value of God to man.* New York: Henry Holt and Company.

Magyar, G. M., Pargament, K. I., & Mahoney, A. (2000, August). *Violating the sacred: A study of desecration among college students.* Paper presented at the annual meeting of the American Psychological Association, Washington, DC.

Mahoney, A. (this issue). Religion and conflict in marital and parent-child relationships. *Journal of Social Issues..*

Mahoney, A., Pargament, K. I., Ano, G., Lynn, Q., Magyar, G. M., McCarthy, S., Pristas, E., Wachholtz, A., & Procidano, M. (2002, August). *The devil made them do it: Desecration and demonization and the 9/11 attacks.* Paper presented at the annual conference of the American Psychological Association, Washington, DC.

Mahoney, A., Pargament, K. I., Murray-Swank, A., & Murray-Swank, N. (2003). Religion and the sanctification of family relationships. *Review of Religious Research, 44*, 220–236.

Mahoney, A., Pargament, K. I., Cole, B., Jewell, T., Magyar, G. M., Tarakeshwar, N., Murray-Swank, N. A., & Phillips, R. (2005). A higher purpose: The sanctification of strivings in a community sample. *The International Journal for the Psychology of Religion, 15*, 239–262.

Mahoney, A., Pargament, K. I., Jewell, T., Swank, A., Scott, E., Emery, E., & Rye, M. (1999). Marriage and the spiritual realm: The role of proximal and distal religious constructs in marital functioning. *Journal of Family Psychology, 13*, 321–338.

McCullough, M. E., Hoyt, W. T., Larson, D. B., Koenig, H. G., & Thoresen, C. (2000). Religious involvement and mortality: A meta-analytic review. *Health Psychology, 19*, 211–222.

Mickley, J. R., Pargament, K. I., Brant, C. R., & Hipp, K. M. (1998). God and the search for meaning among hospice caregivers. *The Hospice Journal, 13*, 1–17.

Murphy, P. E., Ciarrocchi, J. W., Piedmont, R. W., Cheston, S., Peyrot, M., & Fitchett, G. (2000). The relation of religious belief and practices, depression, and hopelessness in persons with clinical depression. *Journal of Consulting and Clinical Psychology, 68*, 1102–1106.

Murray-Swank, N. A., Pargament, K. I., & Mahoney, A. (2005). At the crossroads of sexuality and spirituality: The sanctification of sex by college students. *The International Journal for the Psychology of Religion, 15*, 199–219.

Oxford English Dictionary. (1989). (2nd ed., Vol. *14*). New York: Oxford.

Paden, W. E. (1992). *Interpreting the sacred: Ways of viewing religion.* Boston: Beacon Press.

Paloutzian, R. F. (1996). *Invitation to the psychology of religion* (2nd ed.). Boston: Allyn & Bacon.

Pargament, K. I. (1997). *The psychology of religion and coping: Theory, research, practice.* New York: Guilford Press.

Pargament, K. I. (1999). The psychology of religion *and* spirituality? Yes and no. *International Journal for the Psychology of Religion, 9*, 3–16.

Pargament, K. I. (2002). Is religion nothing but. . .? Explaining religion versus explaining religion away. *Psychological Inquiry, 13*, 239–244.

Pargament, K. I., Cole, B., Vandecreek, L., Belavich, T., Brant, C., & Perez, L. (1999). The vigil: Religion and the search for control in the hospital waiting room. *Journal of Health Psychology, 4*, 327–341.

Pargament, K. I., Koenig, H. G., & Perez, L. (2000). The many methods of religious coping: Initial development and validation of the RCOPE. *Journal of Clinical Psychology, 56*, 519–543.

Pargament, K. I., Koenig, H. G., Tarakeshwar, N., & Hahn, J. (2001). Religious struggle as a predictor of mortality among medically ill elderly patients: A two-year longitudinal study. *Archives of Internal Medicine, 161*, 1881–1885.

Pargament, K. I., Koenig, H. G., Tarakeshwar, N., & Hahn, J. (2004). Religious coping methods as predictors of outcomes of psychological, physical, and spiritual outcomes among medically ill elderly patients: A two-year longitudinal study. *Journal of Health Psychology, 9*, 713–730.

Pargament, K. I., Magyar, G. M., Benore, E., & Mahoney, A. (2005). Sacrilege: A study of sacred loss and desecration and their implications for health and well-being in a community sample. *Journal for the Scientific Study of Religion, 144*, 59–78.

Pargament, K. I., & Mahoney, A. (2002). Spirituality: Discovering and conserving the sacred. In C. R. Snyder & S. J. Lopez (Eds.), *Handbook of positive psychology* (pp. 646–659). Washington, DC: APA Press.

Pargament, K. I., & Mahoney, A. (2005). Sacred matters: Sanctification as a vital topic for the psychology of religion. *The International Journal for the Psychology of Religion, 15*, 179–198.

Pargament, K. I., & Maton, K. I. (2000). Religion in American life: A community psychology perspective. In J. Rappaport & E. Seidman (Eds.), *Handbook of community psychology* (pp. 495–522). New York: Kluwer Academic.

Pargament, K. I., Poloma, M. M., & Tarakeshwar, N. (2001). Methods of coping from the religions of the world: Spiritual healing, karma, and the Bar Mitzvah. In C. R. Snyder (Ed.), *Coping and copers: Adaptive processes and people* (pp. 259–284). Oxford University Press.

Pargament, K. I., Smith, B. W., Koenig, H. G., & Perez, L. (1998b). Patterns of positive and negative coping with major life stressors. *Journal for the Scientific Study of Religion, 37*, 710–724.

Pargament, K. I., Sullivan, M. S., Balzer, W. K., Van Haitsma, K. S., & Raymark, P. H. (1995). The many meanings of religiousness: A policy-capturing approach. *Journal of Personality, 63*, 953–983.

Pargament, K. I., Zinnbauer, B. J., Scott, A. B., Butter, E. M., Zerowin, J., & Stanik, P. (1998a). Red flags and religious coping: Identifying some religious warning signs among people in crisis. *Journal of Clinical Psychology, 54*, 77–89.

Piedmont, R. L. (1999). Does spirituality represent the sixth factor of personality? Spiritual transcendence and the five-factor model. *Journal of Personality, 67*, 985–1013.

Piedmont, R. L. (2001). Spiritual transcendence and the scientific study of spirituality. *Journal of Rehabilitation, 67*, 4–14.

Rappaport, J. (1981). In praise of paradox: A social policy of empowerment over prevention. *American Journal of Community Psychology, 9*, 1–26.

Richards, P. S., & Bergin, A. E. (1997). *A spiritual strategy for counseling and psychotherapy.* Washington, DC: APA Press.

Roof, W. C., & McKinney, W. (1987). *American mainline religion: Its changing shape and future.* New Brunswick, NJ: Rutgers University.

Sethi, S., & Seligman, M. E. P. (1993). Optimism and fundamentalism. *Psychological Science, 4*, 256–259.

Silberman, I., Higgins, E. T., & Dweck, C. S. (2001, August). *Religion and emotional well-being: World and self beliefs as mediators.* Paper presented at annual conference of the American Psychological Association, San Francisco, CA.

Tarakeshwar, N., Swank, A. B., Pargament, K. I., & Mahoney, A. (2001). Theological conservatism and the sanctification of nature: A study of opposing religious correlates of environmentalism. *Journal for the Scientific Study of Religion, 42*, 387–404.

Tetlock, P. E., Kristel, O. V., Elson, S. R., Green, M. C., & Lerner, J. S. (2000). The psychology of the unthinkable: Taboo tradeoffs, forbidden base rates, and heretical counterfactuals. *Journal of Personality and Social Psychology, 78*, 853–370.

Tix, A. P., & Frazier, P. A. (1998). The use of religious coping during stressful life events: Main effects, moderation, and mediation. *Journal of Consulting and Clinical Psychology, 66*, 411–422.

Trenholm, P., Trent, J., & Compton, W. (1998). Negative religious conflict as a predictor of panic disorder. *Journal of Clinical Psychology, 54*, 59–65.

Tyler, F. B., Pargament, K. I., & Gatz, M. (1983). The resource collaborator role: A model for interactions involving psychologists. *American Psychologist, 38*, 388–398.

USA Today. (2001, October 7). Osama bin Laden speech reported from Al-Jazeera TV.

Welch, M. R., & Barrish, J. (1982). Bringing religious motivation back in: A multivariate analysis of motivational predictors of student religiosity. *Review of Religious Research, 23*, 357–369.

KENNETH I. PARGAMENT, PhD is currently Professor of Psychology at Bowling Green State University. He has published extensively in the psychology of religion, stress, and coping. He received the William James Award for excellence in research in the psychology of religion from Division 36 (Psychology of Religion) of the American Psychological Association. A fellow of the American Psychological Association and the American Psychological Society, Dr. Pargament is author of the book, *The Psychology of Religion and Coping: Theory, Research, Practice* and coeditor of the book, *Forgiveness: Theory, Research, and Practice*. He is former president of Division 36 of the American Psychological Association. Dr. Pargament consults with national and international health institutes, foundations, and universities.

GINA M. MAGYAR-RUSSELL, PhD is a post-doctoral fellow in the Department of Psychiatry and Behavioral Sciences at Johns Hopkins University School of Medicine. She received her doctorate in clinical psychology from Bowling Green State University. Her research and clinical interests include studies of the impact of the loss or violation of what individuals perceive as sacred, religious and spiritual coping in medically ill patients, and integrating spirituality into psychotherapy with adults suffering from physical illness and injury and traumatic life events.

NICHOLE A. MURRAY-SWANK, PhD is currently Assistant Professor in the Department of Pastoral Counseling at Loyola College in Maryland. She is also a research faculty with the Center for the Study of Spirituality, Trauma, Loss and Violence. She obtained her PhD in clinical psychology from Bowling Green State University, with a specialty in the psychology of religion. Her research and clinical interests focus on the intersection between trauma, sexuality, and spirituality. She has published on the role of spirituality in coping with sexual abuse, and has developed a spiritually integrative treatment program for female survivors of sexual abuse. She has presented her research at numerous national and international conferences.

Journal of Social Issues, Vol. 61, No. 4, 2005, pp. 689–706

Religion and Conflict in Marital and Parent-Child Relationships

Annette Mahoney[*]
Bowling Green State University

This article discusses how religion can substantively influence the manifestation and resolution of conflict in marital and parent-child relationships. Religious systems of meaning are proposed to influence conflict by promoting which goals and values should be sought in family life and the appropriate means to achieve these ends. Conflict can be amplified or inhibited based on the extent to which family members differ and agree about such religiously based parameters. Religion also offers families strategies that may facilitate or hinder the resolution of conflict after it erupts. The limited amount of empirical research on how religion shapes the manifestation and resolution of marital and parent-child conflict is highlighted, and suggestions are made to advance research and clinical practice on this topic.

Despite expectations that the increasing secularization of human societies over the past century would diminish the impact of religion on family life, studies conducted during the past 25 years clearly indicate that religion is a salient factor in marriage and parenting (for reviews see Mahoney, Pargament, Tarakeshwar, & Swank, 2001; Sherkat & Ellison, 1999). Although ample empirical evidence connects religion to family functioning, most findings involve global and/or single-item indices of religiousness (e.g., religious affiliation, church attendance; Jenkins, 1992; Mahoney et al., 2001). This leaves open many unexplored questions about specific processes that tie religion to family interaction patterns. The purpose of this article is to discuss mechanisms by which religion may substantively (i.e., through its theological content) facilitate or inhibit marital and parent-child conflict, along with related empirical findings. The conceptual underpinnings of the article are first presented. The potential influence of religion on the occurrence of marital conflict then is described, followed by how religion may be tied to methods

---

[*]Correspondence concerning this article should be addressed to Annette Mahoney, Department of Psychology, Bowling Green State University, Bowling Green, OH 43403 [e-mail: amahone@bgnet.bgsu.edu].

of conflict resolution in marriage. Next, the role that religion may play for parent-child conflict and its resolution is discussed within a family-developmental context. Finally, recommendations for social scientists and practitioners are provided.

Conceptual Underpinnings Regarding Substantive Roles of Religion in Family Conflict

Interpersonal conflict can be broadly defined as an incompatibility between individuals or groups in their selection and pursuit of goals (Fincham & Bradbury, 1991). Thus, conflict occurs when people disagree about which goals are most appropriate to pursue or what methods should be used to achieve goals (Silberman, this issue). Applied to families, conflict can occur in marital or parent-child relationships with regard to any topic involved in planning and carrying out a shared life. The first critical conceptual premise made here is that religion is relevant to conflicts that families experience because religion offers people values about appropriate goals pertaining to family life and how to reach them. In turn, the frequency and intensity of conflictual interactions may be exacerbated due to incompatible religiously based views about the selection and pursuit of goals embedded in marital and parent-child relationships. Alternatively, religion may buffer family members from conflict by providing them with a common set of values rooted in a religious system of meaning. Thus, although world religions do not typically encourage family members to have conflicts, underlining (dis)similarities between family members' religious views of values that impact family life could exacerbate or buffer intrafamilial disagreements on a wide range of topics.

Conflict resolution strategies are defined as strategies people use to cope with interpersonal conflict after it emerges (Kerig, 1996). In marital relationships, partners may use adaptive (e.g., reflective listening, collaboration) or maladaptive (e.g., avoidance, verbal attacks, physical violence; Kerig, 1996) methods to deal with conflict. When conflict occurs in parent-child relationships, the developmental status of the child shapes parents' methods of conflict resolution. When children are younger, parents rely more on the assertion of parental authority (e.g., dispensing punishment, setting limits) to curb parent-child conflict over unacceptable child behavior. As children approach adolescence, parents are challenged to shift increasingly toward egalitarianism to deal with parent-child disputes (Steinberg & Silk, 2002). The second key premise of this article is that religiously grounded beliefs and practices could positively or negatively influence the resolution of family conflicts. That is, religiously based values about what constitutes desirable interpersonal processes in marriage and parent-child relationships may affect how family members cope with conflicts after they arise.

The third key premise made here is that religion offers people theologically grounded systems of meaning that can shape family conflict in unique ways. Religion is unique because it incorporates peoples' perceptions of the "sacred" into both the goals and pathways people pursue in life (Pargament, Murray, & Magyar, this issue; Pargament & Mahoney, 2002). Regardless of the different terms that people from different religions use to denote the sacred realm (e.g., God, Higher Power, Christ, karma), religious teachings and practices provide family members with substantive guidelines about desirable parameters of life, grounded in rituals and myths that are tightly interwoven with convictions about transcendental phenomena (Roccas, this issue). Thus, the substantive messages propagated by various religions on the interplay between the spiritual realm and family relations should be taken seriously because such messages may powerfully affect the content and frequency of conflictual family interactions and their resolutions. Moreover, it is important to distinguish between two types of substantive messages found in religious world views. One involves constructs, such as commitment, which are recommended by religions based on theological rationales, yet may also be promoted by nonreligious systems of meaning. In this context, when a familial conflict emerges over a certain topic, religion could exacerbate the dispute due to the spiritual meaning that family members attach to the issue. Alternatively, religion could greatly ameliorate conflict about a given topic because family members share deeply held religious values on the issue. The second type of substantive messages emphasized by religion involves constructs, such as the sanctification of marriage or parenting (Mahoney, Pargament, Murray-Swank, & Murray-Swank, 2003), that are unique to religious systems of meaning because they articulate interpersonal goals and processes that pertain directly to transcendental phenomena.

In sum, the substantive content of religion infuses the goals and processes of family relationships with spiritual significance and meaning. The degree of (dis)similarity between family members about religiously based views of family functioning can influence the manifestation and resolution of intrafamily conflict. Such mechanisms will be illustrated in this article by drawing on common messages found in Western religions about how marital and parent-child relationships should operate. While an exhaustive review of the diverse theological views that exist on family life across the globe is not possible here, drawing attention to the particular dimension of life that religion deals with—namely perceptions of the sacred—will hopefully help researchers uncover religion's continued salience in contemporary family life and highlight important applied implications. Readers are referred elsewhere for discussions of the impact of religion on family functioning via general psychological and sociological mechanisms that are independent of the theological content of religion (Curtis & Alison, 2002; Mahoney et al., 2001).

Marital Conflict

Religion as an Influence on the Manifestation of Marital Conflict

Substantive messages that overlap with secular discourse. Religious systems of meaning routinely delineate guidelines for fundamental aspects of marriage. One category of guidelines are those justified with theological or religious rationales that could also be promoted within purely psychological or "secular" models of marriage. For example, common substantive themes embedded in Judeo-Christian religious literature and tradition about appropriate goals of marriage that can dovetail with nonreligious worldviews include an emphasis on marriage as a lifelong commitment; expectations that partners love, help, and comfort one another; the subjugation of individual desires to the marriage; obligations not to abandon one's spouse if major external stressors occur (e.g., major illness or financial problems); the value of sexual fidelity and heterosexuality; the importance of procreation and raising children; and the proper balance of gender roles in and out of the home (Bartkowski, 1997; Giblin, 1993; Lauer, 1985). Martial conflict could occur, or be intensified, based on the degree to which partners differ in their religiously based interpretations of these issues as well as when one partner violates a presumably shared religious value (e.g., extramarital affairs). Conversely, the extent to which couples adhere to similar religious views of the above goals, and their relative priority over other purposes of marriage, may facilitate harmony.

Substantive messages unique to religious worldviews. The most central substantive message that religion conveys about marriage is the spiritual nature of the relationship itself (Giblin, 1993). Spiritual objectives of marriage involve destinations that fall outside the purview of secular systems of meaning. In traditional and liberal Christian circles alike, for instance, marriage is viewed as a sacred encounter in which transcendental love and grace is experienced (Lauer, 1986; Stanley, Trathen, McCain, & Bryan, 1998). Alternatively, Christians often describe God as a third person in the marriage, a personified being whose purposes are intimately connected to marriage and its developmental history (Butler & Harper, 1994). A study of 97 couples, who mirrored the religious diversity of U.S. couples, confirmed that the construct of "sanctification" applies to marriage. That is, marriage is often perceived as having spiritual meaning, with married persons commonly ascribing sacred, divine qualities to their marriage and reporting the belief that God is manifested in their marriage (Mahoney et al., 1999). Three mechanisms may help create and perpetuate such beliefs: (a) use of religiously oriented language and dialect in daily conversation; (b) annual and daily religious rituals or ceremonies; and (c) narrative reiterations of family history that involve spiritual themes (Butler & Harper, 1984).

Discrepancies in spouses' cognitive or behavioral attempts to integrate spirituality into their marriage may give a uniquely religious impetus to marital conflict. Furthermore, clashes on any topic may carry surplus meaning for couples who view their marriage as a means by which they "touch the Divine" (Lauer, 1985). If spouses deeply believe that a primary purpose of a genuine and authentically loving marriage is to discover what God is (Lauer, 1985), then chronic conflict could carry added psychological threat of losing a connection to God as well as losing one's partner. Accordingly, religious belief systems could exacerbate conflict by heightening feelings of fear, anger, shame, and guilt, particularly if one spouse engages in behavior that clearly violates religious precepts held dear by one or both parties (e.g., engaging in extramarital affairs or homosexuality).

Religion also presents couples with unique opportunities for conflict regarding each partner's expression of his or her personal spirituality. Couples may experience clashes about how to integrate the "sacred" into aspects of life other than marriage, including: (a) each partner's pursuit of a connection with the "sacred" itself (e.g., opposing images of God or unequal desires to participate in organized religion); and (b) roles or activities that may be sanctified by only one spouse (e.g., child rearing; charity work; vocational goals; artistic or athletic pursuits; material wealth; Mahoney et al., 2003). On the other hand, couples' level of unity about the spiritual purposes of marriage may also mediate their level of agreement about key aspects of marriage (e.g., sexuality, gender roles, child rearing). Also, the added psychological threat of losing a connection to God, as discussed above, may help motivate couples to acknowledge and resolve problems.

Empirical findings. Several sources of empirical evidence indirectly suggest that religion influences couples' views of the purposes of marriage and therefore could influence the degree to which partners disagree/agree on certain topics. For example, members of "conservative," "moderate," and "liberal" subcultures in Christianity report different attitudes about gender roles, abortion, homosexuality, and extramarital relationships (Gay, Ellison, & Powers, 1996). Denominational affiliation and/or degree of Christian conservatism are also tied to views on women's labor force participation (Sherkat, 2000), domestic power arrangements and household labor allocation (Ellison & Barkowski, 2002), and fertility rates (Mosher, Williams, & Johnson, 1992). Greater religious devoutness also predicts an avowed preference for a "convenantal" model of marriage that emphasizes individual sacrifice and absolute commitment to marriage, rather than a "contractual" model of marriage marked by individuals' needs taking primacy over the marital bond and an emphasis on negotiation (Sanchez, Nock, Wright, & Gager, 2002). The most direct evidence that religion influences couples' views of marriage is that more religious individuals are more likely to view their marriage as having spiritual qualities (e.g., blessed, holy) and believe God is manifested in their marriage (Mahoney et al., 1999).

Questions remain, however, as to whether religiously based attitudes pertinent to marriage actually trigger or buffer couples from conflict. Studies that link religious heterogamy between partners (i.e., dissimilar religious affiliation, beliefs, and practices) to somewhat higher divorce rates and lower marital satisfaction imply that religiously based differences may increase conflictual interactions (for review, see Mahoney et al., 2001). Further, couples in mixed-faith marriages report more frequent disagreements than same-faith couples (Curtis & Ellison, 2002) as do couples who less often engage in religious activities together (Mahoney et al., 1999). One study appears to have directly explored whether disparities between couples' religious views, specifically about the inerrancy and authority of the Bible, generates greater conflict about particular issues (Curtis & Ellison, 2002). Couples argue more often about how they spend time and about in-laws when the wife holds much more conservative Christian beliefs than her husband, whereas more child-rearing disputes arise for couples when the husband is more conservative than his wife. Discrepancies about the Bible in either direction are linked to more conflicts about housework and money. Thus, conservative Christian views on the Bible in general, not necessarily about marriage, impact the frequency and nature of conflict for couples who do not share this perspective (Curtis & Ellison, 2002). Comparable research on disparities about non-Christian or nonconservative religious orientations and couples' religious views specifically about marriage does not appear to exist.

While the above research suggests that religion may impact the manifestation of marital conflict, the psychological mechanisms that account for these links are unclear. Reliance on global, single-item measures to assess religiousness (e.g., type of denomination, frequency of attendance) obscures whether religion represents a distinct wellspring of marital conflict (or harmony) between partners, or merely signals incompatibilities that have little to do with the substance of religion. To clarify the significance of religion, social scientists need to ask couples direct and in-depth questions about the extent to which each partner embraces messages embedded in various religious systems about the goals of marriage, whether behavioral practices (e.g., religious rituals) reinforce these values, and whether religiously based (dis)similarity about specific aspects of marriage generate (dis)agreements. For example, couples' views on gender roles in marriage deserve far more careful scrutiny. Even spouses who belong to the same religious group (e.g., a particular Conservative Protestant group) can hold strikingly different views on marriage since both nonegalitarian and egalitarian models of domestic task sharing can be defended with Biblical scriptures (Bartkowski, 1997; Ellison & Bartkowski, 2002). A thorough understanding of the role that religion plays in marital conflict requires that researchers devise methods to capture the diversity of messages that religion holds for many aspects of marriage.

Religion as an Influence on Conflict Resolution Processes in Marriage

Substantive messages that overlap with secular discourse. Religious systems of meaning include a variety of prescriptive messages about the strategies that couples should use to resolve disputes. Various religious teachings can be construed to encourage adaptive or maladaptive methods of conflict resolution (Mahoney et al., 2001). For instance, Judeo-Christian literature encourages individuals who encounter marital conflict to engage in self-scrutiny, acknowledge mistakes, relinquish fears of rejection and disclose vulnerabilities, forgive transgressions, inhibit expressions of anger, and be patient, loving, and kind (Giblin, 1993; Stanley et al., 1998). Adherence to such ideals is likely to facilitate adaptive communication methods that secular models of marriage promote (e.g., empathic listening, compromise; Fincham & Bradbury, 1991). On the other hand, the patriarchal structure of many Judeo-Christian traditions, and messages of gender-based inequalities that result therefrom, have been implicated as contributors to maladaptive conflict resolution methods. For instance, a justification of an imbalance of power and control between spouses in conservative Christian groups has frequently been hypothesized to promote husbands' use of physical aggression toward wives (Bartkowski, 1997).

Empirical findings. Few studies have directly investigated links between religion and the types of strategies that couples use to deal with marital conflict (Jenkins, 1992; Mahoney et al., 2001). Greater religiousness has not been associated with greater maladaptive communication between partners (e.g., yelling, stonewalling) in six relevant studies published in the past two decades, including two studies comparing Fundamentalist Protestant couples to non-Fundamentalist couples (for review, see Mahoney et al., 2001; Sullivan, 2001). To the contrary, couples' reports of engaging in more joint religious activities and perceiving marriage as having spiritual meaning have been linked with greater self-reported collaboration during disagreements (Mahoney et al., 1999). Also, couples' higher ratings of general religiousness predict more adaptive communication patterns based on rigorous observations of couples' behavior during video-taped family interactions (Brody, Stoneman, Flor, & McCrary, 1994). In three of the four quantitative studies that have systematically addressed whether religion promotes or discourages domestic violence, greater church attendance has been associated with lower, not higher, rates of marital physical aggression (for review, see Mahoney et al., 2001). This protective effect of religion persists after controlling for other psychosocial mediators, including social support, alcohol/substance abuse, low self-esteem, and depression (Ellison & Anderson, 2001).

Overall, greater involvement in religion appears to dissuade individuals from resorting to maladaptive methods to resolve marital disputes. However, with the exception of Mahoney et al. (1999), the available research relies on one or two items to assess the role of religion in marriage. Clearly, social scientists should develop a better understanding of how religious systems of meaning shape the strategies that couples select to cope with marital conflict. For example, couples with stronger religious convictions about the sanctity of marriage may rely more often on communication processes that researchers have found to be protective of marriages (e.g., empathic listening, compromise, acceptance) and bypass those that intensify distress (e.g., verbal coercion, stalemating, avoidance; Mahoney et al., 2003). In addition, such choices may be moderated by the nature of the goals that couples fight over. Potentially irreconcilable religious views about the purposes of marital life could heighten the use of maladaptive strategies. For example, conflict over ending a marriage or pregnancy may be exacerbated if one spouse believes divorce or abortion is absolutely unacceptable to God and the other spouse holds contrary views.

Substantive messages unique to religious worldviews. While religion may operate as an impetus for couples to adopt adaptive communication processes recommended by secular marital experts (Fincham & Bradbury, 1991; Stanley et al., 1998), religion also offers couples unique strategies to deal with marital conflict which deserve consideration by psychologists. Most notably, several scholars have discussed how couples may triangulate God into the marital system when conflict emerges (Butler & Harper, 1994; Giblin, 1993; Pattison, 1982; Rotz, Russell, & Wright, 1993). Using a Bowenian and structural family systems approach, for example, Butler and Harper (1994) present an insightful delineation of how couples' interpretations of God's role as a third person in the marriage could be a powerful mechanism to help resolve or exacerbate conflict. In the former case, God would be seen as: (a) being intensely interested in maintaining a compassionate relationship with each spouse; (b) taking a neutral stance about each partner's "side" of the story; and (c) insisting that each partner take responsibility for change in the relationship instead of blaming the other. Couples who view God in this way may be more able to disengage emotionally from destructive communication patterns and explore options for compromise or healthy acceptance of one another. However, God could also be psychologically drawn into one of three counter-productive triangles that block resolution of marital conflict: coalition (e.g., God takes one partner's side); displacement (e.g., adversity is God's fault); or substitutive (i.e., partners seek support from God but avoid dealing directly with the conflict). Anecdotal case examples (e.g, Giblin, 1993; Pattison, 1982; Rotz et al., 1993) and qualitative studies of marriage (Butler, Gardner, & Bird, 1998; Kaslow & Robison, 1996) highlight the power of these processes. Couples may also rely on other forms of religious coping (Pargament, 1997) to deal with marital conflict, including intervention from religious community (e.g., pastoral counseling), benevolent reappraisals of conflict (e.g., viewing the personal risks or pain involved in addressing conflict as part of a spiritual journey), and religious rituals (e.g., forgiveness and reconciliation ceremonies). A recent descriptive study found that long-married, highly religious couples often say they turn to prayer to help resolve marital conflict adaptively (Butler, Stout, & Gardner, 2002). However, inferential studies about the effectiveness and general pervasiveness of religious methods to cope with marital conflict need to be conducted.

Parent-Child Relationship Conflict

Religion as an Influence on the Manifestation of Parent-Child Relationship Conflict

Substantive messages that overlap with secular discourse. Many families may turn to religion for guidelines about the appropriate parameters of parent-child relationships. One set of issues involve parents' views regarding the standards of conduct they should instill in their children. For instance, Judeo-Christian traditions discuss, to varying degrees, parents' spiritual duty to achieve certain socialization goals, such as fostering a sense of respect and obedience toward authority figures; encouraging self-discipline and self-esteem; imparting prosocial values (e.g., honesty, altruism); and prohibiting antisocial behavior (e.g., drug or alcohol use, delinquency; Bartkowski & Ellison, 1995; Mahoney et al., 2001; Wilcox, 1998). Religion also addresses whether mothers and fathers should perform different parental roles in the family as a function of gender (Bartkowski & Xu, 2000; Hawkins et al., 2000). Finally, religion frames the parental role as a sacred calling, which requires personal sacrifice and making family life a central priority of life (Bartkowski & Ellison, 1995; Marks & Dollahite, 2001). The degree to which parents adopt (dis)similar religiously based views about appropriate socialization goals for children and parental responsibilities may shape the nature and frequency of conflicts. Failures of parents or children to adhere to religiously based expectations of their roles could become potent sources of discord in family relationships, whereas consensus about such issues could foster family unity.

Substantive messages unique to religious worldviews. Besides framing mothers' and fathers' respective roles in socializing children in terms of a spiritual mission, religion imparts spiritual meaning to aspects of the parent-child relationship not discussed in secular circles. Thus, like marriage, parent-child relationships can serve unique religious purposes. For example, many religions encourage parents to view children themselves as divine, holy gifts to be treasured. In turn, parents are expected to foster their children's connection to the divine and facilitate the development of their spirituality and religious identity (Wallace, 1996). Religion also portrays the burdens and pleasures of parenting as opportunities to model and deepen one's own understanding of God's love, patience, and commitment (Abbot, Berry, & Meredith, 1990). Finally, many religions argue that certain family structures fulfill divine plans, most typically biological parents should be married and provide an example to children of God's love within a permanent relationship.

Empirical findings. Empirical research on the intersection between religion and parents' expectations of the values and behavioral standards to which children should be held accountable is surprisingly sparse (Jenkins, 1992; Mahoney et al., 2001). A few studies indicate that adults (not necessarily parents) affiliated with Catholic and more conservative Christian groups place a higher value on children's obedience to authority figures and less emphasis on children's autonomy than other adults (for review, see Mahoney et al., 2001). Links between religion and parents' attitudes about other socialization goals seem to have attracted little attention. Although some work has addressed the intergenerational transmission of denominational affiliation and church attendance rates (Clark & Worthington, 1990), researchers have not yet directly examined whether parents' religious beliefs about parenting are connected to their perceptions of what specific types of child behavior are acceptable or unacceptable at different ages.

Empirical research also appears to be limited regarding how religion shapes adults' views of the parenting role itself. In two studies, parents of typical preschoolers (Murray-Swank, Mahoney, & Pargament, 2003) and of young children with autism (Tarakeshwar & Pargament, 2001) reported that they often imbue the role of parenting with spiritual meaning. This is consistent with several studies of parents of young children with developmental disabilities, who often describe a spiritual dimension to their job as caretakers (for review, see Mahoney et al., 2001). Other evidence suggests that religiousness influences parents' sense of devotion to parenting. One national survey found that greater church attendance is tied to greater monitoring, supervision, and rule setting of preadolescents by fathers (mothers' behavior was not addressed; Bartkowski & Xu, 2000). Greater involvement in public religious activities also relates to higher involvement of grandparents in their grandchildren's lives (King & Elder, 1999). Insightful qualitative research conducted by Marks and Dollahite (2001) on Latter-day Saint fathers of developmentally disabled and chronically ill children also indicates that religiously grounded expectations heighten a sense of responsibility in parenting. Finally, religion appears to shape general parenting styles. In a large national sample of families, parents' self-reports of greater personal religiousness have been linked with trained observers' ratings of authoritative parenting styles during parent-adolescent discussions (balance of warmth and firmness; Gunnoe, Hetherington, & Reiss, 1999). Conservative Christian views of the Bible have also been related to parents' reports of more affection (Wilcox, 1998) and less verbal hostility (Bartkowski & Wilcox, 2000) toward preadolescents.

Taken together, the above literature hints at the power of religion to shape family members' perceptions of the objectives of parenting. The critical issue here, however, is whether religion influences conflict between family members by promoting agreement or dissension about socialization goals and/or the appropriate roles that parents play in their children's lives. Indirect evidence for this question comes from a study showing that similarity between mothers' and adolescents' church attendance rates and self-rated importance of religion longitudinally predicts more satisfaction by both parties with their relationship (Pearce & Axinn,

1998). Greater general religiousness of family members has also been linked to more cohesiveness during observed family interactions (Brody, Stoneman, & Flor, 1996) and greater self-reported cohesion within the family unit (Abbot et al., 1990). Greater general importance of religion to parents also seems to facilitate better coparenting between parents (Brody et al., 1994).

Hopefully, future research will better elucidate variations in religiously based beliefs and practices that inform the goals of parenting (e.g., socialization outcomes) and more clearly determine whether sharing these values diminishes the occurrence of parent-child conflict while discrepancies heighten parent-child conflict. For example, the Conservative Protestant literature proposes a child-rearing philosophy that holds children to a fairly strict code of socially conventional conduct (Bartkowski & Ellison, 1995). In contrast, more liberal Christian literature suggests parents should aim to relinquish a personal need for or expectation of producing "perfect" children who neatly conform to society's expectations (Krokonko, 1986; Wallace, 1986). Parents are instead encouraged to become a source of unconditional love, trusting that God is doing the work through them, thereby freeing children from pressures to distort their identities. In short, regardless of what processes families use to resolve parent-child conflict (discussed more below), religion may facilitate agreement between parents and children about the types of child behavior that are viewed as acceptable and unacceptable. Given the centrality of child rearing to many religious orientations, clashes between parents and children may take on additional meaning when either party refuses to accept religiously based guidelines. When children violate religiously grounded values, parents may experience this as a personal spiritual failure. Furthermore, children who view their parents as failing to live up to God's mandates for parenting may experience greater anger and disillusionment.

Future research also needs to pay more attention to the developmental context of parent-child conflict. In contrast to marriage, where two adults jointly determine the goals to be pursued, parents inevitably dictate a particular set of norms to shape the parent-child relationship, although their ability to enforce these norms diminishes across time. From early to late childhood, parents possess disproportional resources to impose their expectations upon children about what constitutes desirable parent-child relationships (e.g., degree of intimacy and balance of control between parties) and child behavior (e.g., moral, social, and academic functioning). During adolescence, parents' authority becomes more ambiguous, while youth gain psychological and physical resources to resist parental directives. As youth increasingly gain equal footing in making choices about goals, the nature of parent-adolescent conflict becomes more similar to that between couples (Steinberg & Silk, 2002). Interestingly, religious traditions provide families with formal rituals to acknowledge the developmental transition to adolescence (e.g., Holy Confirmation, Bar Mitzvah) and to validate adolescents' growing autonomy to select their own values. Nevertheless, religion may be an important wellspring of conflict (or harmony) in parent-adolescent relationships. For example, parent-adolescent conflict may escalate to the degree to which adolescents adopt beliefs and behaviors that diverge from parents' religiously prescribed values. The scarcity of research pinpointing the role that religion plays in parent-adolescent conflict leaves open many questions about these issues.

Religion as an Influence on Conflict Resolution Processes in Parent-Child Relationships

Substantive messages that overlap with secular discourse. Social scientists' efforts to understand how religion may guide parents' selection of conflict -resolution strategies have focused heavily on Conservative Protestant theologies that advocate a distinct disciplinary approach to young children who refuse to conform to parental rules. Although scholarship and popular media often portray the disciplinary practices of Conservative Protestants as fitting into an authoritarian style consisting of harsh punishment, arbitrary assertions of power, or otherwise unresponsive child-rearing practices, comprehensive reviews of conservative Christian media and theology paint a far different picture (Bartkowski & Wilcox, 2000). Specifically, this particular religious meaning system relies on Biblical interpretations to encourage parents to use mild corporal punishment judiciously with young children, untainted by anger or verbal outbursts, and in a family context marked by high levels of parental affection and involvement (Bartkowski & Xu, 2000; Bartkowski & Wilcox, 2000). The influence that religious systems of meaning besides Conservative Protestantism have on the strategies that parents select to resolve conflict with young children have received very limited attention by social scientists (Mahoney et al., 2001). Nevertheless, consistent with theological directives to nurture and protect children, some parents may hold deep religious beliefs that discourage physical discipline and encourage "low power" techniques to handle child noncompliance.

Empirical findings. Empirical research confirms that Conservative Protestants are more likely to spank preadolescents than parents from other religious orientations and nonbelievers (Ellison, Bartkowski, & Segal, 1996a, 1996b; Gershoff, Miller, & Holden, 1999). However, well-controlled research has not substantiated concerns that Christian conservatism heightens the risk for severe or abusive methods of physical discipline when parents encounter conflict with children (Mahoney et al., 2001). National surveys also suggest that parents who endorse conservative Christian views about the Bible are more affectionate (Wilcox, 1998), and yell at their children less often than other parents (Bartkowski & Wilcox, 2000). On average, Conservative Protestants would appear to exert control over preadolescents during conflictual interactions in a manner consistent with their religious system of meaning.

The influence of religions other than Conservative Protestantism on parents' disciplinary strategies is not well documented empirically (Mahoney et al., 2001). In addition, the way in which parents from *any* religious orientation choose to deal with conflict with adolescents is far from clear. One study indicates that greater parental religiousness facilitates an authoritative parenting style during stressful problem-solving discussions with adolescents (Gunnoe et al., 1999). Another study links greater importance of religion to parents with greater disapproval of physical discipline in a combined sample of children and adolescents (Jackson et al., 1999). Clearly, more research is needed to better understand how parents with varying levels of commitment to different theological orientations (e.g., liberal, moderate, and conservative views on Christianity) differentially rely on religious beliefs to resolve conflict with children across development.

Substantive messages unique to religious worldviews. As with marital relationships, religion may also offer parents and children unique methods to address conflict. Pattison (1982) points out that parents may incorporate religious figures (e.g., God, Christ, angels or devils) into interactions with their children. An adaptive example of this method is a parent who suggests that both parties take a "time out" from a dispute and temporarily turn the issue over to God. Alternatively, a parent may escalate conflict by threatening a child with the divine punishment. This represents an attempt to heighten parental power by asserting a coalition with God, a potentially common phenomenon. For instance, 27% of school-aged children from mid-western U.S. have reported that at least one parent tells them God will punish them if they are bad (Nelsen & Kroliczak, 1984). Religiously based methods of coping with stressors could also be relevant for parent-child conflict (Pargament, 1997; Mahoney et al., 2001). Effective conflict resolution patterns could be facilitated by both parties looking to God for guidance; seeking input from church members or clergy to mediate conflict; using religious practices and rituals to foster acceptance and forgiveness; and, benevolently reframing conflicts in religious terms. For example, Griffith (1986) describes a case example in which a mother withdrew from counter-productive power struggles with her college-age daughter after the therapist used the New Testament parable of the Prodigal Son. In this story, a father accepts his son's decision to squander his inheritance in a faraway land and later forgivingly welcomes the son when he returned home. The mother used this religious story as a model to help her face her powerlessness in forcing change on her daughter. A single parent of five adopted sisters, age 9–15, describes how her reliance on God helped her overcome urges she referred to as her "crusader complex" to excessively push her spiritual beliefs onto her children (Krokonko, 1986). Empirical research to substantiate the impact of religious strategies to deal with conflict in parent-child relationships across development remains a challenge for the future.

Recommendations for Social Scientists and Clinicians

Social scientists. The well-documented pervasiveness and robustness of links between single-item, global indices of religiousness (e.g., type of denomination; frequency of prayer) and family life (Jenkins, 1992; Mahoney et al., 2001) compels social scientists to conduct in-depth investigations of the mechanisms through which religious systems of meaning may influence conflictual family interactions. The primary assertion made in this article is that religion plays an important role in family conflict by shaping beliefs about the goals and pathways that should be pursued in family life, as well as by providing guidelines for appropriate resolution of conflict in marital and parent-child relationships. The degree to which individual family members find themselves agreeing and disagreeing about theologically grounded guidelines could minimize or heighten conflict over issues. To confirm these suppositions, researchers need to give more attention to the substantive messages that religions have for family relations. More specifically, social scientists need to develop measures that assess different types of religiously based beliefs about the parameters of marriage and parenting as well as various religiously based beliefs and practices invoked to resolve marital and parent-child conflict. The assertion that psychologists should aspire to understand the substantive elements of religion is consistent with calls for a constructive view of the relationship between psychology and religion and with arguments against reducing the determinants of either scientific or religious systems of meaning to social-cultural forces alone (Jones, 1994).

Attention to several other issues would also enhance future research. First, when investigating the impact of religion on well-being, researchers need to distinguish among the multiple levels of a family system, including the functioning of individual family members and relationships within a family system (e.g., marital, parent-child, sibling dyads; extended family relations). For example, substantive messages from some religions may reduce the frequency of conflict within family relationships (desirable outcome), but at what some might consider to be an excessive cost to a given family member's well-being or autonomy (undesirable outcome). Alternatively, the values of a religious systems of meaning could exacerbate conflict in one dyad (e.g., parent-adolescent interactions) while protecting another dyad (e.g., parent-toddler interactions). Second, the diversity of religious systems of meaning deserve far better illumination. This would involve exploring the similarities and differences in both the goals and the interactional processes for family life that are promoted by different theological orientations (e.g., liberal versus conservative; Christian, Jewish, Muslim, or Hindu backgrounds), which are likely to be tied to different outcomes for each relationship and member in a family system. To date, empirical research in this area has exclusively involved Judeo-Christian perspectives, with the overwhelming bulk of research focused on Conservative Protestant theology (Jenkins, 1992; Mahoney et al., 2001). Even in the

United States, this subgroup comprises only about 25% of the population (Hodge, 2000) whereas 53–60% of married Americans attend religious services at least once a month (Heaton & Pratt, 1990). In a similar manner, future research on the role of religion in family relations needs to go beyond studying predominantly Caucasian populations and "traditional" family systems. Research should incorporate non-Caucasian ethnic groups as well as "non-traditional" families, such as single-parent families, blended families, and families headed by same-sex partners. Overall, more pluralistic and multilayered empirical investigations are clearly needed.

Clinicians. For clinicians and clergy who work with families, religion offers rich insight into possible sources and solutions to conflictual family interactions. Although disputes about religious activities (e.g., church attendance) rarely appear to be a primary presenting problem for secular therapists who work with couples (Whisman, Dixon, & Johnson, 1997) or with parents and adolescents (Robin & Foster, 1989), several benefits proceed from addressing connections between religion and family conflict in clinical practice. These include: (1) clarifying underlying assumptions that may contribute to conflict in the family system via an exploration of religiously based language systems and expectations about marriage and parenting (Griffith, 1986; Prest & Keller, 1993); and (2) identifying ways that religious beliefs and rituals could trigger and reinforce family members' use of conflict-resolution methods that are adaptive (Giblin, 1993; Butler & Harper, 1994; Stanley et al., 1998) and maladaptive (Pattison, 1982; Prest & Keller, 1993; Rotz et al., 1993). New tools have been developed to facilitate clinicians' assessment of religion in marriage and family therapy, including "spiritual genograms," that uncover the role of religion throughout multiple generations (Frame, 2000), and "spiritual ecomaps" that diagram a family's integration of religious rituals, God, faith community, spiritual leader(s), parents' spiritual tradition and transpersonal beings (e.g., angels, devils) into their current family functioning (Hodge, 2000). These methods represent initial responses to ethical directives requiring marital and family therapists to develop expertise in addressing religious and spiritual concerns of clients, just as skills and sensitivity are required for other cultural issues (Huag, 1998; Jones, 1994).

In sum, this article advocates that social scientists and practitioners should strive to better understand how religion as a system of meaning may influence the manifestation and resolution of conflict within marital and parent-child relationships. Religion may shape the emergence of marital and parent-child conflict by promoting distinct substantive guidelines that family members are encouraged to embrace about the appropriate goals of marriage and parenting. The degree to which family members (dis)agree about these messages could influence conflict about particular topics. Religion also offer families a variety of methods grounded in religion to employ to resolve conflict after it erupts. While available research hints at the potential power of religion to influence conflictual family interactions, more direct, detailed evidence is needed to confirm the extent and implications of religion's involvement in this dimension of family functioning.

References

Abbot, D. A., Berry, M., & Meredith, W. H. (1990). Religious belief and practice: A potential asset for helping families. *Family Relations, 39*, 443–448.

Bartkowski, J. (1997). Debating patriarchy: Discursive disputes over spousal authority among Evangelical family commentators. *Journal for the Scientific Study of Religion, 36*, 393–410.

Bartkowski, J. P., & Ellison, C. G. (1995). Divergent models of childrearing in popular manuals: Conservative Protestants vs. the mainstream experts. *Sociology of Religion, 56*, 21–34.

Bartkowski, J. P., & Wilcox, W. B. (2000). Conservative Protestant child discipline: The case of parental yelling. *Social Forces, 79*, 263–290.

Bartkowski, J. P., & Xu, X. (2000). Distant patriarchs or expressive dads? The discourse and practice of fathering in conservative Protestant families. *The Sociological Quarterly, 41*, 465–485.

Brody, G. H., Stoneman, Z., & Flor, D. (1996). Parental religiosity, family processes, and youth competence in rural, two-parent, African-American families. *Developmental Psychology, 32*, 696–706.

Brody, G. H., Stoneman, Z., Flor, D., & McCrary, C. (1994). Religion's role in organizing family relationships: Family process in rural, two-parent, African-American families. *Journal of Marriage and the Family, 56*, 878–888.

Butler, M. H., & Harper, J. M. (1994). The divine triangle: God in the marital system of religious couples. *Family Process, 33*, 277–286.

Butler, M. H., Gardner, B. C., & Bird, M. H. (1998). Not just a time-out: Change dynamics of prayer for religious couples in conflict situations. *Family Process, 37*, 451–475.

Butler, M. H., Stout, J. A., & Gardner, B. C. (2002). Prayer as a conflict resolution ritual: Clinical implications of religious couples' report of relationship softening, healing perspective, and change responsibility. *The American Journal of Family Therapy, 30*, 19–37.

Clark, C. A., & Worthington, E. L. (1990). Family variables affecting the transmission of religious values from parents to adolescents: A review. In B. K. Barber & B. C. Rollins (Eds.), *Parent-adolescent relationships* (pp. 167–191). Lanham, MD: University Press of America.

Curtis, K. T., & Ellison, C. G. (2002). Religious heterogamy and marital conflict: Findings from the national survey of families and households. *Journal of Family Issues, 23*, 551–576.

Ellison, C. G., & Anderson, K. L. (2001). Religious involvement and domestic violence among U.S. couples. *Journal for the Scientific Study of Religion, 40*, 269–286.

Ellison, C. G., & Bartkowski, J. P. (2002). Conservative Protestantism and the division of household labor among married couples. *Journal of Family Issues, 23*, 950–985.

Ellison, C. G., Bartkowski, J. P., & Segal, M. L. (1996a). Conservative Protestantism and the parental use of corporal punishment. *Social Forces, 74*, 1003–1028.

Ellison, C. G., Bartkowski, J. P., & Segal, M. L. (1996b). Do conservative Protestants spank more often? Further evidence from the National Survey of Families and Households. *Social Science Quarterly, 77*, 663–673.

Fincham, F. D., & Bradbury, T. M. (1991). Marital conflict: Towards a more complete integration of research and treatment. In J. Vincent (Ed.), *Advances in family intervention, assessment and theory* (Vol. 5, pp. 1–24). London: Kingsley; *Resolution: Theory and Practice* (pp. 163–184). San Francisco: Jossey-Bass Publishers.

Frame, M. W. (2000). The spiritual genogram in family therapy. *Journal of Marriage and Family Therapy, 26*, 211–216.

Gay, D. A., Ellison, C. G., & Powers, D. A. (1996). In search of denominational subcultures: Religious affiliation and "pro-family" issues revisited. *Review of Religious Research, 38*, 3–17.

Gershoff, E. T., Miller, P. C., & Holden, G. W. (1999). Parenting influences from the pulpit: Religious affiliation as a determinant of corporal punishment. *Journal of Family Psychology, 13*, 307–320.

Giblin, R. (1993). Marital conflict and marital spirituality. In R. J. Wicks & R. D. Parsons (Eds.), *Clinical handbook of pastoral counseling* (Vol. 2, pp. 313–328). New York: Paulist Press.

Griffith, J. L. (1986). Employing the God-family relationship in therapy with religious families. *Family Process, 25*, 609–618.

Gunnoe, M. L., Hetherington, E. M., & Reiss, D. (1999). Parental religiosity, parenting style, and adolescent social responsibility. *Journal of Early Adolescence, 19*, 199–225.

Haug, I. E. (1998). Including a spiritual dimension in family therapy: Ethical considerations. *Contemporary Family Therapy, 20*, 181–194.

Hawkins, A. J., Spangler, D. L., Hudson, V., Dollahite, D. C., Klein, S. R., Rugh, S. S. Fronk, C., Draper, R., Sorensen, A. D., Wardle, L. D., & Hill, E. J. (2000). Equal partnership and the sacred responsibilities of mothers and fathers. In D. C. Dollahite (Ed.), *Strengthening our families: An in-depth look at the proclamation on the family* (pp. 63–82). Salt Lake City, UT: Bookcraft.

Heaton, T. B., & Pratt, E. L. (1990). The effects of religious homogamy on marital satisfaction and stability. *Journal of Family Issues, 11*, 191–207.

Hodge, D. R. (2000). Spiritual ecomaps: A new diagrammatic tool for assessing marital and family spirituality. *Journal of Marital and Family Therapy, 26*, 217–228.

Jackson, S., Thompson, R. A., Christiansen, E. H., Colman, R. A., Wyatt, J., Buckendahl, C. W., Wilcox, B. L., & Peterson, R. (1999). Predicting abuse-prone parental attitudes and discipline practices in a nationally representative sample. *Child Abuse and Neglect, 23*, 15–29.

Jenkins, K. W. (1992). Religion and families. In S. J. Bahr (Ed.), *Family research: A sixty-year review, 1930–1990* (Vol. 1, pp. 235–288). New York: Lexington Books.

Jones, S. L. (1994). A constructive relationship for religion with the science and profession of psychology: Perhaps the boldest model yet. *American Psychologist, 49*, 184–199.

Kaslow, F., & Robison, J. A. (1996). Long-term satisfying marriages: Perceptions of contributing factors. *American Journal of Family Therapy, 24*, 153–170.

Kerig, P. K. (1996). Assessing the links between interparental conflict and child adjustment: The conflicts and problem-solving scales. *Journal of Family Psychology, 10*, 454–473.

King, V., & Elder, G. H. (1999). Are religious grandparents more involved grandparents? *Journal of Gerontology: Social Sciences, 54B*, S317–S328.

Krokonko, V. A. (1986). The spiritual journey of a single parent. *Studies in Formative Spirituality, 7*, 45–62.

Lauer, E. F. (1985). The holiness of marriage: Some new perspectives from recent sacramental theology. *Studies in Formative Spirituality, 6*, 215–226.

Mahoney, A., Pargament, K. I., Jewell, T., Swank, A. B., Scott, E., Emery, E., & Rye, M. (1999). Marriage and the spiritual realm: The role of proximal and distal religious constructs in marital functioning. *Journal of Family Psychology, 13*, 1–18.

Mahoney, A., Pargament, K. I., Murray-Swank, A. B., & Murray-Swank, N. (2003). Sanctification of family relationships. *Review of Religious Research, 44*, 220–236.

Mahoney, A., Pargament, K. I., Tarakeshwar, N., & Swank, A. B. (2001). Religion in the home in the 1980s and 90s: Meta-analyses and conceptual analyses of links between religion, marriage, and parenting. *Journal of Family Psychology, 15*, 559–596.

Marks, L. D., & Dollahite, D. C. (2001). Religion, relationships, and responsible fathering in Latter-day Saint Families of children with special needs. *Journal of Social and Personal Relationships, 18*, 625–650.

Mosher, W. D., Williams, L. B., & Johnson, D. P. (1992). Religion and fertility in the United States: New patterns. *Demography, 29*, 199 214.

Murray-Swank, A. B., Mahoney, A., & Pargament, K. I. (2003). Sanctification of parenting: Influences on corporal punishment and warmth by liberal and conservative Christian mothers. Manuscript submitted for publication.

Nelsen, H. M., & Kroliczak, A. (1984). Parental use of the threat "God will punish": Replication and extension. *Journal for the Scientific Study of Religion, 23*, 267–277.

Pargament, K. I. (1997). *The psychology of religion and coping: Theory, research, practice*. New York: Guilford Press.

Pargament, K. I., & Mahoney, A. (2002). Spirituality: Discovering and conserving the sacred. In C. R. Snyder (Ed.), *Handbook of positive psychology* (pp. 646–675). Washington, DC: American Psychological Association.

Pargament, K. I., Murray, N., & Magyar, G. (this issue). The sacred and the search for significance: Religion as a unique process. *Journal of Social Issues.*

Pattison, E. M. (1982). Management of religious issues in family therapy. *International Journal of Family Therapy, 4*(3), 140–163.

Pearce, L. D., & Axinn, W. G. (1998). The impact of family religious life on the quality of mother-child relations. *American Sociological Review, 63*, 810–828.

Prest, L. A., & Keller, J. F. (1993). Spirituality and family therapy: Spiritual beliefs, myths, and metaphors. *Journal of Marital and Family Therapy, 19*, 137–148.

Robin, A. L., & Foster, S. L. (1989). *Negotiating parent-adolescent conflict: A behavioral-family systems approach.* New York: Guilford.

Roccas, S. (this issue). Religion and value systems. *Journal of Social Issues.*

Rotz, E., Russell, C., & Wright, D. (1993). The therapist who is perceived as "spiritually correct": Strategies for avoiding collusion with a "spiritually one–up" spouse. *Journal of Marital and Family Therapy, 19*, 369–375.

Sanchez, L., Nock, S. L., Wright, J. D., & Gager, C. T. (2002). Setting the clock forward or back? Covenant marriage and the "divorce revolution." *Journal of Family Issues, 23*, 91–120.

Sherkat, D. E. (2000). "That they be keepers of the home": The effect of conservative religion on early and late transitions into housewifery. *Review of Religious Research, 41*, 344–358.

Sherkat, D. E., & Ellison, C. G. (1999). Recent developments and current controversies in the sociology of religion. *Annual Review of Sociology, 25*, 363–394.

Silberman, I. (this issue). Religion as a meaning-system: Implications for the new millennium. *Journal of Social Issues.*

Stanley, S. M., Trathen, D., McCain, S., & Bryan, M. (1998). *A lasting promise: A Christian guide to fighting for your marriage.* San Francisco: Jossey-Bass Publishers.

Steinberg, L., & Silk, J. S. (2002). Parenting adolescents. In M. E. Bornstein (Ed.), *Handbook of parenting* (2nd ed., Vol. 1, pp. 103–134). Hillsdale, NJ: Lawrence Erlbaum.

Tarakeshwar, N., & Pargament, K. I. (2001). Religious coping in families of children with autism. *Focus on Autism and Other Developmental Disabilities, 16*, 247–260.

Wallace, A. T. (1986). Christian parenting as anticipation of the mystery. *Studies in Formative Spirituality, 7*, 91–102.

Whisman, M. A., Dixon, A. E., & Johnson, B. (1997). Therapists' perspectives of couple problems and treatment issues in couple therapy. *Journal of Family Psychology, 11*, 361–366.

Wilcox, W. B. (1998). Conservative Protestant childrearing: Authoritarian or authoritative? *American Sociological Review, 63*, 796–809.

ANNETTE MAHONEY, PhD, is Professor at Bowling Green State University. She graduated Rice University in 1984 with dual degrees in Religious Studies and Psychology. She received her PhD in Clinical Psychology from the University of Houston in 1992. Her research interests focus on religion and spirituality in family life, marriage, parenting and child behavior problems, and physical aggression in families. She has received research funding from the Templeton Foundation, the Fetzer Foundation, and the Ohio Department of Mental Health. She is a member of the Association for the Advancement of Behavior Therapy and the American Psychological Association's Division 36 (Psychology of Religion) and 43 (Family Psychology). She conducts clinical work with children, families, and adults. She is an adhoc reviewer for the *Journal of Family Psychology, Journal of Marriage and Family, Journal of Consulting and Clinical Psychology, The International Journal for the Psychology of Religion, and Journal for the Scientific Study of Religion.*

Journal of Social Issues, Vol. 61, No. 4, 2005, pp. 707–729

Religion as a Meaning-Making Framework in Coping with Life Stress

Crystal L. Park
University of Connecticut

This article explores how religion, as a meaning system, influences coping with adversity. First, a model emphasizing the role of meaning making in coping is presented. Next, religion as a meaning system is defined, and theory and research on the role of religion in the coping process are summarized. Results from the author's study of 169 bereaved college students are then presented to illustrate some of the pathways through which religious meaning can influence the coping process in making meaning following loss. Findings indicate that associations between religion and adjustment vary across time since loss, and that these associations are mediated by meaning-making coping. Finally, implications for individual and societal well-being and suggestions for future research are discussed.

The pervasive effects of religion on well-being have recently garnered a great deal of attention, and books, articles, and seminars on this subject have proliferated (Baumeister, 2002; Hill & Pargament, 2003). While this work is ongoing, findings to date are unequivocal: Various aspects of religion are strongly related to physical and psychological well-being in everyday life in general, and in the context of coping with adversity in particular (Oman & Thoresen, in press; Pargament, Ano, & Wachholtz, in press). With these empirical links established, the intriguing question of *how* religion gets translated into well-being has moved to the forefront (Dull & Skokan, 1995; Powell, Shahabi, & Thoreson, 2003). The pathways through which religion exerts its influence are many: As exemplified in this issue, religion may influence the everyday lives of individuals by influencing their experiences (Pargament, Magyar, & Murray-Swank, this issue), ultimate goals (Emmons, this issue), and values and attitudes (Roccas, this issue; Silberman, Higgins, & Dweck,

*Correspondence concerning this article should be addressed to Crystal L. Park, Department of Psychology, University of Connecticut, 406 Babbidge Road, Box U-1020, Storrs, CT 06269, [e-mail: crystal.park@uconn.edu].

Thanks to Ken Pargament, J. Conrad Schwartz, Israela Silberman, and four anonymous reviewers for their comments on earlier versions of this article.*

707

this issue), as well as by shaping family dynamics and childhood experiences (Mahoney, this issue).

The present article focuses on the pathways through which religion as a meaning system influences well-being when an individual encounters stressful situations. First, a conceptual model of coping is presented and religion as a meaning system is defined. Next, theory and research regarding the role of religion as a meaning system in the coping process are summarized. A study of bereaved college students is presented to illustrate some of the many ways that religious meaning can influence the coping process, particularly in making meaning following loss. Finally, implications for individual and societal well-being and suggestions for future research are discussed.

Conceptual Models of the Coping Process

The complexity of the coping process has given rise to the development of several models that attempt to describe this process. Two of them are described in this section, the *transactional stress and coping model* and an expanded version of this model, the *meaning-making coping model*, which focuses more explicitly on aspects of meaning in coping.

The Transactional Stress and Coping Model

The transactional stress and coping model proposes that adaptation to a stressor is influenced by the coping processes in which people engage following that stressor (Lazarus & Folkman, 1984). This model focuses on cognitive appraisals of the situation and the coping strategies that follow from this appraisal. Cognitive appraisal involves making initial attributions about why the event occurred; determining the extent to which the event is threatening, controllable, and predictable (primary appraisal); and deciding what can be done (secondary appraisal). These appraisals, in turn, influence the coping efforts put forth by the individual. Coping researchers often distinguish between problem-focused coping strategies (attempts to directly change the problem) and emotion-focused coping strategies (attempts to regulate the distress). Research indicates that although some types of emotion-focused coping, particularly talking with others about the stressful experience, are helpful in coping (Nolen-Hoeksema & Larson, 1999), other emotion-focused strategies, such as avoidance, tend to be related to continued distress, while problem-focused coping tends to be more consistently related to better adjustment outcomes (Aldwin, in press).

A Meaning-Making Coping Model

Some theorists have argued that the transactional stress and coping model is of limited usefulness in studying adjustment to major traumas and loss (Mikulincer &

Florian, 1996). In such events, which are not amenable to "problem solving" strategies, coping involves a great deal of intrapsychic cognitive processes or "meaning-making," since only through cognitive adaptation can individuals transform the meaning of the stressful experience. To describe this dynamic meaning-making aspect of coping, Park and Folkman (1997) integrated the work of numerous coping and meaning theorists (Greenberg, 1995; Rothbaum, Weisz, & Snyder, 1982; Taylor, 1983) into a meaning-making model of coping. This model distinguishes between two levels of meaning: Systems of global meaning and the appraised meaning of specific events. Global meaning includes global beliefs and global goals. Global beliefs are the basic internal cognitive structures that individuals construct about the nature of the world. These structures guide people throughout life by influencing their fundamental ways of construing reality and by structuring their global goals (Silberman, this issue). Global goals are the basic internal representations of desired outcomes that motivate people in their lives (Emmons, this issue; Park & Folkman, 1997). Appraised meaning of events include appraisals of events as a loss, threat, or challenge, as well as initial causal attributions explaining why the events occurred (e.g., God's will, coincidence), determination of the extent to which the events are discrepant with one's global system of meaning, and decisions regarding what can be done to cope with the event.

This model, depicted in Figure 1, suggests that events such as loss of a loved one may cause distress because their appraised meaning may challenge people's

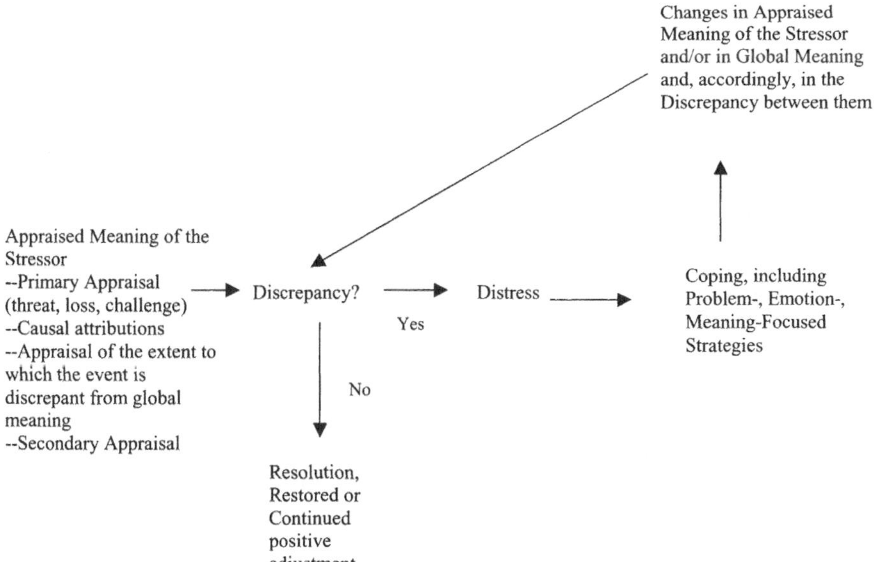

Fig. 1. Model of meaning-making coping with stressful events.

global beliefs or goals. According to this model, to decrease their distress, people must adjust their views of the event or revise their goals and beliefs about the world to accommodate the new information (Parkes, 1993). More specifically, when individuals encounter potentially stressful events, they appraise the meaning of the event (i.e., "What has happened?") and determine the extent to which this appraised meaning is discrepant from their global meaning system. The extent of this discrepancy (i.e., the extent to which the appraised meaning violates the person's global beliefs and goals) determines the level of distress that the event causes. For example, an "off-time" death may cause more distress than an "on-time" death because it is more likely to violate beliefs about the benevolence or justness of the world, and the death of a close friend may be more disturbing than the death of a stranger because it violates the person's global goals of having support or companionship to a greater degree (Kitson, 2000).

The meaning-making coping model posits that this discrepancy between appraised and global meaning is a highly uncomfortable state, involving a sense of loss of control, predictability, or comprehensibility of the world. To recover, the discrepancy between the appraised meaning of the event and the basic beliefs and goals that have been disrupted by it (in the example above, beliefs in the fairness of the world and goals such as companionship) must be reduced (see Park & Folkman, 1997, for a review). The processes through which people reduce this discrepancy involve changing the appraised meaning of the situation, changing their global beliefs and goals, or both. Such changes of either the appraised meaning of situations or of global meaning facilitate integration of the appraised (or eventually reappraised) meaning of the event into their global meaning system (Parkes, 1993; Klinger, 1998). Such integration should lead to adjustment to the event (Rothbaum et al., 1982), reflected in lower levels of depression or higher levels of subjective well-being and stress-related growth (McIntosh, Silver, & Wortman, 1993; Park, Cohen, & Murch, 1996).

Meaning-making coping is often characterized as attempting to see the event in a better light (Pearlin, 1991), or as cognitively "working through" the event (Creamer, Burgess, & Pattison, 1992). It may involve meaning-making mechanisms such as reappraising events as more positive or creating more benign reattributions [i.e., finding more acceptable reasons why an event occurred and who or what is responsible for its occurrence (Baumeister, 1991; Taylor, 1983)]. For example, following the death of a loved one, a person may come to see the hand of a loving God in the event or may redefine the event as an opportunity to learn new coping skills or develop new sources of social support.

This meaning-making coping model expands the transactional model by emphasizing the dynamic, meaning-making aspects of coping, which are particularly relevant in situations that are not solvable or reparable, such as trauma and loss. Specifically, this model emphasizes the interaction between situational appraisals and people's global beliefs and goals, and highlights the centrality of reappraisals.

As will be discussed below, religion is a meaning system that can significantly influence the process of meaning-making coping (Park, in press).

Religion as a Primary Meaning System

Religion, which can be defined as "a search for significance in ways related to the sacred" (Pargament, 1997, p. 32), is central to the meaning systems of many people, although its centrality varies greatly from individual to individual (Pargament et al., this issue). Religious meaning systems can be comprehensive, ubiquitously informing both global beliefs and goals. Some theorists have argued that religion grows out of a human need for comprehension of the deepest problems of existence (Geertz, 1966). Regardless of whether religion arises specifically out of this need for meaning or simply helps to establish it for people who embrace religion for other reasons, it is often characterized as the prime example of a belief system that provides ways to understand suffering and loss (Kotarba, 1983). Clearly, for many people, religion is an important philosophical orientation that affects their understanding of the world, and that makes reality and suffering understandable and bearable (Pargament, 1997). Religion frequently serves as an individual's core schema, informing beliefs about the self, the world, and their interaction (McIntosh, 1995), and providing understanding of both mundane and extraordinary occurrences (Spilka, Hood, Hunsberger, & Gorsuch, 2003). In terms of goals, religion is central in the life purpose of many people (Baumeister, 1991; Pargament, 1997), providing the ultimate motivation and goals for living as well as prescriptions and guidelines for achieving those goals. The following section examines the roles of religious meaning systems throughout the coping process, with a particular emphasis on meaning-making coping.

Religion and Coping

Because religion serves as the basis for the global beliefs and goals of many individuals, religious meaning often plays crucial roles throughout the coping process (Pargament, 1997), including the kinds of initial appraised meaning that people give to events, the extent to which this appraised meaning is discrepant with their global meaning, and the types of resources and coping strategies that they have available to reduce their distress. The extent to which religion is involved in a given individual's coping with a particular event is largely predicated on the extent to which religion is part of his or her orienting system: Religion is far more likely to be used in the coping of those for whom religion is a highly salient aspect of their understanding of self and world than in the coping of those who are less devout (see Pargament, 1997, for a review).

The nature of the event also determines the likelihood of religious involvement. As was mentioned above, if the stressful event is one that is not amenable to being "repaired" (i.e., problem-solved), such as illness or death, meaning-making efforts become more central (Mattlin, Wethington, & Kessler, 1990). It is in these situations that religion may have its greatest impact, by helping to restore beliefs that the world is safe, predictable, fair, and controllable, and that there is, perhaps, a benevolent God in charge of it all (Dull & Skokan, 1995; Pargament, 1997).

Religion and Appraised Meaning of Stressors

Research indicates that religion commonly influences the appraised meanings of stressors (Pargament, 1997). For example, religion is often involved in *causal attributions* following traumatic events (Spilka, Shaver, & Kirkpatrick, 1997). In their classic study of spinal cord injury victims, Bulman and Wortman (1977) found that over a third of the sample spontaneously mentioned God's will as the reason for their injury. Similarly, in a study of bereaved college students, most attributed the death at least partially to a loving or purposeful God (Park & Cohen, 1993).

Beyond that, the same event can be viewed quite differently depending on an individual's specific religious views. Some individuals may believe that God would not harm them or visit upon them more than they could handle, whereas others may believe that God is trying to communicate something important through the event, or that the event is a punishment from God (Furnham & Brown, 1992). For example, a study of hospice caregivers found that some appraised their situation as part of God's plan or as a means of gaining strength or understanding from God, while others viewed their situation as an unfair punishment or as desertion by God (Mickley, Pargament, Brant, & Hipp, 1998).

Religion and Reappraising Situational Meaning

Religion can influence the specific coping options available to individuals confronted with difficult situations (Pargament, 1997). In addition to prayer, individuals frequently report using a wide variety of other religious coping strategies, including benevolent religious reappraisals, "punishing God" reappraisals, religious forgiveness, seeking of religious support, and spiritual discontent (Pargament, Koenig, & Perez, 2000). Thus, it appears that making religious reappraisals are a major form of religious coping.

Religion can be involved in changing the appraised meaning of a stressful situation by (a) helping the individual to see the positive aspects that have come from the stressful situation, and (b) providing a means to make more benign reattributions (Park, in press). Positive reinterpretation is a very common, and adaptive, coping response (Aldwin, in press) that involves construing the situation in a positive way and identifying the benefits that may follow from a stressful encounter (Carver, Scheier, & Weintraub, 1989). Many religious traditions emphasize the necessity of, and possible good outcomes of, enduring the difficulties in life (Aldwin, in press). Religion also offers many avenues for making positive reattributions. For example, people often come to see the stressful event as the will of a loving or purposeful God, even if it is a God who is inscrutable and beyond human understanding (Park & Cohen, 1992). Other reattributions involve coming to see the event as a spiritual opportunity, as the result of a punishing God, or as the result of human sinfulness (Pargament, 1997). Pargament (1997) described the power of religion to transform the meaning of events: "When the sacred is seen working its will in life's events, what first seems random, nonsensical and tragic is changed into something else—an opportunity to appreciate life more fully, a chance to be with God, a challenge to help others grow, or a loving act meant to prevent something worse from taking place" (p. 223). While conceptually, these additional insights can be either positive or negative, research suggests that religion often facilitates the perception of positive aspects of stressful situations and encourages more benign reattributions (Frazier, Tashiro, Berman, Steger, & Long, 2004; Kunst, Bjorck, & Tan, 2000).

Because religious beliefs, like other basic beliefs, tend to be relatively stable, people confronting crises are more likely to change their perceptions of situations to fit their preexisting beliefs than to change their religious beliefs (Pargament, 1997). In fact, reappraisals of traumatic events may sustain religious beliefs, even if the logic of these reappraisals may appear somewhat convoluted. For example, in a study of the attributions that bereaved college students made for their friends' deaths, one participant explained that her friend, who had been killed by a drunken driver who ran over the curb and struck her on the sidewalk, was entirely responsible for her own death and that God was not at all responsible. Another student explained that her friend, who had been severely disabled, was not at all responsible for her own death, a suicide, because God had made her the way she was and had given her no other options (Park & Cohen, 1992).

Religion and Changing Global Meaning

Sometimes events are too traumatic or the discrepancy between appraised and global meaning is too great for individuals to bring the reappraised meaning into line with preexisting beliefs and goals. Making meaning of such events can involve changing one's fundamental philosophical, religious, or existential belief systems or construing drastically altered goal hierarchies (Lehman et al., 1993). More specifically, meaning making following traumatic events may involve changes in global beliefs about the world or about the self, such as coming to view God as less powerful (Kushner, 1981), or ceasing to believe in the existence of God, or perhaps seeing the devil as more powerful, or one's self as sinful, or as being unable to know or understand everything that happens in the world (Pargament, 1997). In terms of changes in global goals, people may, for example, rededicate themselves to their religious commitments or pledge to be more devout (Emmons, Colby, & Kaiser, 1998).

Such changes in global beliefs and goals may entail the development of new models for the world, the self, or their interaction. When people experience extreme stress and have difficulty coping, they may end up switching their congregations or denominations, or even undergoing a religious conversion—a far more radical religious transformation (Paloutzian, Richardson, & Rambo, 1999). Their new-found denomination or religion may provide alternative frameworks of meaning that help people answer their difficult questions and solve their life problems as well as a new system of purposes and goals (Pargament, 1997).

Adjustment Outcomes of Religious Meaning-Making Coping

Research suggests that the adjustment outcomes of religious meaning-making coping are often positive. For example, beliefs in a fair, just world and a benevolent, loving God—beliefs that are endorsed by many major religions—are associated with greater well-being (Janoff-Bulman, 1989; Pargament, 1997). In a study of adjustment following a major personal loss, renewed commitment to spiritual and religious goals, including pleasing God, achieving salvation, and engaging in religious traditions, was strongly related to recovery (Emmons et al., 1998).

Stress-related growth (e.g., positive changes in coping skills, relationships, and life perspectives; Schaefer & Moos, 1992), which is quite common following stressful events, is often of a religious nature (Park et al., 1996). Research has found, for example, that following a stressful encounter, many people report feeling closer to God, more sure in their faith, and more religious; they often report using more religious coping and increasing their involvement in their religious community (Emmons et al., 1998; Pargament, 1997). Further, those who report higher levels of religiousness report more growth following stressors (Pargament et al., 2000; Park et al., 1996), and such religious growth is often related to other measures of adjustment (Emmons et al., 1998).

The above analysis of religion and coping suggests that relations between religion and adjustment following stressful events are complex. On the one hand, it suggests that religion might be initially related to higher levels of distress due to greater disturbances of global religious-based beliefs. On the other hand, it suggests that religion may facilitate positive reappraisals, which might decrease long-term distress. Taken together, these predictions suggest that the impact of religion on adjustment may be contingent on the time since the event. Religion may have some negative consequences at the initial stages of coping, when individuals are struggling to understand negative events that seem to contradict their religiously oriented beliefs about how good people should not suffer (Hall & Johnson, 2001). Yet, religion may have long-term positive impact since many religious systems encourage making meaning of negative events in benign ways. Further, the above analysis, which emphasizes the role of religion as a source of both appraised meaning and global meaning also suggests that the impact of religion on adjustment may be mediated by meaning-making coping. The results of the SIDS study, cited earlier (McIntosh et al., 1993), demonstrated that parents higher on religiousness engaged in more meaning-making coping (defined as thinking about the child and the death, which, they posited, reflected attempts to integrate the death into their existing schemas) 3 weeks after the death. Meaning-making coping was cross-sectionally related to more distress but longitudinally related to less distress and higher levels of well-being. Further, religiousness was only indirectly related, through meaning making coping, to adjustment.

An Illustration of Religious Meaning in the Process of Making Meaning Following Bereavement

To illustrate the influence of religion and making meaning, a study is presented that examines relations among religion, meaning-making coping, and adjustment, focusing explicitly on the perception of discrepancy between global beliefs and goals and the potential of meaning-making coping to mediate the influence of religion on adjustment. Specifically, the following hypotheses were examined: (1) Religion will be related to the appraised meaning of the death, based on the notion that the more religious a person is, the more that religion will influence their understanding of events. In particular, higher religion scores will be related to (a) more religious attributions, and (b) more initial discrepancy between global and situational beliefs and goals. (2) Religion will be related to more meaning-making coping. In this study, meaning-making coping was conceptualized as deliberate efforts to see the stressful situation in a less distressing way (Sears, Stanton, & Danoff-Burg, 2003; Carver et al., 1989). (3) Since meaning-making coping might facilitate long-term adjustment while inhibiting short-term adjustment, religion will, accordingly, be related to better long-term adjustment following bereavement, but may be positively related to higher levels of initial distress. (4) Beyond that, the relation between religion and adjustment will be mediated by meaning-making coping.

These data are part of a longitudinal study of bereaved college students. Presented here are analyses of a subset of data gathered during the initial data collection period. To capture the bereavement processes closest to the death, the present analyses are limited to those participants who had been bereaved within the past year.

Method

Participants

Participants were 169 college students (121 women, 44 men, and 4 students who did not identify their gender) at a medium-sized Midwestern public university.

Selected as participants were those students who had reported that they had experienced the death of a significant other within the past year (mean time since loss = 5.8 months, *SD* = 3.5), to whom they reported being at least moderately close (at least 4 on a scale ranging from 1 [*not at all close*] to 7 [*extremely close*]). Mean age of participants was 19.2 years (range = 17–25), and racial composition was 93.5% Caucasian, 4% African-American, 1% Latino, and 1.5% Asian. Participants were primarily Christian: Religious affiliations reported were Catholic (*n* = 70), Protestant (*n* = 46), nondenominational Christian (*n* = 21), Jewish (*n* = 8), and none (*n* = 12). Twelve students reported other affiliations (e.g., Muslim, Mormon).

Procedures

Participants were drawn from the Psychology Department participant pool. They completed packets of questionnaires in a small group setting and received research credit for their participation.

Measures

Religion was assessed using the intrinsic scale (which measures the extent to which religion is held as the respondent's master motive) of the Age-Universal Intrinsic/Extrinsic Scale-Revised (Gorsuch & McPherson, 1989). Participants rated each of seven items (e.g., "My whole approach to life is based on my religion") from 0 (*not at all*) to 4 (*very much*) (α = .87).

Appraisals included measures of attributions for the death and appraisals of the extent to which the participant's global beliefs and goals were disrupted by the death. *Attributions* were assessed using rating scales that asked the participant, "In your view, how much did the death occur as a result of . . ." both nonreligious ("his or her own behavior," "chance"), and religious ("God's will or purpose") attributions, each rated on scales from 1 (*not at all*) to 7 (*very much*) (Park & Cohen, 1993).

Discrepancy between global and situational meaning was assessed using scales designed specifically for this study, to assess the extent to which participants appraised the death, currently, as discrepant with their global beliefs ("Now, how much does the death interfere with the way you understood the world to work and the way things happen?") and goals ("Now, how much does the death interfere with your daily goals and the everyday things that are important to you?) rated from 1 (*not at all*) to 7 (*very much*).

Meaning-making coping. There is currently no scale designed to specifically assess meaning-making coping, although some tap similar constructs. In the present study, meaning-making coping was measured with the *positive reinterpretation and growth scale* of the COPE (Carver et al., 1989). The COPE asked participants to rate the extent to which they used each of 60 coping activities in "response to the death" from 1 (*never*) to 5 (*very often*). The positive reinterpretation and growth scale consists of four items pertaining to attempting to see the situation in a less distressing way or to find something positive in it (e.g., "I looked for something good in what was happening") ($\alpha = .82$).

Adjustment. Because researchers have indicated that it is important to assess both positive and negative aspects of adjustment (Folkman & Moskowitz, 2003) and both general and event-specific aspects of adjustment (Pargament et al., 2000), these dimensions of adjustment were assessed in the present study. Two negative aspects of adjustment, *depressed mood* (Center for Epidemiological Studies-Depression Scale; CES-D; Radloff, 1977) and *intrusive and avoidant symptomatology* (Impact of Events Scale; Horowitz, Wilner, & Alvarez, 1979), and two positive aspects of adjustment, *subjective well-being* (Satisfaction with Life Scale; SWLS, Diener, Emmons, Larsen, & Griffin, 1985) and *stress-related growth* (Stress-Related Growth Scale; SRGS, short form; Park et al., 1996) were assessed. The CES-D, a measure of general symptomatology, asked participants to rate the extent to which they experienced each of 20 depressive symptoms in the past week (e.g., "I felt sad") on a scale from 0 (*rarely or none of the time*) to 3 (*most or all of the time*), ($\alpha = .91$). The IES measures distress regarding a specific event, and consisted of 15 items asking participants about the extent to which, in the past week, they experienced intrusive thoughts of the death (e.g., "I thought about it when I didn't mean to") and deliberate avoidance of reminders of the death (e.g., "I tried not to talk about it"). Each item was scored from 0 (*not at all*) to 3 (*often*); ($\alpha = .88$ for the intrusion subscale and .83 for the avoidance subscale). The SWLS, a measure of general life satisfaction, consisted of five questions regarding the extent to which the participant was satisfied with his or her life (e.g., "In most ways, my life is close to my ideal"), rated from 1 (*strongly disagree*) to 7 (*strongly agree*), ($\alpha = .92$). The SRGS consisted of 15 positive changes that the respondent may have experienced because of or following a particular stressor (in this case, the death) (e.g., "I rethought how I want to live my life"), rated as 0 (*not at all*), 1 (*somewhat*), or 2 (*a great deal*), ($\alpha = .92$).

Results

Religiousness of the Sample

The sample was fairly religious, with an item mean of the intrinsic scale of 2.30 (*SD* = 1.07). Only 7% of the sample scored 0, and a total of 13% scored less than 1.

*Relations among Religion and Appraisals, Meaning-Making Coping,
and Adjustment*

Bivariate correlations were conducted to examine relations among study variables (see Table 1). As expected, religion was positively related to appraised discrepancies in beliefs and goals, and to attributions to God, and was negatively related to attributions to chance. Religion was positively related to meaning-making coping. Also, as expected, religion was related to subjective well-being and stress-related growth, but contrary to predictions, religion was not significantly related to depressed mood, intrusions, or avoidance.

The Time Factor in Religion, Meaning Making, and Adjustment Links

Based on previous research suggesting that meaning-making coping had differential effects on adjustment based on the length of time following the loss (McIntosh et al., 1993), a finer-grained analysis examined participants in the early middle, and latter parts of the first year postbereavement. The three sets of bivariate correlations corresponding to these analyses are reported in Table 2. These results indicate that, for those early in bereavement, religion is associated with more appraised discrepancies between global and situational beliefs and goals, and that for those later in bereavement, this association diminishes. Further, religion is indeed related to more meaning-making coping as reflected in positive reinterpretation, and is related to depressed mood and avoidant and intrusive symptomatology, but that by the latter part of the year, the effect on depressed mood disappears, while the relation between religion and intrusion and avoidance were in the reverse direction. The findings regarding subjective well-being suggest that its relation with religion is more strongly positive for people further from bereavement, while religion is consistently related to higher levels of stress-related growth.

*Meaning-Making Coping as a Mediator of the Relationship Between Religion
and Adjustment*

To examine whether meaning-making coping mediated the effects of religion on adjustment, path analyses were conducted for those adjustment variables that had significant zero-order correlations with religion (Baron & Kenny, 1986). Two sets of regressions were conducted, one set for subjective well-being and one set for stress-related growth. In the first path analysis, regressions were conducted to examine the direct effect of religion on subjective well-being and then to examine the effect of religion and meaning-making coping on subjective well-being. Results indicated that religion was a significant predictor of subjective well-being (Figure 2A) and that its effect was mediated through meaning-making coping (Figure 2B). A second path analysis was conducted with stress-related growth as the

Table 1. Bivariate Correlations among Study Variables

	2.	3.	4.	5.	6.	7.	8.	9.	10.	11.	12.
1. Religion	−.05	−.16*	.48***	.13†	.14†	.31***	.11	.05	.01	.21**	.32***
2. Attributions to deceased	−	−.17*	−.14†	.14†	.06	.02	.14†	.05	.03	−.10	−.02
3. Attributions to chance		−	−.04	.13†	.04	−.03	−.02	.05	.04	−.08	.04
4. Attributions to God			−	.04	.06	.28***	.08	.11	.03	.08	.18*
5. Discrepancy with beliefs now				−	.47***	−.17*	.33***	.29***	.28***	−.07	.27***
6. Discrepancy with goals now					−	−.05	.45***	.41***	.27***	−.14†	.31***
7. Meaning-making coping						−	.04	−.13†	−.26***	.30***	.35***
8. Intrusive thoughts							−	.61**	.18*	−.03	.21**
9. Avoidance								−	.27***	−.12	.13†
10. Depressed mood									−	−.54***	−.17*
11. Subjective well-being										−	.30***
12. Stress-related growth											−

Note. $N = 169$. $^\dagger p < .10$. *$p < .05$. **$p < .01$. ***$p < .001$.

Table 2. Correlations of Religion with Disruption, Coping, and Adjustment Variables Across Time since Death

	Time Since Death		
	0–4 Months	5–8 Months	9–12 Months
Disruption of global meaning			
Interfere with beliefs	.35**	.04	−.09
Violate goals	.31**	.09	−.21
Meaning-making coping	.33**	.26*	.34*
Adjustment			
Depressed mood	.24*	−.19	.04
Intrusive thoughts	.38**	.07	−.29†
Avoidance	.23†	.09	−.37*
Subjective well-being	.07	.27*	.29†
Stress-related growth	.34**	.38**	.16

Note. †*p* < .10. **p* < .05. ***p* < .01.
For 0–4 months, *N* = 66, for 5–8 months, *N* = 60, and for 9–12 months, *N* = 42.

(A)

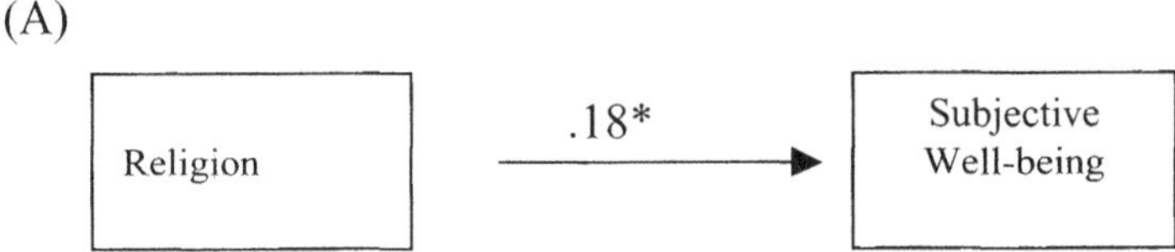

(B)

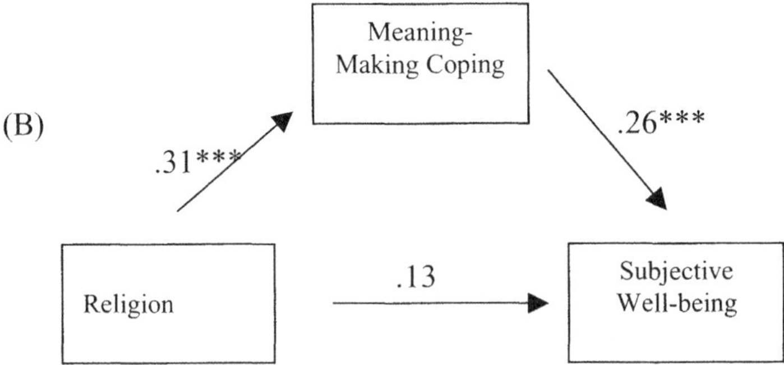

Fig. 2. Path models predicting subjective well-being, using (A) religion, and (B) religion and meaning-making coping.

(A)

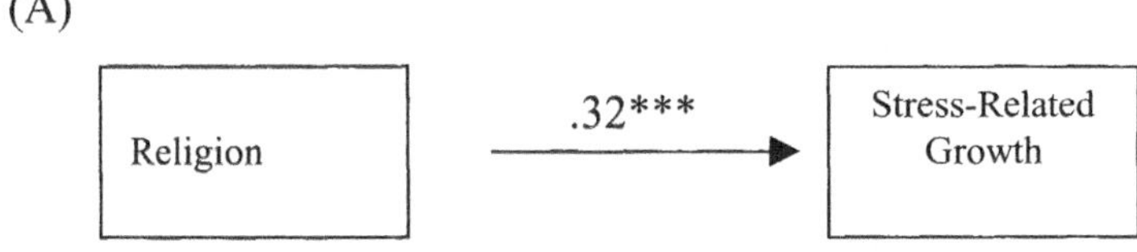

(B)

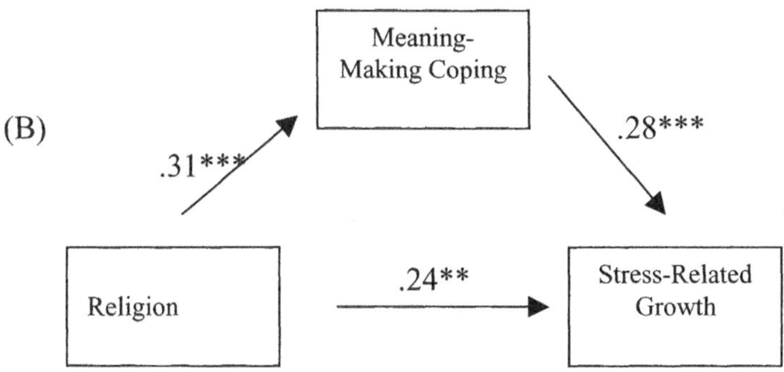

Fig. 3. Path models predicting stress-related growth, using (A) religion, and (B) religion and meaning-making coping.

outcome. Results indicated that religion was a significant predictor of stress-related growth (Figure 3A) and that its effect was partially mediated through meaning-making coping (Figure 3B).

Discussion

These results demonstrate how religion may serve as a meaning system within which the bereaved can reframe their loss, look for more benign interpretations, find coping resources, and, perhaps, identify areas of personal growth. Most participants reported being at least somewhat religious, and religion was related to their understanding of the death's occurrence. Religion was related to meaning-making coping, as reflected in positive reappraisal coping, and to adjustment in terms of subjective well-being and stress-related growth. Further, the association of religion with these adjustment outcomes was mediated by positive reappraisal coping. When subgroups of participants who were in earlier versus later stages of bereavement were examined, a more complex picture emerged. Religion appeared to be initially related to the extent of the appraised discrepancy between global beliefs and goals and the occurrence of the death. These findings indicate that those with a stronger religious meaning system may have initially experienced more disruption in their global meaning system, although these effects disappeared rapidly. Consistent with these findings, religion was associated with more distress for those earlier in the bereavement experience, as reflected in higher levels of intrusive thoughts and avoidance, as well as with higher levels of depressed mood. For people with more time since bereavement, these effects disappeared or even reversed, suggesting a positive association between religion and long-term adjustment. These results are consistent with prior research showing that those higher in religion may experience more initial disruption (McIntosh et al., 1993; Park & Cohen, 1993), as well as with the large body of research indicating that, in general, intrinsic religiousness tends to be positively related to several aspects of mental health and well-being (Ventis, 1995).

Several caveats should be noted with respect to interpreting these findings. First, they are based on cross-sectional data, and future work is needed to follow the adjustment of the same people across time. Second, the measures of discrepancies with global beliefs and goals used were developed specifically for this study and future research is needed to develop more refined measures of global meaning and meaning violation. For example, it would be desirable to measure global goals, in terms of larger life goals and purpose, as well as daily goals. Finally, a better measure of meaning-making coping needs to be developed. Some researchers have argued that the IES scale reflects not only distress, but cognitive processing or meaning-making as well (Greenberg, 1995; Lutgendorf & Antoni, 1999). Such a view would be consistent with the findings of the present study that indicate that relations between religion and this aspect of distress—or attempts at making meaning—is positive for those closer to bereavement and negative for those further from their loss.

Implications for Individual and Societal Well-Being

That religious meaning often exerts strong and diverse influences on individuals' well-being and functioning has important implications for clinical work. Religion plays important roles throughout the lifespan, and may be particularly important when people confront stressful life experiences. Mainstream clinicians have recently begun to recognize the importance of the religious meaning systems of their clients (Richards & Bergin, 2000), a promising trend.

It is important to recognize that religious meaning making is not only a personal, intrapsychic phenomenon, but is part of a reciprocal and ongoing process between individuals and the societies in which they live. Not only do individuals acquire their religious meaning systems from the larger culture, particularly their family and subculture, but the larger cultural and religious institutions provide a great deal of support and structure within which individuals conduct themselves, and to which they turn in times of crisis (Maton, Dodgen, Domingo, & Larson, this issue). These institutions reinforce and facilitate the application of religious meaning systems by individuals when they are coping with stressful situations. Finally, individuals' application of religious meaning systems in understanding and dealing with their stressful situations supports and reinforces the societal provision of these larger structures; individuals create and maintain these institutions, and their needs and desires thereby shape them.

This interplay between individual and institutional levels of religion in coping can be seen in the context of the national crisis in the United States following the September 11th terrorist attacks. The disruptions in beliefs and goals were both personal and public, creating a shared sense of grief and a collective search to make sense out of what had happened and what might happen next (Schuster et al., 2001). Religion was highly involved in many individuals' ways of understanding this traumatic experience and responding to it. The fact that the terrorists framed their attack in religious terms added to the need for religious explanations to assist people in their efforts to create meaning from the attacks (Nielsen, 2002). Prayer services, for example, were very prominent in the weeks following the attacks as people struggled to recover. Many of these services included preaching by religious leaders about the meaning of the situation and about the ways in which religion could facilitate coping with it. Recognizing the need, religious institutions offered increased spiritual support on both individual and communal levels.

Religious meaning systems can influence broader societal well-being as well. For example, religious cohesion (commonality of religious beliefs and purposes) may be related to better societal functioning (Pargament & Maton, 2000; Turner, 1991). Maton and his colleagues have identified a number of ways through which religious meaning systems may influence the functioning of individuals through prevention and treatment, and have also described some of the ways that individuals contribute back to their religious communities (Maton & Wells, 1995).

It should be noted that the relationships between individual and societal meaning making are not always compatible. The meanings that individuals make of their stressful situations, for example, may converge or diverge from those of the larger social system; in fact, this level of congruence may in itself be an important indicator of individual and societal well-being. Certain forms of meaning making, including religious ones, may lead to changes in beliefs that affect not only individuals, but society as a whole. For example, blaming natural catastrophes on Jews has led to wholesale slaughters over the centuries (Caroll, 2001). Gopin (2000) describes religion as influential in the formation of a mythic meaning of reality, which in turn shapes the psychological worlds of millions of individuals and the relations between them. Such myths may create deep intergroup conflicts but may also carry the potential for conflict resolution and peace.

Future Research Directions

More Sophisticated Research on Meaning

First, research on meaning must continue to increase in methodological so-phistication. In concluding their review article on meaning and meaning-making coping, Park and Folkman (1997) laid out a series of issues to advance research in this area. Recommendations included (a) using longitudinal, prospective designs, (b) measuring appraised and global meaning more concisely, distinguishing be-tween different meaning making constructs such as *meaning-making, searching for meaning,* and *finding meaning,* (c) emphasizing the role of goals as well as beliefs in this meaning, (d) developing measures of discrepancy between appraised and global meaning, and (e) devising ways to assess and track cognitive processing across time to capture the dynamic process of meaning making (see Park, in press).

Attention to the Differences in Theodicies among Groups

Theodicies refer to the belief systems of particular religions, particularly the justification of God's goodness in the face of evil (Donahue, 1989). For example, in Buddhism, suffering is considered to be caused by craving or grasping for wrong things or for right things in wrong ways (Drumont, 1994), while for Christian Scientists, disease, sin, sickness, and death are considered illusions of a mortal mind and not a cause for grief (Allen, 1994). The analysis of different theodicies as meaning systems may illuminate the role of religion in coping in the lives of individuals who come from different religions or from different groups within the same religion (Donahue, 1989). Currently, most research on religion and coping is limited to Christian populations. While this research has revealed important information on the role of religion in the coping process, comparisons across religious groups are necessary to distinguish between general effects of religion on coping and the unique impact of specific theodicies on the coping process. For example, several studies have demonstrated how religiousness and religious coping function differently in the coping processes of Catholics and Protestants (Park, Cohen, & Herb, 1990; Tix & Frazier, 1998).

Examination of Negative as well as Positive Religious Meaning

It is important to note that while the meaning-making model emphasizes the discrepancy between global and situational meaning as a source of stress, adjust-ment to stressful events is contingent not only on the extent to which the discrep-ancy is resolved, but also on the *content* of the changes that have occurred through the process of meaning making. Changes in appraised meaning or global meaning may have favorable or unfavorable effects on adjustment, depending on the specific content of that meaning (Thompson & Janigian, 1988). For example, in a study of elderly medical patients, making negative religious meaning of their illness (e.g., seeing it as the work of the devil or a result of God's abandonment) were related to higher rates of mortality, even after controlling for sociodemographic variables and physical and mental health (Pargament, Koenig, Tarakeshwar, & Hahn, 2001). Research is needed to examine whether different ways of dealing with meaning discrepancy (i.e., by changing global and situational meaning in positive or negative ways) has different impacts on well-being. Attending to both positive and negative aspects of religious meaning promises to provide a more accurate picture regarding the influences of religious meaning (Exline, 2002).

Examination of the Roles of Nonreligious and Spiritual in the Coping Process

One way to explore the uniqueness of religion in coping is by comparing it to other meaning systems (e.g., the nonreligious and the spiritual) in this context. Earlier, it was noted that religion serves as a source of meaning for many people (Gallup & Lindsay, 2000). However, the group of people who consider themselves to be nonreligious is growing rapidly. Worldwide, it is estimated that 768 million people consider themselves "nonbelievers" (Barrett, 2000). Some of these nonbelievers may consider themselves "spiritual but not religious" (Zinnbauer et al., 1997; Averill, 1998). Interesting questions can be raised about how our understanding of philosophical meaning systems applies to those who are not religious (or spiritual) (Benzein, Saveman, & Norberg, 2000). Comparing religious meaning systems with these alternatives may also shed light on those aspects of religion that distinguish it from other types of philosophical systems in the context of individual and societal well-being in general, and in the context of coping with adversity, in particular.

Concluding Comments

This article presents a framework for conceptualizing meaning systems and religion as a meaning system, and describes pathways through which religion as a meaning system may be involved in coping with stressful life experiences. Potential applications to individual and societal well-being were also described. It is hoped that this article will serve as a springboard for more thoughtful and more conceptually and methodologically sophisticated research on the roles of religion in the processes of coping with stress. This area of research, while challenging, promises to illuminate a central aspect of human adaptation.

References

Aldwin, C. M. (in press). *Stress, coping, and development* (2nd ed.). New York: Guilford.

Allen, J. (1994). The spiritual search. In R. P. Beaver (Ed.), *Gerdman's handbook to the world's religions* (pp. 399–405). Grand Rapids, WY: W. B. Gerdman's Publishing Co.

Averill, J. R. (1998). Spirituality: From the mundane to the meaningful—and back. *Journal of Theoretical and Philosophical Psychology, 18*, 101–126.

Baron, R. M., & Kenny, D. A. (1986). The moderator-mediator variable distinction in social psychological research: Conceptual, strategic and statistical considerations. *Journal of Personality and Social Psychology, 51*, 1173–1182.

Barrett, D. B. (2000). *World Christian encyclopedia*. New York: Oxford University Press.

Baumeister, R. F. (1991). *Meanings of life*. New York: Guilford.

Baumeister, R. F. (2002). Religion and psychology: Introduction to the special issue. *Psychological Inquiry, 13*, 165–167.

Benzein, E. G., Saveman, B., & Norberg, A. (2000). The meaning of hope in healthy, religious Swedes. *Western Journal of Nursing Research, 22*, 303–319.

Bulman, R. J., & Wortman, C. B. (1977). Attributions of blame and coping in the "real world": Severe accident victims react to their lot. *Journal of Personality and Social Psychology, 35*, 351–363.

Caroll, J. (2001). *Constantine's sword: The Church and the Jews—A history*. Boston and New York: Houghton Mifflin.

Carver, C. S., Scheier, M. G., & Weintraub, J. G. (1989). Assessing coping strategies: A theoretically-based approach. *Journal of Personality and Social Psychology, 56*, 267–283.

Creamer, M., Burgess, P., & Pattison, P. (1992). Reaction to trauma: A cognitive processing model. *Journal of Abnormal Psychology, 101*, 452–459.

Diener, E., Emmons, R. A., Larsen, R. J., & Griffin, S. (1985). The satisfaction with life scale. *Journal of Personality Assessment, 49*, 71–75.

Donahue, M. J. (1989). Disregarding theology in the psychology of religion: Some examples. *Journal of Psychology and Theology, 17*, 329–335.

Drumont, R. (1994). The Buddha's teaching. In R. P. Beaver (Ed.), *Gerdman's handbook to the world's religions* (p. 231). Grand Rapids, WY: W. B. Gerdman's Publishing Co.

Dull, V. T., & Skokan, L. A. (1995). A cognitive model of religion's influence on health. *Journal of Social Issues, 51*, 49–64.

Emmons, R. A. (this issue). Striving for the Sacred: Personal goals, life meaning and religion. *Journal of Social Issues*.

Emmons, R. A., Colby, P. M., & Kaiser, H. A. (1998). When losses lead to gains: Personal goals and the recovery of meaning. In P. T. P. Wong & P. S. Fry (Eds.), *The human quest for meaning* (pp. 163–178). Mahwah, NJ: Erlbaum.

Exline, J. J. (2002). Stumbling blocks on the religious road: Fractured relationships, nagging vices, and the inner struggle to believe. *Psychological Inquiry, 13*, 182–189.

Folkman, S., & Moskowitz, J. T. (2003). Positive psychology from a coping perspective. *Psychological Inquiry, 14*, 121–125.

Frazier, P., Tashiro, T., Berman, M., Steger, M., & Long, J. (2004). Correlates of levels and patterns of positive life changes following sexual assault. *Journal of Consulting and Clinical Psychology, 72*, 19–30.

Furnham, A., & Brown, L. B. (1992). Theodicy: A neglected aspect of the psychology of religion. *International Journal for the Psychology of Religion, 2*, 37–45.

Gallup, G., Jr., & Lindsay, D. M. (2000). *Surveying the religious landscape: Trends in U.S. beliefs*. Harrisburg, PA: Morehouse Publishing.

Geertz, C. (1966). Religion as a cultural system. In M. Banton (Ed.), *Anthropological approaches to the study of religion* (pp. 1–46). London: Tavistock.

Gopin, M. (2000). *Between Eden and Armageddon: The future of world religions, violence, and peacemaking*. Oxford: Oxford University Press.

Gorsuch, R. L., & McPherson, S. E. (1989). Intrinsic/Extrinsic measurement: I/E–Revised and single item scales. *Journal for the Scientific Study of Religion, 28*, 348–354.

Greenberg, M. A. (1995). Cognitive processing of traumas: The role of intrusive thoughts and reappraisals. *Journal of Applied Social Psychology, 25*, 1262–1296.

Hall, M. E. L., & Johnson, E. L. (2001). Theodicy and therapy: Philosophical/ethological contributions to the problem of suffering. *Journal of Psychology and Christianity, 20*, 5–17.

Hill, P. C., & Pargament, K. I. (2003). Advances in the conceptualization and measurement of religion and spirituality. *American Psychologist, 58*, 64–74.

Horowitz, M., Wilner, N., & Alvarez, W. (1979). Impact of Event Scale: A measure of subjective distress. *Psychosomatic Medicine, 41*, 209–218.

Janoff-Bulman, R. (1989). Assumptive worlds and the stress of traumatic events: Applications of the schema construct. *Social Cognition, 7*, 113–136.

Kitson, G. C. (2000). Adjustment to violent and natural deaths in later and earlier life for black and white widows. *The Journals of Gerontology Series B: Psychological Sciences and Social Science, 55*, S341–S351.

Klinger, E. (1998). The search for meaning in evolutionary perspective and its clinical implications. In P. T. P. Wong & P. S. Fry (Eds.), *The human quest for meaning* (pp. 27–50). Mahwah, NJ: Erlbaum.

Kotarba, J. A. (1983). Perceptions of death, belief systems and the process of coping with chronic pain. *Social Science and Medicine, 17*, 681–689.

Kunst, J. L., Bjorck, J. P., & Tan, S. (2000). Causal attributions for uncontrollable negative events. *Journal of Psychology and Christianity, 19*, 47–60.

Lazarus, R. S., & Folkman, S. (1984). *Stress, appraisal, and coping.* New York: Springer.

Lehman, D., Davis, C., DeLongis, A., Wortman, C., Bluck, S., Mandel, D., & Ellard, J. (1993). Positive and negative life changes following bereavement and their relations to adjustment. *Journal of Social and Clinical Psychology, 12*, 90–112.

Lutgendorf, S. K., & Antoni, M. H. (1999). Emotional and cognitive processing in a trauma disclosure paradigm. *Cognitive Therapy and Research, 23*, 423–440.

Mahoney, A. (this issue). Religion and conflict in marital and parent-child relationships. *Journal of Social Issues.*

Maton, K. I., Dodgen, D., Domingo, M. R. S., & Larson, D. B. (this issue). Religion as a meaning system: Policy implications for the new millennium. *Journal of Social Issues.*

Maton, K. I., & Wells, E. A. (1995). Religion as a community resource for well-being: Prevention, healing, and empowerment pathways. *Journal of Social Issues, 51*, 177–193.

Mattlin, J. A., Wethington, E., & Kessler, R. (1990). Situational determinants of coping and coping effectiveness. *Journal of Health and Social Behavior, 31*, 103–122.

McIntosh, D. N. (1995). Religion as schema, with implications for the relation between religion and coping. *International Journal for the Psychology of Religion, 5*, 1–16.

McIntosh, D. N., Silver, R. C., & Wortman, C. B. (1993). Religion's role in adjustment to a negative life event: Coping with the loss of a child. *Journal of Personality and Social Psychology, 65*, 812–821.

Mickley, J. R., Pargament, K. I., Brant, C. R., & Hipp, K. M. (1998). God and the search for meaning among hospice caregivers. *Hospice Journal, 13*, 1–17.

Mikulincer, M., & Florian, V. (1996). Coping and adaptation to trauma and loss. In M. Zeidner & N. S. Endler (Eds.), *Handbook of coping: Theory, research, applications* (pp. 554–572). New York: Wiley.

Nielsen, M. E. (2002). Religion's role in the terroristic attack of September 11, 2001. *North American Journal of Psychology, 3*, 377–384.

Nolen-Hoeksema, S., & Larson, J. (1999). *Coping with loss.* Mahwah, NJ: Erlbaum.

Oman, D., & Thoresen, C. (2005). Religion and health. In R. F. Paloutzian & C. L. Park (Eds.), *Handbook of the psychology of religion and spirituality* (pp. 435–459). New York: Guilford.

Paloutzian, R. F., Richardson, J. T., & Rambo, L. R. (1999). Religious conversion and personality change. *Journal of Personality, 67*, 1047–1079.

Pargament, K. I. (1997). *The psychology of religion and coping.* New York: Guilford.

Pargament, K. I., Ano, G. G., & Wacholtz, A. B. (2005). The religious dimension of coping: Advances in theory, research, and practice. In R. F. Paloutzian & C. L. Park (Eds.), *Handbook of the psychology of religion and spirituality* (pp. 479–495). New York: Guilford.

Pargament, K., I., Koenig, H. G., & Perez, L. M. (2000). The many methods of religious coping: Development and initial validation of the RCOPE. *Journal of Clinical Psychology, 56*, 519–543.

Pargament, K. I., Koenig, H. G., Tarakeshwar, N., & Hahn, J. (2001). Religious struggle as a predictor of mortality among medically ill elderly patients: A two-year longitudinal study. *Archives of Internal Medicine, 161*, 1881–1885.

Pargament, K. I., Magyar, G. M., & Murray-Swank, N. (this issue). The Sacred and the search for significance: Religion as a unique process. *Journal of Social Issues.*

Pargament, K. I., & Maton, K. (2000). Religion in American life: A community psychology perspective. In J. Rappaport & E. Seidman (Eds.), *Handbook of community psychology* (pp. 495–522). New York: Plenum.

Park, C. L. (2005). Religion and meaning. In R. F. Paloutzian & C. L. Park (Eds.), *Handbook of the psychology of religion and spirituality* (pp. 295–314). New York: Guilford.

Park, C. L., & Cohen, L. H. (1992). *Attributions for the death of a friend: God's involvement personal responsibility and chance.* Poster presented at the Annual Convention of the American Psychological Association, Washington, DC.

Park, C. L., & Cohen, L. H. (1993). Religious and nonreligious coping with the death of a friend. *Cognitive Therapy and Research, 6,* 561–577.

Park, C. L., Cohen, L. H., & Herb, L. (1990). Intrinsic religiousness and religious coping as life stress moderators for Catholics versus Protestants. *Journal of Personality and Social Psychology, 52,* 562–574.

Park, C. L., Cohen, L. H., & Murch, R. (1996). Assessment and prediction of stress-related growth. *Journal of Personality, 64* 71–105.

Park, C. L., & Folkman, S. (1997). Meaning in the context of stress and coping. *General Review of Psychology, 1,* 115–144.

Parkes, C. M. (1993). Bereavement as a psychosocial transition: Processes of adaptation to change. In M. S. Stroebe, W. Stroebe, & R. O. Hansson (Eds.), *Handbook of bereavement: Theory, research, and intervention* (pp. 91–101). New York: Cambridge University Press.

Pearlin, L. I. (1991). The study of coping: An overview of problems and directions. In J. Eckenrode (Ed.), *The social context of coping* (pp. 261–276). New York: Plenum.

Powell, L. H., Shahabi, L., & Thoresen, C. E. (2003). Religion and spirituality: Linkages to physical health. *American Psychologist, 58,* 36–52.

Radloff, L. S. (1977). The CES-D Scale : A self-report measure of depressive symptoms for use in the general population. *Applied Psychological Measurement, 1,* 385–401.

Richards, P. S., & Bergin, A. E. (Eds.) (2000). *Handbook of psychotherapy and religious diversity.* Washington, DC: American Psychological Association.

Roccas, S. (this issue). Religion and value systems. *Journal of Social Issues.*

Rothbaum, F., Weisz, J. R., & Snyder, S. S. (1982). Changing the world and changing the self: A two-process model of perceived control. *Journal of Personality and Social Psychology, 42,* 5–37.

Schaefer, J. A., & Moos, R. H. (1992). Life crises and personal growth. In B. Carpenter (Ed.), *Personal coping* (pp. 149–170). Westport, CT: Praeger.

Schuster, M. A., Stein, B. D., Jaycox, L. H., Collins, R. L., Marshall, G. N., Elliott, M. N., et al. (2001). A national survey of stress reactions after the September 11, 2001, terrorist attacks. *New England Journal of Medicine, 345,* 1507–1512.

Sears, S. R., Stanton, A. L., & Danoff-Burg, S. (2003). The yellow brick road and the emerald City: Benefit-finding, positive reappraisal coping, and posttraumatic growth in women with early-stage breast cancer. *Health Psychology, 5,* 487–497.

Silberman, I. (this issue). Religion as a meaning-system: Implications for the new millennium. *Journal of Social Issues.*

Silberman, I., Higgins, E. T., & Dweck, C. S. (this issue). Religion and world change: Violence and terrorism versus peace. *Journal of Social Issues.*

Spilka, B., Hood, R. W., Jr., Hunsberger, B., & Gorsuch, R. (2003). *The psychology of religion: An empirical approach* (3rd ed.). Guilford: New York.

Spilka, B., Shaver, P. P., & Kirkpatrick, L. A. (1997). A general attribution theory for the psychology of religion. In B. Spilka & D. N. McIntosh (Eds.), *The psychology of religion: Theoretical approaches* (pp. 153–170). Boulder, CO: Westview Press.

Taylor, S. E. (1983). Adjustment to threatening events: A theory of cognitive adaptation. *American Psychologist, 38,* 1161–1173.

Thompson, S. C., & Janigian, A. S. (1988). Life schemes: A framework for understanding the search for meaning. *Journal of Social and Clinical Psychology, 7,* 260–280.

Tix, A. P., & Frazier, P. A. (1998). The use of religious coping during stressful life events: Main effects, moderation, and mediation. *Journal of Consulting and Clinical Psychology, 66,* 411–422.

Turner, B. S. (1991). *Religion and social theory* (2nd ed.). London: Sage.

Ventis, W. L. (1995). The relationships between religion and mental health. *Journal of Social Issues, 51*, 33–48.
Zinnbauer, B. J.,Pargament, K.I., Cole, B., Rye, M. S., Butter, E. M., Belavich, G., Hipp, K. M., Scott, A. B., & Kadar, J. L. (1997). Religion and spirituality: Unfuzzying the fuzzy. *Journal for the Scientific Study of Religion, 36*, 549–564.

CRYSTAL L. PARK is Associate Professor of Psychology at the University of Connecticut. She received her PhD in Clinical Psychology from the University of Delaware. Her research focuses on stress, coping, and adaptation, particularly on how people's beliefs, goals, and values affect their ways of perceiving and dealing with stressful events, especially health-related problems and loss. Most recently, this research has been applied to studies of people living with congestive heart failure, myocardial infarction, and cancer. She has published articles on the roles of religious beliefs and religious coping in response to stressful life events, the phenomenon of stress-related growth, and people's attempts to find meaning in or create meaning out of negative life events. She received the Margaret Gorman Early Career Award from Div. 36 (Psychology of Religion) of APA in 1999, and is former president of that Division.

Journal of Social Issues, Vol. 61, No. 4, 2005, pp. 731–745

Striving for the Sacred: Personal Goals, Life Meaning, and Religion

Robert A. Emmons*

University of California, Davis

Religion invests human existence with meaning by establishing goals and value systems that potentially pertain to all aspects of a persons' life. A goals approach provides a general unifying framework to capture the dynamic aspect of religion in people's lives. Empirical research on the measurement of spirituality and religion through personal goals is described. To illustrate the application of the goals framework, data from the author's research program on personal goals and quality of life in persons with neuromuscular diseases are described. Framing subjective quality-of-life outcomes in terms of goals can lead to new possibilities for understanding adaptation to physical disabilities and in particular, the understanding of the religious and spiritual dimensions of disability and rehabilitation.

> Faith, classically understood, is not a separate dimension of life, a compartmentalized specialty. Faith is an orientation of the total person, giving purpose and goal to one's hopes and strivings, thoughts and actions...as such, faith is an integral part of one's character or personality (Fowler, 1981, pp. 14 & 92).

The recent completion of the sequencing of the human genome has rekindled interest in the degree to which human beings are both similar to and distinct from other species. Though in fact anthropologists and primatologists regularly remind us that approximately 98% of our DNA is identical with our nearest phylogenetic cousin, as far as we know humans are the only meaning-seeking species on the planet. Meaning-making is an activity that is distinctly human, a function of how the human brain is organized (Rue, 2000). The many ways in which humans conceptualize, create, and search for meaning has become a recent focus of behavioral science research on quality of life and subjective well-being (Wong & Fry, 1998).

---

*Correspondence concerning this article should be addressed to Robert A. Emmons, Department of Psychology, University of California, One Shields Avenue, Davis, CA 95616-8686 [e-mail: raemmons@ucdavis.edu].

731

This article will review the recent literature on meaning-making in the context of religious and spiritual personal goals. My intention will be to document how the pursuit of personally significant goals in general, and goals of a religious and spiritual nature in particular, can contribute to positive experience and the construction of life meaning.

Over the past two decades, psychologists have learned how goals, as key integrative and analytic units in the study of human motivation (see Austin & Vancouver, 1996; Karoly, 1999, for reviews), contribute to long-term levels of well-being. Subjective well-being (SWB) refers to long–term affective states of emotional well–being as well as cognitive states of life satisfaction and meaning in life. Research on the structure of well-being has reliably identified three components: Positive affect or pleasant emotions, negative affect or unpleasant emotions, and a cognitive component of life satisfaction (Diener, Suh, Lucas, & Smith, 1999). Positive affect reflects a person's level of pleasurable engagement with the world, and negative affect is an indicator of a person's level of subjective distress. A primary focus in this line of inquiry has been to understand how personal goals are related to long-term levels of happiness and life satisfaction, and how ultimately to use this knowledge for well-being interventions. How do goals contribute to SWB? Of all the goals that people strive for, which really matter? Which goals most provide a sense of meaning and purpose?

Personal Goal Strivings as Units of Analysis

Personal strivings are consciously accessible and personally meaningful objectives that people pursue in their daily lives (see Emmons, 1999, for a review). Personal strivings refer to the typical goals that a person characteristically is trying to accomplish. Several points need to be made with respect to the term "personal strivings" and their conceptual nature. First, an emphasis on the concept of striving implies an action-oriented perspective on human motivation. It stresses the behavioral movement toward identifiable endpoints as can be seen in the following definition of goals as "an imagined or envisaged state condition toward which a person aspires and which drives voluntary activity" (Karoly, 1993, p. 274). Second, strivings provide information not only on what a person is trying to do, but also on who a person is trying to be—the relatively high-level goals that are central aspects of a person's identity. Third, goals are highly personal—they reflect subjective experience, values, and commitments as uniquely identified by the person. Fourth, they represent potentialities rather than actualities in that they are never fully satisfied. They reflect what a person is trying to do, not necessarily what they are actually doing. To strive also implies that meaning comes from the "journey" and not just arriving at the "destination." However, one can also strive toward particular modes of being without necessarily making a strenuous effort; for instance, in Eastern philosophies, which emphasize a cessation of striving and

Table 1. Examples of Personal Strivings

Avoid letting anything upset me
Work toward higher athletic capabilities
Meet new people through my present friends
Promote happiness and hope to others
Accept others as they are
Be myself and not do things to please others
Not eat between meals to lose weight
Not be a materialistic person
Appear intelligent to others
Always be thankful, no matter what the circumstances
Reciprocate kindnesses
Keep my beagles happy and healthy
Do what is pleasing to God

Note. Examples come from personal strivings data archive collected by Robert A. Emmons.

nonattachment to goals (e.g., being at peace with oneself, being at one with the universe). Certainly the notion of strivings (as a noun) would include these latter examples, in that they reflect desired endpoints or objectives to be realized. Spiritual concerns are reflected in both "doing" as well as in "being" goals; indeed, perhaps that is an important distinction between the types of goals that adherents to Western and Eastern religious systems aspire toward. Examples of strivings are shown in Table 1.

The Centrality of Goals in Human Functioning

People spend significant amounts of their daily lives reflecting on, deciding between, and pursuing personally important and meaningful goals, goals that lend order and structure to their lives (Emmons, 1986). Goals, according to Klinger (1998), serve as "the linchpin of psychological organization" (p. 44). As internal representations of desired outcomes, they determine the contents of consciousness, including most thoughts and accompanying emotional states. Klinger (1998) has demonstrated that our preoccupations and the emotions we feel are tied to the nature of our goals and the status of their pursuits. Goals are the concretized expression of future orientation and life purpose, and provide a convenient and powerful metric for examining these vital elements of a positive life. More explicitly, goal attainment seems to be a major benchmark for the experience of well-being. When asked what makes for a happy, fulfilling, and meaningful life, people spontaneously discuss their life goals, wishes, and dreams for the future. For many people, of course, the primary goal in life *is* to be happy. Yet research indicates that happiness is most often a byproduct of participating in worthwhile projects and activities that do not have as their primary focus the attainment of happiness. Whether they focus primarily on basic research or intervention, psychologists also see goal striving as vital to "the good life." Psychological well-being has been defined as "the self-evaluated level of the person's competence and the self, weighted in terms of the person's hierarchy of goals" (Lawton, 1996, p. 328). Frisch (1998) defined happiness as "the extent to which important goals, needs, and wishes have been fulfilled" (p. 35). A rapidly expanding database now exists demonstrating that personal goals are a valid representation of how people structure and experience their lives—they are critical constructs for understanding the ups and downs of everyday life, and they are key elements for understanding both the positive life as well as psychological dysfunctions (Karoly, 1999). People's priorities, goals, and concerns are key determinants of their overall quality of life. The possession of and progression toward important life goals are essential for long–term well–being. Several investigators have found that individuals who are involved in the pursuit of personally meaningful goals possess greater emotional well-being and better physical health than do persons who lack goal direction (see Emmons, 1999, for a review). Along with researchers, therapists are increasingly advocating a motivational analysis of life trajectories. For example, quality-of-life therapy (Frisch, 1998) advocates the importance of revising goals, standards, and priorities as a strategy for boosting life happiness and satisfaction. Similarly, the development of goals that allow for a greater sense of purpose in life is one of the cornerstones of well-being therapy (Fava, 1999), meaning-centered counseling (Wong, 1998), and goal-focused group psychotherapy (Klausner et al., 1998).

Goals and Life Meaning

Goals are thought to produce well-being by serving as important sources of meaning. According to Reker and Wong (1988), goals and values, as the motivational component of meaning, provide guidelines for living, orienting a person to that which is valuable, meaningful, and purposeful. Whereas values are more abstract orientations that may or may not be reflected in concrete actions (Roccas, this issue) goals represent the desired outcomes that a person is currently committed to working toward. The goals construct has given form and substance to the amorphous concept of "meaning in life" that humanistic psychology has long understood as a key element of human functioning. For example, a generative goal to "teach my son to make a difference in his community" lends meaning and direction to the role of parenthood. Some have argued that the construct of "meaning" has no meaning outside of a person's goals and purposes, that is, what a person is trying to do. Psychologists are beginning to warm to the concept of personal meaning (Wong & Fry, 1998), and are gradually recognizing that despite its somewhat vague and boundless nature, the topic can be seriously and fruitfully investigated (Debats, 1996; Ryff, 1989; Wong & Fry, 1998).

In the context of well-being, contemporary psychological research, consistent with the existentialist perspective, has shown that *meaning matters*. The explanations that a person offers concerning ultimate issues—the nature of life and death, the meaning of suffering and pain, of what really matters in life—have profound implications for individual well-being. Without meaning and purpose, there is little reason to do what is necessary to live and to endure the inevitable suffering and trials that come with life. The scientific and clinical relevance of the personal meaning construct has been demonstrated in the adjustment literature, in which indicators of meaningfulness (e.g., purpose in life, a sense of coherence) predict positive functioning (French & Joseph, 1999; Robak & Griffin, 2000), while indicators of meaninglessness (e.g., anomie, alienation) are regularly associated with psychological distress and pathology (Baumeister, 1991; Keyes, 1998; Seeman, 1991). Recent empirical research has demonstrated that a strong sense of meaning is associated with life satisfaction and happiness, while a lack of meaning is predictive of depression and disengagement (Reker & Wong, 1988; Wong & Fry, 1998). Meaning is conceptualized in most research as a relatively independent component of well-being, and researchers have recently advocated including it in conceptual models of well-being, quality of life, and personal growth (Compton, Smith, Cornish, & Qualls, 1996; Ryff & Keyes, 1995).

A consensus is emerging on what can be considered to be at least a preliminary *taxonomy of meaning*. Table 2 shows the major categories of life meaning that have emerged across three different research programs on personal meaning. The four life meaning categories of *achievement/work, relationships/intimacy, religion/spirituality,* and *self-transcendence/generativity* appear to encompass most of the domains in which people strive for a sense of meaning. Achievement includes being committed to one's work, believing in its worth, and liking challenge. The relationships/intimacy category includes relating well to others, trusting others, and being altruistic and helpful. Having a personal relationship with God, believing in an afterlife, and contributing to a faith community are expressions of religion/spirituality. Finally, generativity encompasses contributing to society, leaving a legacy, and transcending self-interests. What makes the robustness of these findings of meaning factors especially impressive is that the results are based on diverse methodologies (including rating scales, surveys, and interviews)

Table 2. A Consensual Taxonomy of Life Meaning

Author: Wong (1998) Method: Personal Meaning Profile	Emmons (1999) Personal Strivings	Ebersole (1998) Life Narratives
Achievement	Achievement	Life work
Relationship	Intimacy	Relationships
Religion	Religion/spirituality	Religious beliefs
Self-transcendence	Generativity	Service

Note. Achievement includes being committed to one's work, believing in its worth, and liking challenge. The relationships/intimacy category includes relating well to others, trusting others, and being altruistic and helpful. Religion/spirituality encompasses having a personal relationship with God, believing in an afterlife, and contributing to a faith community. Generativity refers to contributing to society and leaving a legacy.

in heterogeneous populations. For example, the Personal Strivings methodology (Emmons, 1999) utilizes a semi-projective sentence completion task; the Personal Meaning Profile developed by Wong (1998) resembles Q-sort items; and Ebersole (1998) employed narrative methodology in asking people to write about the central personal meaning in their life.

Ultimate Concerns: Religious and Spiritual Goals

When it comes to contributing to well-being, not all goals are equal. In order to explore the contours of goals and well-being, we developed a coding system for classifying personal strivings into 12 thematic content categories (Emmons, 1999, Appendix B). Three types of goal strivings consistently relate to well-being: intimacy, generativity, and spirituality. These three goal types correspond to three of the four major categories of personal meaning from Table 2. Of these, we have recently focused on spiritual strivings as primary elements of people's goal-based meaning systems.

Spiritual strivings refer to goals that are oriented toward the sacred. They are those personal goals that are concerned with ultimate purpose, ethics, commitment to a higher power, and a seeking of the divine in daily experience. By identifying and committing themselves to spiritual goals, people strive to develop and maintain a relationship with the sacred. In other words, spiritual strivings are strivings that reflect a desire to transcend the self, that reflect an integration of the individual with larger and more complex units, or that reflect deepening or maintaining a relationship with a higher power. Strivings are coded as spiritual if they reflect concern for an integration of the person with larger and more complex units: with humanity, nature, with the cosmos ("to achieve union with the totality of existence," "to immerse myself in nature and be part of it," "to live my life at all times for God," "to approach life with mystery and awe"). As implied above, spiritual strivings contain both conventional religious themes as well as more personalized expressions of spiritual concern. Although my focus in this article is primarily with "religious spirituality," it is certainly the case that other, nonreligious, humanistic versions of the concept can be detected in personal strivings as well. Coding strivings in this manner allows for greater inclusivity than do many existing measures of spirituality or religiosity and is sensitive to the diversity of spiritual expression in a religiously pluralistic culture.

Such a conception of spirituality is consistent with a number of authors who, while acknowledging the diversity of meaning, affirm that a common core meaning of spirituality/religion is the recognition of a transcendent, metaempirical dimension of reality (see Emmons, 1999, chapter 5). For example, Tillich (1957), in his classic analysis of the affective and cognitive bases of faith, contended that the essence of religion, in the broadest and most inclusive sense, is *ultimate concern.* Faith, according to Tillich, is the state of being ultimately concerned—concerns that have a sense of urgency unparalleled in human motivation. Ultimate concern is "a passion for the infinite" (p. 8), and religion "is the state of being grasped by an ultimate concern, a concern which qualifies all other concerns as preliminary and which itself contains the answer to the question of the meaning of our life" (Tillich, 1963, p. 4). In religious behavior, "man seeks the largest values in their utmost completion . . . the ultimate relationships" (Johnson, 1959, p. 102).

Concerns over ultimate questions of meaning and existence, purpose and value, do find expression in one form or another through personal goals. In attempting to answer questions such as "Does life have any real meaning?" or "Is there any ultimate purpose to human existence?" implicit worldview beliefs give rise to goal concerns that reflect how people "walk with ultimacy" in daily life. In personal goals that participants have generated in past research studies, they report the ultimate concerns of trying to "be aware of the spiritual meaningfulness of my life," "discern and follow God's will for my life," "bring my life in line with my beliefs," and "speak up on issues concerning people who have been wronged."

The use of goal language in discussions of spirituality and religion may seem foreign. Yet religion is about goals. One of the basic functions of a religious belief system and a religious worldview is that it provides "an ultimate vision of what people should be striving for in their lives" (Pargament & Park, 1995, p. 15) and the strategies to reach those ends. In addition to the prescriptive nature of religion, there is also a long history of using goal language metaphorically to depict spiritual growth. In devotional writings, spiritual growth and spiritual maturity are viewed as a process of goal attainment, with the ultimate goal being intimacy with the divine.

In our own research, we have found that people differ in their tendency to attribute spiritual significance to their strivings, with percentages of spiritual strivings ranging from 0% to nearly 50%, depending upon the nature of the sample studied. College males have the lowest level of avowed spiritual strivings, whereas elderly, church-going females tend to have the highest levels. In both community-based and college student samples, we have found that the presence of intimacy strivings, generativity strivings, and spiritual strivings within a person's goal hierarchy predict greater SWB, particularly higher positive affect. In each case, we examine the proportion of striving in that category relative to the total number of strivings generated. This provides a rough index of the centrality of each motivational theme within the person's overall goal hierarchy. Spiritual strivings are related to higher levels of SWB, especially to greater positive affect and to both marital and overall life satisfaction (Emmons, Cheung, & Tehrani, 1998). In the Emmons et al. (1998) study, these relations were stronger for women than for men, in accord with the literature on gender differences in religion and SWB (Stark, 2002). Spiritual strivings were also rated as more important, requiring more effort, and engaged in for more intrinsic reasons than were nonspiritual strivings. Investing goals with a sense of sacredness confers upon them a power to organize experience and to promote well-being that is absent in nonsacred strivings (Mahoney

& Pargament, 2000). In their sample of 150 community adults, Mahoney and Pargament (2000) found that people tended to place a high priority on strivings that they viewed as sacred. They devoted more time and energy to spiritual strivings and derived greater satisfaction and sense of meaning from them relative to strivings that were more self-focused and materially oriented (see also Pargament, Magyar, & Murray-Swank, this issue).

The Power of Spiritual Strivings

What accounts for the unique ability of spiritual strivings to predict well-being outcomes? As Pargament (2002) has convincingly argued, identifying that which is sacred and striving to protect and preserve the sacred lends deep significance to human existence, a significance that is difficult to explain through more basic psychological or social levels of description. Spiritual strivings may have a unique empowering function; people are more likely to persevere in these strivings, even under difficult circumstances. This empowering function may be stronger in groups that have limited access to other resources, such as racial minorities, the elderly, and the chronically ill (Pargament, 1997). People are more likely to take measures to protect and preserve strivings that focus on the sacred, and devote time and effort toward their realization. People admit that in today's secular culture, whether their spiritual strivings are socially accepted or socially sanctioned, they derive tremendous meaning and purpose from them. Spiritual strivings are also likely to provide stability and support in times of crisis by reorienting people to what is ultimately important in life (Emmons, Colby, & Kaiser, 1998).

The unique ability of spiritual strivings on well-being may be partially explained by the ability of religion to provide a unifying philosophy of life and to serve as an integrating force (Allport, 1950; Tillich, 1957). Conflict or fragmentation is a source of stress that can undermine meaning-making, and, thus well-being. Research has documented the deleterious effect of goal conflict on well-being (Emmons & King, 1988). Although meaning is forged out of the many possibilities that life presents, these same choices can be experienced as paralyzing (see also Schwartz, 2000). Johnson (1959) describes this predicament:

> Out of the very contradictions that provide freedom come the distresses of conflict. Life can never be simple or easy for a conscious person. He must forever contend with the competing demands of a complicated world that give him no rest. Like Adam, the prototype of every man, he is lured by the unknown, tempted by untasted possibilities, seduced by the one he loves, forbidden by highest authority, caught in conflicts of desire, overcome with guilty remorse and driven forth to wrestle and sweat in a world of contradiction and uncertainty (p. 104).

Some support for the integrative role of religious striving comes from a recent study of ours (Emmons et al., 1998), which found that the presence of theistic spiritual strivings in particular were related to low levels of inter-goal conflict, and to greater levels of goal integration. Spiritual strivings appeared to have a greater number of positive, excitatory connections with other goals, and fewer negative, inhibitory connections within people's overall goal systems. Without an overall organizational framework that unites separate goal strivings into a coherent structure, a person would have a very difficult time living a life that is meaningful. Religion, then, has the potential to invest human existence with meaning by establishing goals and value systems that pertain to all aspects of a person's life with the potential to confer unity upon disparate experiences. At the same time, not all religious or spiritual goals facilitate other goals or even one another. For example, in our research we found that desires to share one's faith with others were often not consonant with other goals in the person's hierarchy, indicating that certain spiritual strivings may be associated with greater overall conflict.

Spiritual Goals in the Lives of Persons with Neuromuscular Disease

Having documented that there are substantial and replicable relationships between spiritual goals and indicators of SWB in healthy populations, we wished to demonstrate the value of a goals approach in clinical health populations. Goals and goal-system variables have been utilized in several lines of research to examine positive and negative functioning in the area of health psychology. Goal variables have been identified as a key determinant of both health promotion and health endangerment (Ewart, 1991; Karoly, 1993) and have been linked to conditions as diverse as heart disease, cancer, diabetes, alcohol and tobacco abuse, chronic pain, and hypochondriasis. For example, Affleck et al. (1998; see also Affleck et al., 2001) found that perceived progress toward personal goals attenuated the effect of pain on well-being in women with fibromyalgia. Women who reported more progress toward their goals on a given day experienced an increase in emotional well-being for that day that was independent of pain or fatigue levels. Thus, a personal goals approach has potential to lead to new insights into understanding the effects of chronic illness on emotional and psychological well-being.

We have recently begun a project to examine how a personal goals perspective can be applied to understanding issues related to the quality of life and SWB of people with neuromuscular diseases (NMDs). NMDs are estimated to affect approximately 4 million people in the United States (National Institute of Health, 1998). The majority of participants in our study had post-polio disease (PPS). PPS is a condition that can strike polio survivors anywhere from 10 to 40 years after recovery from an initial attack of the poliomyelitis virus, and occurs in approximately 70% of persons infected with polio. It is characterized by a further weakening of muscles that were previously injured by polio infection. Symptoms include fatigue, slowly progressive muscle weakness, muscle and joint pain, and muscular atrophy. Some patients experience only minor symptoms, while others develop spinal muscular atrophy or what appears to be, but is not, a form of amyotrophic lateral sclerosis. PPS is a very slowly progressing condition marked by long periods of stability and an unpredictable course, although it is rarely life-threatening. Other neuromuscular diseases that were represented in our sample included Charcot-Marie-Tooth Disease, Limb Girdle Muscular Dystrophy, and Facioscapulohumeral Dystrophy (for a detailed description of each disease, see http://www.rehabinfo.net/resources/diseases/list/).

Few studies have systematically examined what determines the quality of life of individuals with neuromuscular disease. Objective indicators, such as functional ability in daily living, occupational status, and social activities, are typically the focus of rehabilitation specialists. These indices, however, fail to account for much variance in SWB (Abresch, Seyden, & Wineinger, 1998). By assisting people in the identification of their current priorities and commitments, by examining the sense of meaning and purpose that goals provide as well as their manageability, stressfulness, and support, a personal goals approach serves to clarify what is possible and desirable to obtain. Framing subjective quality-of-life outcomes such as personal well-being in terms of goals may lead to new possibilities for understanding adaptation to physical disabilities.

While little is known about the spiritual lives of individuals with neuromuscular disease, the general literature on religion and coping suggests that spiritual needs are especially strong in people coping with chronic diseases. Some authors have remarked that a spiritual or religious worldview can be a source of empowerment for people with disabilities, and a means of moving beyond physical limitations to embrace a more holistic vision of life (Selway & Ashman, 1998). A pair of recent review articles (Kilpatrick & McCullough, 2000; Selway & Ashman, 1998) on religion, disability, and health lamented the dearth of empirical research in this area and called for additional research to understand the religious and spiritual dimensions of disability and rehabilitation. The studies that do exist have tended to examine the reactive role of religion in coping with disability. The possible proactive role of religious orientation in setting direction and purpose in people's lives has yet to be considered.

With this rationale in mind, we administered a lengthy survey consisting of the Personal Strivings Assessment Packet (Emmons, 1999), measures of SWB, health status, functional ability, and a variety of other variables relevant to quality of life to over 200 individuals with neuromuscular disease. Participants were obtained through the University of California, Davis, Medical Center Neuromuscular Disease Clinic. Because of the special needs of this population with respect to achieving integration into their communities, specific measures were created to assess the degree to which their personal goals enabled them to feel connected to and integrated into their communities. Strivings were appraised for their personal meaningfulness, difficulty, likelihood of attainment and other attributes (see Emmons, 1999, for a full description of striving dimensions). We also examined a number of social ecological goal variables, including the degree to which others were aware of the striving (visibility), were supportive of the striving (support), hindered the striving (hindrance), and whether the striving causes strain or tension in everyday interactions (strain).

Regression analyses indicated that the goal-based measure of integration was the strongest predictor of overall levels of well-being (a composite of life satisfaction, positive affect, and vitality) of any of the goal variables. Community integration through goals, perceived meaningfulness, and low goal difficulty were the strongest predictors of life satisfaction. Goal meaningfulness and low goal difficulty were the strongest predictors of positive affect. In other words, as goals increased in meaningfulness and attainability, persons with NMD felt more satisfied with their lives. We created a goal-based measure of spirituality based on the concept of sanctification (see Pargament, Magyar, & Murray-Swank, this issue). Self-ratings of the degree to which the goal brings the person closer to God were positively associated with life satisfaction and positive affect. The degree to which pain interfered with the person's ability to work toward his or her goals was predictive of psychological distress (negative affect), as was the amount of interpersonal strain perceived by the person to be caused by the striving. In contrast, a global rating of pain was unrelated to well-being, suggesting that the goal-relevant pain measure is a more sensitive indicator of quality of life than is a global rating of overall degree of pain. Overall, the goal variables accounted for 39% to 44% of the variance in SWB ratings. This finding dovetails with the research by Affleck et al. (1998), who found that goal pursuit is a key motivational-cognitive construct for chronic pain in patients with fibromyalgia. Interestingly, in their study, effort toward health and fitness goals was not diminished on days with increasing pain, but effort and progress toward interpersonal goals was, indicating that pain does not affect all goals equally.

Improving the quality of life of persons with neuromuscular disease has been a long-standing concern of rehabilitation medicine (Abresch et al., 1998). Yet little information has been provided as to what factors are critical for achieving a high quality of life. Facilitating patients' identification of personally meaningful, attainable strivings and developing workable strategies for their accomplishment becomes a priority for rehabilitation providers, enabling them to "live happily and productively on the same level as their neighbors" (Krusen, 1994). Frisch (1998) has demonstrated that goals' setting and values clarification provide meaning and clarity to a client's life, and that changing one's goals through a process of reprioritization is a key strategy for increasing quality of life. Determining a person's interest in spiritual or religious goals should be part of any person-centered planning process (Gaventa, 2001/02). The results of the research presented here suggest that rehabilitation providers will need to take seriously their patient's spiritual beliefs and goals, and to develop methods for assessing their clients' spiritual and religious functioning and its impact on their well-being. A personal strivings assessment can be easily integrated with existing tools designed to assess patient spirituality (Fitchett, 1993).

Conclusions

Motivational constructs such as goals have been under-appreciated by researchers as sources of meaning in people's lives. People often define themselves and their lives by what they are trying to do and by who they are trying to be. Spiritual and religious goals, above all others, appear to provide people with significant meaning and purpose. As Silberman (this issue) points out, an analysis of religion as a goal-based meaning system facilitates an understanding of the dynamic, process-oriented function of religion and could provide a unifying framework for the psychological study of religion. To the extent that their meaning-making systems contain religious and spiritual goals to strive for, they are likely to experience life as fulfilling, meaningful, and purposeful, even in the face of a deteriorating and disabling physical condition. Religion is, thus, able to serve as a general unifying framework to bring about harmony and connection among a person's diverse strivings.

While spiritual strivings tended to be associated with higher levels of well-being, it should not be assumed that spiritual goals necessarily guarantee emotional well-being. There are many possible ways in which spiritual goals might not contribute to well-being, and may even be detrimental for well-being. For example, spirituality that results in excessive self-preoccupation, can discourage generative actions such as responsible parenting (Dollahite, 1998). High-level religious strivings, if not accompanied by concrete plans and strategies for attainment, might be experienced as a source of frustration. Like other high-level strivings, successful self-regulation hinges on the identification of progress indicators. Unlike other high-level strivings, however, spiritual strivings might provide sufficient meaning and purpose to offset the uneasiness associated with other forms of abstract strivings. Serious religious mindfulness can make a person increasingly uneasy about his or her shortcomings, particularly when the person is strongly committed to a goal of living a virtuous life. Although religions are often accused of burdening a person with guilt, dissatisfaction can be desirable if it is used as fuel for constructive life change. Even usually positive characteristics can have harmful consequences.

More significantly, what contributes to the self-perceived well-being of an individual might be detrimental to the well-being of others. It is quite likely that the terrorists who perpetrated the September 11 atrocities would have considered themselves successful in attaining their spiritual strivings. On both national and international levels the spiritual strivings of certain groups can be in conflict with those of others, facilitating intergroup conflicts and wars. Little (1983) has suggested ways of measuring inter-goal conflict at an institutional level. Such research would be an important extension of the individually based goals approach to well-being described in this article. Goals that fulfill individualistic, but not collective or societal needs may ultimately lead to lower quality of life and to a worsening of interpersonal relationships.

To know which goals are out of reach, which are not in our best interest, and which really matter is essential for constructing a meaningful life. Nozick (1989) defined wisdom as "being able to see and appreciate the deepest significance of whatever occurs . . . knowing and understanding not merely the proximate goods but the ultimate ones, and seeing the world in this light" (p. 276). A wise person knows which goals are ultimately fulfilling and which offer only the illusion of fulfillment, and will appropriate this information into his or her life, as well as transmit this knowledge to future generations.

References

Abresch, R. T., Seyden, N. K., & Wineinger, M. A. (1998). Quality of life: Issues for persons with neuromuscular disease. *Physical Medicine and Rehabilitation Clinics of North America, 9,* 233–248.

Affleck, G., Tennen, H., Urrows, S., Higgins, P., Abeles, M., Hall, C., Karoly, P., & Newton, C. (1998). Fibromyalgia and women's pursuit of daily goals: A daily process analysis. *Health Psychology, 17,* 40–47.

Affleck, G., Tennen, H., Zautra, A., & Urrows, S. (2001). Women's pursuit of personal goals in daily life with fibromyalgia: A value-expectancy analysis. *Journal of Consulting and Clinical Psychology, 69,* 587–596.

Allport, G. W. (1950). *The individual and his religion.* New York: Macmillan.

Austin, J. T., & Vancouver, J. B. (1996). Goal constructs in psychology: Structure, process, and content. *Psychological Bulletin, 120,* 338–375.

Baumeister, R. F. (1991). *Meanings of life.* New York: Guilford Press.

Compton, W. C., Smith, M. L., Cornish, K. A., & Qualls, D. L. (1996). Factor structure of mental health measures. *Journal of Personality and Social Psychology, 71,* 406–413.

Debats, D. L. (1996). Meaning in life: Clinical relevance and predictive power. *British Journal of Clinical Psychology, 35,* 503–516.

Diener, E., Suh, E. M., Lucas, R. E., & Smith, H. L. (1999). Subjective well-being: Three decades of progress. *Psychological Bulletin, 125,* 276–302.

Dollahite, D. C. (1998). Fathering, faith and spirituality. *The Journal of Men's Studies, 7,* 3–15.

Ebersole, P. (1998). Types and depth of written life meanings. In P. T. P. Wong & P. S. Fry (Eds.), *The human quest for meaning* (pp. 179–191). Mahwah, NJ: Erlbaum.

Emmons, R. A. (1986). Personal strivings: An approach to personality and subjective well-being. *Journal of Personality and Social Psychology, 51,* 1058–1068.

Emmons, R. A. (1999). *The psychology of ultimate concerns: Motivation and spirituality in personality.* New York: Guilford Press.

Emmons, R. A., Cheung, C., & Tehrani, K. (1998). Assessing spirituality through personal goals: Implications for research on religion and SWB. *Social Indicators Research, 45,* 391–422.

Emmons, R. A., & King, L. A. (1988). Conflict among personal strivings: Immediate and long-term implications for psychological and physical well-being. *Journal of Personality and Social Psychology, 54,* 1040–1048.

Emmons, R. A., Colby, P. M., & Kaiser, H. A. (1998). When lossses lead to gains: Personal goals and the recovery of meaning. In P. T. P. Wong & P. S. Fry (Eds.), *The human quest for meaning* (pp. 163–178). Mahwah, NJ: Erlbaum.

Ewart, C. (1991). Social action theory for a public health psychology. *American Psychologist, 46,* 931–946.

Fava, G. A. (1999). Well-being therapy: Conceptual and technical issues. *Psychotherapy and Psychosomatics, 68*, 171–179.

Fitchett, G. (1993). *Assessing spiritual needs: A guide for caregivers.* Minneapolis, MN: Augsburg Press.

Fowler, J. W. (1981). *Stages of faith: The psychology of human development and the quest for meaning.* New York: HarperCollins.

French, S., & Joseph, S. (1999). Religiosity and its association with happiness, purpose in life, and self-actualisation. *Mental Health, Religion & Culture, 2*, 117–120.

Frisch, M. B. (1998). Quality of life therapy and assessment in health care. *Clinical Psychology: Science and Practice, 5*, 19–40.

Gaventa, B. (2001/02). Using spiritual needs assessment with persons with disabilities: Ideas for agencies. *Impact, 14*, 11.

Johnson, P. E. (1959). *The psychology of religion.* New York: Abington Press.

Karoly, P. (1993). Goal systems: An organizational framework for clinical assessment and treatment planning. *Psychological Assessment, 3*, 273–280.

Karoly, P. (1999). A goal systems-self-regulatory perspective on personality, psychopathology, and change. *Review of General Psychology, 3*, 264–291.

Keyes, C. L. M. (1998). Social well-being. *Social Psychology Quarterly, 61*, 121–140.

Kilpatrick, S. D., & McCullough, M. E. (2000). Religion and spirituality in rehabilitation psychology. *Rehabilitation Psychology, 44*, 388–402.

Klausner, E. J. et al. (1998). Late-life depression and functional disability: The role of goal-focused group psychotherapy. *International Journal of Geriatric Psychiatry, 13*, 707–716.

Klinger, E. (1998). The search for meaning in evolutionary perspective and its clinical implications. In P. T. P. Wong & P. S. Fry (Eds.), *Handbook of personal meaning: Theory, research, and application* (pp. 27–50). Mahwah, NJ: Erlbaum.

Kottke, F. J., & Lehmann, J. F. (Eds.) (1990). *Krusen's handbook of physical medicine and rehabilitation* (4th Ed.). Philadelphia: Saunders.

Lawton, M. P. (1996). Quality of life and affect in later life. In C. Magai & S. H. McFadden (Eds.), *Handbook of emotion, adult development, and aging* (pp. 327–348). San Diego, CA: Academic Press.

Little, B. R. (1983). Personal projects: A rationale and method for investigation. *Environment and Behavior, 12*, 73–109.

Mahoney, A., & Pargament, K. I. (2000, August). *The sanctification of striving: Implications for personal commitment and health.* Presented at the Annual Convention of the American Psychological Association, Washington, DC.

National Institute of Health. (1998). *Post-polio syndrome fact sheet.* Bethesda, MD: National Institute of Neurological Disorders and Stroke.

Nozick, R. (1989). *The examined life.* New York: Simon and Schuster.

Pargament, K. I. (1997). *The psychology of religion and coping.* New York: Guilford Press.

Pargament, K. I. (2002). Is religion nothing but...? Explaining religion versus explaining religion away. *Psychological Inquiry, 13*, 239–244.

Pargament, K. I., Magyar, G. M., & Murray-Swank, N. (this issue). The sacred and the search for significance: Religion as a unique process. *Journal of Social Issues.*

Pargament, K. I., & Park, C. L. (1995). Merely a defense? The variety of religious means and ends. *Journal of Social Issues, 51*, 13–32.

Reker, G. T., & Wong, P. T. P. (1988). Aging as an individual process: Toward a theory of personal meaning. In J. E. Birren & V. L. Bengston (Eds.), *Emergent theories of aging* (pp. 214–246). New York: Springer.

Robak, R W., & Griffin, P. W. (2000). Purpose in life: What is its relationship to happiness, depression, and grieving? *North American Journal of Psychology, 2*, 113–119.

Roccas, S. (this issue). Religion and value systems. *Journal of Social Issues.*

Rue, L. (2000). *Everybody's story: Wising up to the epic of evolution.* Albany, NY: SUNY Press.

Ryff, C. D. (1989). Happiness is everything, or is it? Explorations on the meaning of psychological well-being. *Journal of Personality and Social Psychology, 57*, 1069–1081.

Ryff, C., & Keyes, C. L. M. (1995). The structure of psychological well–being revisited. *Journal of Personality and Social Psychology, 69,* 719–727.

Schwartz, B. (2000). Self-determination: The tyranny of freedom. *American Psychologist, 55,* 79–88.

Seeman, J. (1991). Person-centered assessment: Reaction. *Journal of Counseling and Development, 69,* 462.

Selway, D., & Ashman, A. F. (1998). Disability, religion and health: A literature review in search of the spiritual dimensions of disability. *Disability and Society, 13,* 429–439.

Silberman, I. (this issue). Religion as a meaning system. *Journal of Social Issues.*

Stark, R. (2002). Physiology and faith: Addressing the universal gender difference in religious commitment. *Journal for the Scientific Study of Religion, 41,* 495–507.

Tillich, P. (1957). *Dynamics of faith.* New York: Harper & Row.

Tillich, P. (1963). *Christianity and the encounter of world religions.* New York: Columbia University Press.

Wong, P. T. P. (1998). Meaning-centered counseling. In P. T. P. Wong & P. S. Fry (Eds.), *The human quest for meaning* (pp. 395–435). Mahwah, NJ: Erlbaum.

Wong, P. T. P., & Fry, P. S. (Eds.). (1998). *Handbook of personal meaning: Theory, research, and application.* Mahwah, NJ: Erlbaum.

ROBERT A. EMMONS, is Professor of Psychology at the University of California, Davis. He received his PhD in Personality and Social Ecology from the University of Illinois at Urbana–Champaign. He is the author of nearly 80 original publications in peer–reviewed journals or chapters in edited volumes, including the acclaimed book *The Psychology of Ultimate Concerns: Motivation and Spirituality in Personality* (Guilford Press). His research focuses on personal goals, spirituality, the psychology of gratitude and thankfulness, and SWB. He has received research funding from the National Institute of Mental Health, the John M. Templeton Foundation, and the National Institute for Disability Research and Rehabilitation.

Journal of Social Issues, Vol. 61, No. 4, 2005, pp. 747–759

Religion and Value Systems

Sonia Roccas*

The Open University of Israel

Uncovering the complex relationships between religiosity and values may provide a better understanding of what it means to be religious or nonreligious. This article reviews research on values and religiosity across cultural and religious groups. Although religious groups differ in the importance they attribute to different values, the pattern of correlations between religiosity and values is strikingly consistent across monotheistic religions: Persons more committed to religion attribute relatively high importance to values expressing motivation to avoid uncertainty and change and relatively low importance to values expressing motivations to follow one's hedonistic desires, or to be independent in thought and action.

Political discourse all over the world is rife with the issue of the relationship between church and state: different perceptions of this relationship often leading to conflicts between individuals with secular versus religious orientations. These conflicts cross ethnical and denominational boundaries: They are found among Muslims, Jews, and Christians, in individualistic and collectivistic cultures, and in countries with high and low GNP (e.g., see Arat, 1998, for Turkey; Kimmerling, 1999, for Israel; Michel, 1990, for Eastern Europe; Welch, Leege, & Woodberry, 1998, for the United States). Sometimes conflicts between less and more religious individuals are fierce. However, even in societies where there is no overt warfare, the issue of the proper impact of religious values on society remains central.

These ideological conflicts seem to be based on the assumption that there are real basic differences between religious and nonreligious individuals. Is this assumption correct? Religious people differ from nonreligious people in many aspects of behavior, including the rituals they abide by, some of their daily practices, and the public figures they admire (see Hood, Spilka, Hunsberger, & Gorsuch,

---

*Correspondence concerning this article should be addressed to Sonia Roccas, The Open University of Israel, The Dorothy de Rothschild Campus, 108 Ravutski Street, P. O. Box 808 Raanana 43107, Israel [e-mail: soniaro@oumail.openu.ac.il].

This article was prepared during the author's residence as Visiting Scholar at the Solomon Asch Center for Study of Ethnopolitical Conflict at the University of Pennsylvania.

1996, for a review). While these differences are readily observed, the underlying basis for them is far less obvious.

One promising line of inquiry in this regard involves uncovering the potentially complex relationships between religiosity and values. As discussed here, values are conceptions of the desirable that guide the way persons select actions, evaluate people and events, and explain their actions and evaluations (Rohan, 2000; Rokeach, 1973; Schwartz, 1992). Values express what people believe to be good or bad, and what they think should or should not be done. Reviewing recent research that examined self-reported value differences between individuals who vary in their degree of religiosity may give us a better conception of what it means to be religious as compared with being secular. Extensive research has been dedicated to this issue, enabling the comparison of the associations of values and religiosity across different cultural and religious groups (e.g., Bilsky & Peters, 1999; Fontaine, Luyten, & Corveleyn, 2000; Kusdil & Kagitcibasi, 2000; Roccas & Schwartz, 1997; Schwartz & Huismans, 1995).

The continuing interest in the relations of values and religiosity has resulted in many empirical studies. Until recently, researchers reported relations between religiosity and the importance of many single values, without attempting any broader organization of these results. For example, Rokeach (1969a, 1969b, 1973) found that religious people attributed relatively high importance to the values "family security," "forgiveness," and "obedience," while attributing relatively low importance to the values "pleasure" and "an exciting life." These studies resulted in complex findings that lacked a coherent theory or structure that would help integrate them.

Schwartz (1992, 1994) addressed this shortcoming by proposing a theory of the content and structure of values. His approach has enabled examining the relationships between values and religiosity within an integrative framework. Schwartz's value theory represents an important advance because it organizes a multitude of separate values into a limited set of value types that are universally recognized across different cultures and religious groups. Because of its potential for understanding the value implications of religiosity, this theory merits extended consideration here.

Schwartz's Value Theory

Schwartz defines values as desirable, trans-situational goals, varying in importance and serving as guiding principles in people's lives (see Schwartz, 1992). The crucial aspect that distinguishes among values is the type of motivational goal they express. Schwartz derived 10 distinct motivational goals that are expressed as the following types of values: power, achievement, hedonism, stimulation, self-direction, universalism, benevolence, tradition, conformity, and security. Table 1 presents the definition of each value type in terms of its motivational goal.

Table 1. Definitions of the 10 Types of Values

POWER: Social status and prestige, control or dominance over people and resources.
ACHIEVEMENT: Personal success through demonstrating competence according to social standards.
HEDONISM: Pleasure and sensuous gratification for oneself.
STIMULATION: Excitement, novelty, and challenge in life.
SELF–DIRECTION: Independent thought and action–choosing, creating, exploring.
UNIVERSALISM: Understanding, appreciation, tolerance, and protection for the welfare of all people and for nature.
BENEVOLENCE: Preservation and enhancement of the welfare of people with whom one is in frequent personal contact.
TRADITION: Respect, commitment, and acceptance of the customs and ideas that traditional culture or religion provide.
CONFORMITY: Restraint of actions, inclinations, and impulses likely to upset or harm others and violate social expectations or norms.
SECURITY: Safety, harmony, and stability of society, of relationships, and of self.

The theory also explicates the dynamic structure of relations among values (Schwartz, 1992). Some values are incompatible, in the sense that actions undertaken in order to fulfill a certain value may conflict with the pursuit of other values. For example, behaviors engaged in the pursuit of stimulation values, which emphasize experiencing excitement, novelty, and challenge, are likely to impede the attainment of security values, which emphasize safety and stability. The total pattern of relations of conflict and compatibility among values yields the structure represented in Figure 1. Competing values emanate in opposing directions from the center; complementary values are in close proximity going around the circle.

The circular structure can be summarized into two basic conflicts. The first conflict is *self-enhancement versus self-transcendence*: Power and achievement values are in conflict with benevolence and universalism values. Both of the former emphasize pursuit of self-interests, even at the expense of others, whereas both of the latter involve concern for the welfare and interests of others, close and distant. The second conflict is *openness to change versus conservatism*: Self-direction and stimulation values are in conflict with security, conformity, and tradition values. Both of the former emphasize independent action, thought and feeling, and readiness for new experience, whereas all of the latter emphasize self-restriction, order, and resistance to change. Hedonism values share elements of both openness and self-enhancement and are in conflict with both self-transcendence and conservatism values.

This theory has been thoroughly investigated in a series of studies. Data have been collected in more than 65 countries from more than 210 samples. In each country at least two samples completed the Schwartz Value Survey (SVS; Schwartz, 1992): a sample of teachers and a sample of students. In the vast majority of samples, the distinctiveness of the 10 value types and their structural relations has been verified (Schwartz, 1992; Schwartz & Sagiv, 1995; unpublished data).

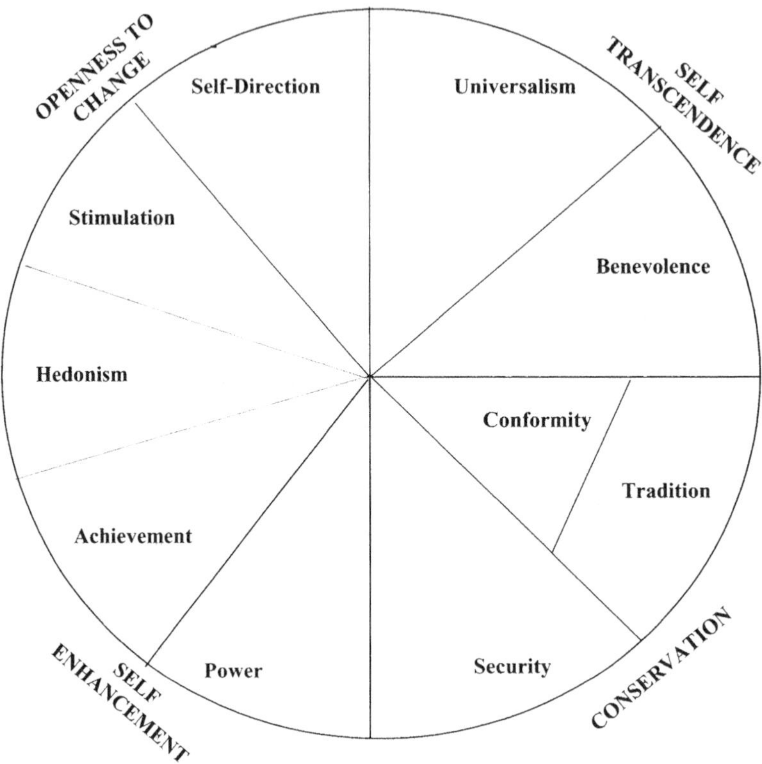

Fig. 1. Structure of the 10 types of values (from Schwartz, 1992).

Examining Associations of Values with Religiosity

Schwartz and Huismans (1995) were the first to examine the relations of values and religiosity within the integrative framework of Schwartz's theory. In developing hypotheses, they considered psychological, sociological, and theological analyses of religiosity. Their sociological analysis suggested that religion provides a consecrated basis for prevailing norms and social structure, and thus encourages the acceptance of the social order and discourages questioning and innovation. In their psychological analysis, they suggested that degree of religiosity reflects, at least in part, the intensity of the need to reduce uncertainty. In their theological analysis, Schwartz and Huismans argued that religion emphasizes feelings of awe, respect, and humility and opposes seeking happiness through the pursuit of material goods.

On the basis of these analyses Schwartz and Huismans (1995) derived the following hypotheses on the relation of religiosity with the 10 types of values:

1. A positive correlation between religiosity and the importance attributed to *conservatism* values because the focus of these values on self-restriction, order, and resistance to change is highly compatible with religiosity. Tradition, in particular, was expected to be most strongly correlated with religiosity, because its central goals of submission to transcendental authority, and protecting individuals from uncertainty are most compatible with religiosity.

2. A negative correlation between religiosity and *openness to change* values because these values conflict with accepting religious dogmas and resigning gratification of material desires. Hedonism values, in particular, were expected to be most negatively related to religiosity because in addition to being a possible threat to existing social order, they also directly oppose a primary function of religion—to temper self-indulgent tendencies.

3. The self-interested focus of *self-enhancement* values is opposed to religious teachings, yet they may also serve to maintain the social order, which is favored by religious institutions. Therefore, Schwartz and Huismans hypothesized that correlations of religiosity with the priority given to power and achievement values would be less positive than those for *conservatism* values, and less negative than those for *openness to change* values.

4. Schwartz and Huismans had different hypotheses for the two types of *self-transcendence* values. They expected a positive correlation of religiosity with benevolence because these values emphasize selflessness in relations with close others. Universalism values emphasize selflessness too. The emphasis of these values, however, on accepting diversity should conflict with the particularism of Western religions. Therefore, the correlation of *universalism* with religiosity was expected to be less positive than that for benevolence values and less negative than the correlations for *openness to change* values.

This set of hypotheses was unified into an integrated set of predicted correlations that represents the circular structure of value systems. Schwartz and Huismans hypothesized that religiosity would be most positively correlated with giving priority to tradition values and most negatively correlated with giving priority to hedonism values. The associations with each of the other types of values were expected to decrease monotonically as one moves around the circular structure of value types in both directions from tradition to hedonism.

Schwartz and Huismans expected that the basic pattern of association of values and religiosity would be found in any Western religion. They tested their hypotheses in four religious groups: Spanish Roman Catholics, Dutch Calvinist Protestants, Greek Orthodox, and Israeli Jews. In all groups, participants reported their values and the extent of their religiosity. The correlations of values and subjective religiosity largely corresponded to the hypothesized pattern in each of the groups. In a total sample, based on averaging across the four religious groups, the correlations ranged from .54 for tradition values to −.39 for hedonism values. The rest of the correlations fell in between, and matched the order expected according to the structure of conflicts and compatibilities among the 10 types of values.

In recent years, the relations of values and religiosity have been examined in several additional cultural and religious groups: Among them are Catholics from Belgium (Duriez, Fontaine, & Luyten, 2001; Fontaine et al., 2000), Catholics from Mexico (Bilsky & Peters, 1999), Muslims from Turkey (Kusdil & Kagitcibasi, 2000), Catholics from Italy, Portugal, and Spain (Roccas & Schwartz, 1997), and additional samples of Israeli Jews (Roccas, Sagiv, Schwartz, & Knafo, 2002; see Saroglu, Delpierre, & Dernelle, 2004, for a meta-analysis of the relationships of values and religiosity). In these studies the relations of values and religiosity generally followed the pattern predicted by Schwartz and Huismans. For example, among Israeli Jewish students subjective religiosity was most positively correlated with tradition values (.59), also positively correlated with benevolence (.22) and conformity values (.18), negatively correlated with stimulation (−.33), self-direction (−.24), and universalism (−.22) values, and most negatively correlated with hedonism values (−.44).

These studies lend additional support to the validity of Schwartz and Huismans' analysis, not only because they extend the variety of cultures in which the model has been tested, but also because they varied in the measures of religiosity: In some studies religiosity was measured by a single item measuring self-rating of subjective religiosity; in others religiosity was measured using multiple-items scales of religious commitment, or by self-reported frequency of church attendance. Thus, in studies in which religiosity is conceptualized as a unidimensional construct the relations of religiosity to values are consistent, regardless the particular measure of religiosity employed. Below I describe studies examining the relations of values and multiple dimensions of religiosity.

Examining the Relations of Values with Multiple Dimensions of Religiosity

Much of the research on the relationship between values and religiosity used a unidimensional conception of religiosity, often based on a single self-report item. A notable exception is the work of Fontaine et al. (2000) and Duriez et al. (2001), who used the conceptualization of religiosity proposed by Wulff (1991). Wulff proposed that approaches to religion could be organized along two dimensions: Exclusion versus inclusion of transcendence, and literal versus symbolic interpretation of religion. The two dimensions define four possible attitudes toward religion: Both "literal affirmation" and "restorative interpretation" reflect embracing religious belief, while both "literal disaffirmation" and "reductive interpretation" reflect a rejection of the religious realm. However, "restorative interpretation" and "reductive interpretation" differ from "literal affirmation" and "literal disaffirmation" in that they try to find symbolic meanings of the religious language.

Hutsebaut and his colleagues developed a scale that captures these four approaches (Fontaine, Duriez, Luyten, & Hutsebaut, 2003; Hutsebaut, 1996) and used it in a series of studies to examine the relations of values and religiosity among Catholics (Duriez et al., 2001; Fontaine et al., 2000, 2005). In general, the dimension of exclusion versus inclusion of transcendence related to values very similarly to the unidimensional conceptualizations of religiosity: Tradition values related most positively and self-direction or hedonism values related most negatively to the inclusion of transcendence. The dimension of literal versus symbolic interpretation was related to values in a way not captured in studies based on unidimensional conceptualizations of religiosity: In general, endorsing a symbolic interpretation was positively related to universalism and negatively to security and power values. This series of studies underscores the importance of studying multiple facets of religiosity, and its contributions to better understanding the psychological dynamics associated with different approaches to religion.

Differences Among Religions

The similarity in the pattern of correlations of values and religiosity across various denominations does not imply that different religious groups hold identical value hierarchies. These patterns of correlation reflect differences within each religious group, but they do not exclude the existence of value differences across religions. For example, although religiosity is related to preference for conservative values among both Protestants and Catholics, Protestants may emphasize somewhat different values than Catholics.

Extensive cross-cultural research on values indicates that religious groups do differ in their values and goals. For example, American Jews and nonbelievers tend to place relatively low value on "salvation" and "forgiving." In contrast, Christians from all denominations tend to rank them considerably higher (Rokeach, 1973). A major study comparing values of different religious groups has been conducted by Inglehart (2000; Inglehart & Baker, 2000). In his analysis of 63 societies, two main value dimensions emerged: survival versus self-expression values and traditional versus secular-rational values. Survival values emphasize giving priority to economic and physical security over self-expression and quality of life; opposition to signing petitions; self-description as not very happy; strong opposition to homosexuality; and mistrust of people. Self-expression values emphasize the opposite. Tradition values emphasize the importance of God in respondent's life; the importance that children learn obedience and religious faith rather than independence and determination; strong opposition to abortion; a strong sense of national pride; and respect for authority. Secular-rational values emphasize the opposite.

Inglehart found that the religion dominant in each society is related to the types of values considered to be most important in it. For example, Protestant European countries attributed very high importance both to self-expression and to secular-rational values, while Catholic European countries attributed only moderate importance to both types of values.

In the studies reviewed above, the relations of values and religiosity have been examined only in the context of monotheistic religions. Would the same relations of values and religiosity be expected in other religions as well? The answer may be somewhat complex and contingent upon the specific value type. In the context of hedonism values, the relations of values and religiosity are likely to hold because Eastern religions view unrestrained pursuing of hedonistic pleasure as moral infractions (Shweder, Mahapatra, & Miller, 1987; Shweder, Much, Mahapatra, & Park, 1997). In the context of conservatism and openness to change values, however, Judaism, Christianity, and Islam may differ deeply from other religions: In contrast to Western religions, Eastern religions do not emphasize the existence of one truth. They offer ways in which a person can improve himself, without precluding belief in other doctrines (Hofstede, 1991). This difference of emphasis fits in with the general tolerance for inconsistencies found repeatedly among people from East Asia (e.g., Choi & Nisbett, 2000).

These differences suggest that Eastern religions may play a lesser role in reducing uncertainty, and thus associations with religiosity may be less positive for conservatism values and less negative for openness to change values. Consistent with this prediction, Miller's (2000) study on the relationship between religiosity and risk preference indicated that in Western societies religiosity was negatively related with risk preference, while in Eastern societies there was no such relation.

The Effects of Social Context on the Relationships Between
Values and Religiosity

An additional type of extension of the research on the relationship between values and religiosity involves examining the conditions that may produce variation in the pattern of relationship proposed by Schwartz and Huismans. One possible factor that has been examined is the relationship between the state and the religious institutions in the country. In all the countries studied by Schwartz and Huismans (1995), church-state relations were cordial and commitment to religion was compatible with holding pro-establishment values. How do antagonistic relations between church and state affect the relationship between values and religiosity? Roccas and Schwartz (1997) postulated that the association of values and religiosity is affected by the standing of the religious institutions because it influences the social and psychological functions of religiosity in society. Data from samples in six Roman Catholic countries were collected during 1988 to 1994. Findings confirmed that in countries with oppositional relations between church and state during the years that preceded data gathering (Poland, Czech Republic, Hungary), religiosity correlated less positively with valuing conformity and security, more negatively with valuing power and achievement, and more positively with valuing universalism than in countries with cordial separation of church and state (Italy, Spain, Portugal). The three Eastern European countries in this study have undergone important political changes in recent years. An analysis of data from these countries in future years will provide a natural experimental test of theorizing about the role of church-state relations as a moderator of religiosity-value associations.

The effect of socioeconomic development on the relationships of values and religiosity has been examined in a recent meta-analysis of 21 samples from 15 countries (Saroglu et al., 2004). Findings supported the pattern of relationships of values and religiosity described above. They indicate, however, that high socioeconomic development attenuates the relationships of values and religiosity.

Future research could also examine additional social context variables. For example, the percentage of the population that is religious may moderate the relation between religiosity and conformity values: The correlation between religiosity and conformity is expected to be higher in countries where most of the population is religious than in countries where most of the population is secular.

Values and the Uniqueness of Religion

Pargament et al. (this issue) discuss the many ways in which religion is unique. Can the findings regarding relations of values and religiosity point to the uniqueness of religion? The answer is somewhat complicated. On the one hand, the pattern of correlations between values and religiosity is not unique: It resembles closely the pattern of correlations found between values and identification with one's nation (Roccas & Schwartz, 2003). Both religiosity and identification with one's national group are positively correlated with conservatism values and negatively correlated with openness to change values. Roccas and Schwartz suggest that the relations between value priorities and identification with a group (one's nation, occupation, religion, etc.) depend on the type of group in question: Identification with any group that helps reducing uncertainty is expected to relate positively to conservatism values. In this sense, religiosity is not unique, because it is not different from identification with one's national group. On the other hand, religiosity may have unique relations with values that are not captured by the Schwartz measure. Schwartz designed his survey to measure values that have similar meaning across cultures and it does not include a set of values specifically designed to tap the importance attributed to things deemed sacred.

Religiosity and Perception of Values of Multiple Ingroups

The studies reviewed so far explored the associations between religiosity and values by examining the correlations of religiosity with the importance individuals attribute to different types of values (e.g., Schwartz & Huismans, 1995). A different approach to the study of religiosity and values involves examining the perceptions individuals have of the values that are endorsed by members of their multiple ingroups.

Religiosity does not exist in a social vacuum: people are simultaneously members of many groups, and the perceptions of the values that characterize these ingroups may have implications for the meaning of being religious. The perceived prototypical features of the groups with which people identify are part of their self-concept, and affect their feelings, attitudes, and behavior (Hogg & Mullin, 1999). The values perceived to be dominant in one's ingroup delimit the goals that an individual feels he or she can successfully pursue in that group (Sagiv & Schwartz, 2000). Therefore, such perceptions help individuals ascertain the perceived likelihood of implementing their valued goals within their religious and nonreligious ingroups. Situations in which different ingroups are perceived as holding different or even contrasting values may be challenging in general, and may pose a special challenge for religious individuals because of the high value they place on adherence to social expectations.

The study of religiosity and value stereotyping of one's ingroups has only just begun, and only preliminary research has been conducted (Roccas, 2003). The perceptions of values important to Christians and to college students were examined among undergraduate students. Participants indicated which group memberships were particularly important to them. In a second session they reported their value priorities, responded to a survey examining identification with their multiple important ingroups, and selected the five values they thought were most important to each of their ingroups. These data enabled comparing which values participants thought were most important to Christians, and which values they thought were most important to college students.

Participants perceived Christians as holding values considerably different from students. The stereotype of Christians included more conservatism and self-transcendence values and less openness to change and self-enhancement values than the stereotype of students. These perceptions are consistent only in part with actual differences in self-reported value priorities of persons differing in religiosity—they are consistent in the dimension of openness versus conservatism, but inconsistent in the dimension of self-transcendence versus self-enhancement. More specifically, participants thought that Christians pursue benevolence and universalism values more than college students. These perceptions contrasted with the actual correlations of religiosity with benevolence, which were positive but very low in most groups. The range in the studies reviewed above was from $-.09$ to $.29$, and in 17 of the 20 samples the correlation was lower than $.20$. These perceptions were also inconsistent with the correlations with universalism, which were even lower than those with benevolence. The range in the studies reviewed above was from $-.39$ to $.17$, and in 15 of the 20 samples the correlation was negative.

Conclusions

People who vary in their religiosity are guided by different value priorities—those who are more committed to religion attribute relatively high importance to values that express the motivation to avoid uncertainty, and relatively low importance to values that express the motivations to follow one's sensuous hedonistic desires, and the motivation to be independent in thought and action. This pattern of correlations has been found in many monotheistic religious groups that varied in their economic strength, as well as in their ethnic and cultural composition and history.

The consistent correlations found between religiosity and values indicate that within various Western religions, religiosity is associated with the same type of motivations. Differences between religious groups have been found as well: members of different religious groups differ in the importance they attribute to values.

Examining the perceptions of the values most important to one's own religious group within the context of simultaneous membership in another group provides a new perspective on the meaning of religiosity. Participants were highly identified both with their religion and as college students, yet they perceived the two groups to hold very different values. When two important reference groups are perceived to hold contrasting values, a discrepancy between the normative expectations of the two groups is inevitable because meeting the standards of one group implies not meeting the standards of the other. Individuals use varied identity management strategies to cope with simultaneous membership in multiple groups (Phinney & Devich-Navarro, 1997; Roccas & Brewer, 2002). Students may cope with the contrasting values that characterize their student and religious groups by compartmentalizing their different identities so that each is "switched on" in the appropriate situation, or by identifying only with the intersection of the two identities (i.e., students who are also religious). Others may represent their nonconvergent group memberships in a merged identity in which the student and religious group are embraced in their most inclusive form.

Both directions of causality between values and religiosity are very likely (Roccas & Schwartz, 1997; Schwartz & Huismans, 1995). On the one hand, religious socialization encourages the adoption of value priorities that express and support the theological doctrines and interests of religious institutions. Thus, the more a person is committed to religion, the more likely he is to accept values endorsed by his religious group. On the other hand, values are only in part the result of socialization. They are also grounded in personal needs, and related to personality traits (e.g., Luk & Bond, 1993; Roccas, Sagiv, Schwartz, & Knafo, 2002). Individuals' value priorities may lead them to become more or less religious depending on the extent to which religion offers opportunities to pursue their valued goals.

An understanding of the meaning of being religious or secular based on the relationship between religion and values may have important applied implications for both intrapersonal and group processes. In the context of intergroup relations, research on value stereotypes and actual value differences between groups may shed light on sources of aggression (e.g., Struch & Schwartz, 1989). In the context of intrapersonal processes, such an understanding may illuminate how individuals resolve conflicts that result from simultaneous membership in groups that endorse potentially contrasting values.

References

Arat, Y. (1998). Feminists, Islamists, and political change in Turkey. *Political Psychology, 19*, 117–131.

Bilsky, W., & Peters, M. (1999). Estructura de los valores y la religiosidad. Una investigacion comparada realizada en Mexico. *Revista Mexicana de Psicologia, 16*, 77–88.

Choi, I., & Nisbett, R. E. (2000). Cultural psychology of surprise: Holistic theories and recognition of contradiction. *Journal of Personality and Social Psychology, 79*, 890–905.

Duriez, B., Fontaine, J. R. J., & Luyten, P. (2001). Does religiosity still influence our lives? New evidence for discriminating value patterns of different types of religiosity. In V. Saroglou & D. Hutsebaut (Eds.), *Religion et développement humain: Questions psychologiques* (pp. 93–113). Paris: L'Harmattan.

Fontaine, J. R. J., Duriez, B., Luyten, P., & Hutsebaut, D. (2003). The Internal Structure of the Post-Critical Belief Scale. *Personality and Individual Differences, 35*, 501–518.

Fontaine, J. R. J., Duriez, B., Luyten, P., Corveleyn, J., & Hutsebaut, D. (2005). Consequences of a multi-dimensional approach to religion for the relationship between religiosity and value priorities. *International Journal for the Psychology of Religon, 15*, 123–143.

Fontaine, J. R. J., Luyten, P., & Corveleyn, J. (2000). Tell me what you believe and I'll tell you what you want. Empirical evidence for discriminating value patterns of five types of religiosity. *The International Journal for the Psychology of Religion, 10*, 65–84.

Hofstede, G. (1991). *Cultures and organizations*. London: McGraw-Hill.

Hogg, M. A., & Mullin, B. A. (1999). Joining groups to reduce uncertainty: Subjective uncertainty and group identification. In D. Abrams & M. Hogg (Eds.), *Social identity and social cognition* (pp. 249–279). Oxford, UK: Blackwell.

Hood, R. W., Spilka, B., Hunsberger, B., & Gorsuch, R. (1996). *The psychology of religion*. London: Guilford Press.

Hutsebaut, D. (1996). Post-critical belief. A new approach to the religious attitude problem. *Journal of Empirical Theology, 9*, 48–66.

Ingelhart, R. (2000). Culture and democracy. In L. E. Harrison & S. P. Huntington (Eds.), *Culture matters. Human values shape human progress* (pp. 80–97). New York: Basic Books.

Inglehart, R., & Baker, W. E. (2000). Modernization, cultural change, and the persistence of traditional values. *American Sociological Review, 65*, 19–51.

Kimmerling, B. (1999). Religion, nationalism and democracy in Israel. *Constellations, 6*, 3, 339–363.

Kusdil, M. E., & Kagitcibasi, C. (2000). Value orientations of Turkish teachers and Schwartz's theory of values. *Turk Psikoloji Dergisi, 15*, 59–80.

Luk, C. L., & Bond, M. H. (1993). Personality variation and values endorsement in Chinese university students. *Personality and Individual Differences, 14*, 429–437.

Michel, P. (1990). Legitimation et regulation etatique de la religion dans les systemes de type sovietique: L'example du Catholocisme en Pologne, Tchecoslovaquie et Hongrie. *Social Compass, 37*, 117–125.

Miller, A. S. (2000). Going to hell in Asia: The relationship between risk and religion in a cross cultural setting. *Review of Religious Research, 42*, 5–18.

Phinney, J. S., & Devich-Navarro, M. (1997). Variations in bicultural identification among African American and Mexican American adolescents. *Journal of Research on Adolescence, 7*, 3–32.

Roccas, S. (2003). *Religiosity and value stereotyping.* Unpublished manuscript.

Roccas, S., & Brewer, M. (2002). Social identity complexity. *Personality and Social Psychology Review, 6,* 88–106

Roccas, S., Sagiv, L., Schwartz, S., & Knafo, A. (2002). The big five personality factors and personal values. *Personality and Social Psychology Bulletin, 28,* 789–801.

Roccas, S., & Schwartz, S. H. (1997). Church-state relations and the associations of religiosity with values: A study of Catholics in six countries. *Cross-Cultural Research, 31,* 356–375.

Roccas, S., & Schwartz, S. H. (2003). *Individual differences in identification with consensual versus nonconsensual groups.* Manuscript submitted for publication.

Rohan, M. J. (2000). A rose by any name? The values construct. *Personality and Social Psychology Review, 4,* 255–277.

Rokeach, M. (1969a). Value systems and religion. *Review of Religious Research, 11,* 2–23.

Rokeach, M. (1969b). Religious values and social compassion. *Review of Religious Research, 11,* 24–38.

Rokeach, M. (1973). *The nature of human values.* New York: Free Press.

Sagiv, L., & Schwartz, S. H. (2000). Value priorities and subjective well-being: Direct relations and congruity effects. *European Journal of Social Psychology, 30,* 177–198.

Saroglu, V., Delpierre, V., & Dernelle, R. (2004). Values and religiosity: A meta-analysis of studies using Schwartz's model. *Personality and Individual Differences, 37,* 721–734.

Schwartz, S. H. (1992). Universals in the content and structure of values: Theoretical advances and empirical tests in 20 countries. In M. P. Zanna (Ed.), *Advances in experimental social psychology,* (Vol. 25, pp. 1–65). Orlando, FL: Academic Press.

Schwartz, S. H. (1994). Are there universal aspects in the structure and contents of human values? *Journal of Social Issues, 50,* 19–45.

Schwartz, S. H., & Huismans, S. (1995). Value priorities and religiosity in four Western religions. *Social Psychology Quarterly, 58,* 88–107.

Schwartz, S. H., & Sagiv, L. (1995). Identifying culture specifics in the content and structure of values. *Journal of Cross-Cultural Psychology, 26,* 92–116.

Shweder, R. A., Mahapatra, M., & Miller, J. (1987). Culture and moral development. In J. Kagan & S. Lamb (Eds.), *The emergence of morality in young children* (pp. 1–83). Chicago: University of Chicago Press.

Shweder, R. A., Much, N. C., Mahapatra, M., & Park, L. (1997). The "Big Three" of morality (autonomy, community, divinity) and the "Big Three" explanations of suffering. In A. Brandt & P. Rozin (Eds.), *Morality and health* (pp. 119–169). New York: Routledge.

Struch, N., & Schwartz, S. H. (1989). Intergroup aggression: Its predictors and distinctness from in-group bias. *Journal of Personality and Social Psychology, 56,* 364–373.

Welch, M. R., Leege, D. C., & Woodberry, R. (1998). Pro-life Catholics and support for political lobbying by religious organizations. *Social Science Quarterly, 79,* 649–663.

Wulff, D. M. (1991). *Psychology of religion: Classic and contemporary views.* New York: John Wiley & Sons.

SONIA ROCCAS is Senior Lecturer at the Open University of Israel. She received her PhD in social psychology from the Hebrew University of Jerusalem in 1997 and was a post-doctoral fellow at the Ohio State University and a Visiting Scholar at the Solomon Asch Center for Study of Ethnopolitical Conflict at the University of Pennsylvania. Her main research interests are in the areas of identity and group processes, and human values.

Journal of Social Issues, Vol. 61, No. 4, 2005, pp. 761–784

Religion and World Change: Violence and Terrorism versus Peace

Israela Silberman,* **E. Tory Higgins, and Carol S. Dweck**
Columbia University

Our article portrays religion as a double-edged sword that can both encourage and discourage world change, and can facilitate both violent and peaceful activism. The article demonstrates how the meaning system approach to religion can shed light on the complicated relationship between religion and world change by illuminating the meaning of world change and the means to achieve it, inherent differences across religious groups, the complexity and malleability of religious meaning systems, and processes that can facilitate either the status quo or violent and peaceful activism. The article discusses context and personality variables that may determine whether religion supports world change and either violent or peaceful activism. It recommends intensive collaboration between researchers, policy–makers, and religious leaders in the contexts of national and international conflicts and religious terrorism.

> *Obedience to God may involve submission to any number of well-established earthly authorities which claim to speak in God's name; it may also describe the spontaneous heroism of a conscientious individual who challenges the powers that be (Walzer, 1982, p. 57).*

> *Paradoxically, religions support both peace and the sword (Appleby, 2000, p. 27).*

The violent message of Osama bin Laden, and his al Qaeda network, which suggests that a positive divine-guided world change can be achieved by religious holy war (jihad) against the infidel West, as well as against "apostate" regimes in

---

*Correspondence concerning this article should be addressed to Israela Silberman, Department of Psychology, 406 Schermerhorn Hall, 1190 Amsterdam Ave., MC 5510, Columbia University, New York, NY 10027 [e-mail: silbermandaytime@yahoo.com or struch@netvision.net.il].

The writing of this article was supported by a grant from the Memorial Foundation for Jewish Culture to the first author. Many thanks to Benjamin Beit Hallahmi, Jonathan Fox, Irene Frieze, Paul Martin, Evelyn Novello, Shalom Schwartz, and several anonymous reviewers for their helpful comments on earlier versions of this article. Special thanks to Miriam Frankel, Aviad Shragai, Nechama and Eliezer Silberman, and Naomi Struch for their continuous encouragement and support.*

the Middle East, has encouraged intensive activism beyond the religious/spiritual realm. It has been transmitted via modern electronic devices to millions of people, motivating many of them in a wide range of places (e.g., Sudan, Egypt, Saudi Arabia, Yemen, Somalia, Afghanistan, Pakistan, Bosnia, Croatia, Algeria, Tunisia, Lebanon, the Philippines, Kenya, Tanzania, India, Russia, United States, and the United Kingdom) to political and military actions, which include self-sacrifice and murder in the name of Islam (Bergen, 2002).

The global activism of the al Qaeda network is only one example of the intensive religious activism that has captured the attention of the world in recent years. Our article starts with a description of religion as a double-edged sword that can both encourage and discourage the goal of world change, and can facilitate both violent and peaceful activism as means to achieve this goal. The article demonstrates how the meaning system approach to religion can illuminate the complicated relationship between religion and world change. It discusses variables that may determine whether religion supports world change and either violent or peaceful activism, and concludes with recommendations for intensive collaboration between researchers, policy makers and religious leaders and communities in efforts to solve national and international conflicts and to prevent religious terrorism.

The Complicated Relationship between Religion and World Change

The relationship between religion and world change has been a challenging issue for both the social sciences and the humanities. Historically, the dominant view in social science has emphasized the role of religion in tradition maintenance and in preserving and justifying the existing social structure (e.g., Durkheim, 1954/1912; Glock, 1973; see Schwartz & Huismans, 1995, for a review). Within this view, Marx (1964/1848), for example, described religion as an opiate for the masses, undermining any motivation to change society for the better. Machiavelli (1940), in a similar manner, advised leaders to uphold the foundations of the religions of their countries in order to keep their people religious and consequently well conducted.

An alternative view of the relationship between religion and change describes religion as encouraging change in the world. The religious call for world change and repair is expressed clearly in the biblical imperative "Justice, justice you shall pursue" (Deuteronomy 16:20), and in the vision of the biblical prophets of a peaceful and harmonious society, e.g., "and they shall beat their swords into plowshares, and their spears into pruning hooks: nation shall not lift up sword against nation, neither shall they learn war any more" (Isaiah 2:4). Many theologians view the struggle for political and social equality as a spiritual struggle attempting to realize God's kingdom on earth (Spilka & Bridges, 1992; Walzer, 1982). Within this view, the Dalai Lama (1999) is calling for a spiritual/ethical revolution, Islam defines the creation of a moral order in human society as one of its main goals

(Nasr, 2003), Judaism calls intensively for world repair (Shakdiel & Shalvi, 1998; Silberman, 1999; Silberman, Higgins, & Dweck, 2000), and Fundamentalist movements across religions are very active in their effort to create a new person and a new society (Einsenstadt, 2002, p. 12; Marty & Appleby, 1991–1995). Consistent with this view, King (1958, p. 36) claimed that, "any religion that professes to be concerned with the souls of men and is not concerned with the slums that damn them, the economic conditions that strangle them and the social conditions that cripple them is a dry-as-dust religion," and Heschel saw the role of religion to "re-create the world in the likeness of the vision of God," and stated that "the liturgical movement must become a revolutionary movement, seeking to overthrow the forces that continue to destroy the promise, the hope, the vision" (Heschel, 1975, p. 217).

Religious and spiritual leaders, such as Martin Luther King, Jr., Abraham Joshua Heschel, Mohandas Gandhi, and Mother Teresa, have tried to put this theology into practice (Pargament & Park, 1995). Under the leadership of such figures, organizations of faith attempting to transform the world closer to a religious ideal and to realize "God's kingdom" on earth, have contributed significantly to social change that aims at the correction of injustice (Spilka & Bridges, 1992). Religiously based social action to change the society for the better can be shown in numerous examples of religiously based charitable activities (e.g., Evans, 1979; Spilka & Bridges, 1992) and in political activism. The latter is exemplified in the significant contribution of people and organizations of faith to the mobilization of major movements such as the Black Civil Rights movement, Poland's Solidarity movement, the South African Antiapartheid movement, and the movement for Indian independence (Smith, 1996). It can also be seen in interfaith dialogues among religious leaders and activists in both international and national arenas in order to facilitate the resolution of conflicts and bring about world peace (Appleby, 2000; Carroll, 2002; Gopin, 2000). For example, during August 2000, 2000 of the world's preeminent religious and spiritual leaders gathered at the United Nations for a Millennium Peace Summit ("World religions converge at U.N. conference," 2000), and during December 2001, Christian, Jewish, and Muslim leaders met in Brussels to try to curb conflicts ("Religious leaders meet on terror," 2001).

Unfortunately, intensive activism in the name of religion has also been demonstrated in numerous historical and recent acts of violence, wars, and terrorism across the world (Hoffman, 1998; Juergensmeyer, 2003; Kimball, 2002) such as the Crusades, the Inquisition, the conflicts between Jews and Muslims in the Middle East, Hindus and Muslims in India, Catholics and Protestants in Ireland, Christians and Muslims in the former Yugoslavia, East Timor, Lebanon, Russia, and many countries in Africa, such as Nigeria, the global activism of the al Qaeda network, and the killing of physicians and nurses by Christian anti-abortion groups (Appleby, 2000; Carroll, 2001; Fox, 2002; Huntington, 2003; Silberman, this issue). This description of violent activism in the name of religion is consistent with the assertion that more destruction perpetrated in the name of religion than by any other institutional force in human history (Allport, 1966; Kimball, 2002). It is also consistent with the description of religious violence by experts on terrorism as being more intense and leading to more fatalities than the relatively more discriminating violence committed by secular terrorist organizations (Appleby, 2000; Hoffman, 1998), and as being an existential danger to modern civilization and the entire world (Ganor, 2005).

The Relationship between Religion and World Change: A Meaning System Perspective

The above description suggests that a comprehensive description of the relationship between religion and world change needs to acknowledge the role of religion as a double-edged sword that can facilitate either the status quo or world change (Berger, 1969; Fox, 2002; Walzer, 1982) and both violent and peaceful activism (Appleby, 2000; Gopin, 2000; Silberman, this issue). We would like to suggest that the meaning system approach to religion (Geertz, 1973; James, 1982/1902; see Silberman, 2003, 2005a, this issue, for reviews) could shed important light on the complicated relationship between religion and world change. The meaning system approach describes religion as an individual or collective meaning system that is similar to other systems in its structure, malleability, and functioning, yet is unique in centering on what is perceived to be the sacred, and in the comprehensive and special way in which it can serve to fulfill the quest for meaning (Silberman, this issue). This approach can contribute significantly, as demonstrated in the following sections, to the understanding of the complicated relationship between religion and world change by illuminating the following four issues: (1) The meaning of world change and of the means to achieve it; (2) inherent differences across religious groups; (3) the complexity and the malleability of religious meaning systems; and (4) the processes through which religion can facilitate either the status quo or violent and peaceful activism.

The Meaning of Change: Goals and Means

One way to summarize the complicated relationship between religion and world change in historical and recent events is by saying that throughout history religion has encouraged both the goals of preserving the status quo and of achieving world change, and any means to achieve these goals, i.e., both violent and peaceful activism (Fox, 1999; Pargament, 1997). The first way in which the meaning system approach to religion can shed light on this relationship is by exploring carefully the meaning that is given within different religious systems to goals, such as world change and tradition maintenance, and to the means that are used to achieve these goals.

The relationship between religion and world change within Judaism is an excellent demonstration of the importance of understanding the meaning of goals and means within a given religious system of meaning. Sociological analyses of the major religious trends within Judaism, which tend to focus on the openness of the participants to changing *tradition*, consistently show that the more traditionally religious trends tend to submit to the authority of the Jewish law, which they accept as divinely inspired, while the less traditionally religious trends try to change the Jewish law in an effort to adjust Judaism to the spirit of the time (Wertheimer, 1993). This information regarding tradition change, which is consistent with the historical view of religion as opposing change, is clearly important. However, the meaning system approach to religion, by exploring carefully the religious meaning of world change and of means to achieve it, has the potential to reveal a more comprehensive and accurate picture of the relationship between Judaism and world change. This potential of the meaning system approach to religion has been demonstrated in the following research, which asked students from the five major trends within Judaism (Ultra-Orthodox (a fundamentalist group), Orthodox, Conservative, Reform, and Secular) to fill out questionnaires in which they described their level of traditional religiosity, their beliefs regarding world change and the mechanisms that they endorse for world change (for detailed descriptions see Silberman, 1999; Silberman, Higgins, & Dweck, 2000).

The results suggested that more traditionally religious individuals are *both* less likely to accept changes in the tradition *and* yet more likely to believe in and encourage radical world change. More specifically, the more traditionally religious participants predicted that the world is more likely to become the way that they ideally wish it to be, and that this future world change will happen sooner. In addition, they believed that they had more power to change the world and reported investing more effort in bringing about the change. In terms of means to achieve the world change, the more traditionally religious participants endorsed more strongly the mechanism of religious practices and evaluated religious practices as being more instrumental for bringing about world change. In contrast, the less traditionally religious participants endorsed more the mechanism of environmental protection and evaluated it as being more instrumental for world change. The groups did not differ significantly in endorsement of strategies that aim at fighting injustice.

This research, which is, thus far, the most direct illustration of the potential utility of the meaning system approach for understanding the relationship between religion and world change, illustrates how religion can oppose tradition change and modernization and yet be interpreted psychologically as motivating revolution and world change. It explains this phenomenon by showing that traditional religiosity contains the belief that tradition maintenance, through religious practices, *is itself a strategic means* for bringing about the desired world change.

The importance of understanding the meaning of world change and the means to achieve it can be demonstrated in the context of other Western and non-Western religions as well. Within Islam, for example, the goal of world change may mean political goals such as social justice and democratic governments. However, the Islamic call for world change can also mean a call for more discrimination against religious minorities, Muslim dissidents, and women. Shari'a (the Islamic law) has been interpreted within different Islamic meaning systems as a means to achieve both types of goals (Mayer, 1993). Within Buddhism, which is often perceived by Western thinkers as socially apathetic, the enlightenment process has actually been interpreted and recommended as a unique means for bringing about revolutionary world change. The principle that is at the heart of the Buddha's social revolution is that helping individuals transform themselves is what transforms society. More specifically, Tibetan Buddhism suggests that through the enlightenment process each individual becomes aware of her/his potential and learns how to free oneself from suffering. This individual enlightenment can stimulate similar experiences for other individuals, and can bring spiritual growth, goodness, and social liberty to the world (Thurman, 1998).

The above discussion suggests that understanding the meaning of world change and the means to achieve it requires explorations of issues such as whether desired world changes involve changes in the tradition or not, whether the change is conducted in the spiritual or the social political realm, and whether the means to achieve the change are perceived as effective or not within given religious or nonreligious systems. Understanding the meaning of world change may also require illumination of the positive or the negative evaluations of relevant goals and means within different meaning systems. This issue may underlie many academic and nonacademic discussions on the nature of religious terrorism. Such discussions often mention disagreements about the definition of terrorism and about the appropriate evaluation of terrorists' goals and means. These disagreements can be expressed in the controversial claim that "one person's terrorist is another person's freedom fighter." However, such discussions also tend to emphasize the need for working definitions for terrorism that could help international and interfaith efforts to deal with this dangerous phenomenon (Ganor, 2005; Moghaddam, 2005).

The meaning system approach to religion can contribute to such discussions in two ways. First, it can illuminate the meaning systems of religious terrorists (Silberman, 2005b). Research suggests that those who commit acts of cruelty, destruction, and violence in the name of religion usually believe that through their actions they create a better world. In the words of Stern (2003, p. 281) about religious terrorists that she interviewed: "From their perspective, they are purifying the world of injustice, cruelty, and all that is antihuman." Second, because of its ability to systematically compare religious and nonreligious systems in terms of psychological constructs such as goals (Silberman, this issue, 2005a), the meaning system approach may be helpful in the challenging effort to develop international working definitions for religious terrorism that define terrorism in terms of goals and means to achieve these goals. The following definition, which emphasizes the goals of terrorists (political goals), the means they endorse in order to achieve their goals (violent actions), and their targets (civilians) could be viewed as an important step in that direction: "Terrorism is a form of violent struggle in which violence is deliberately used against civilians in order to achieve political goals (nationalistic, socioeconomic, ideological, religious, etc.)" (Ganor, 2005, p. 17).

In sum, the above discussion on the meaning of world change within Judaism, Islam, and Buddhism and on religious terrorism illustrates how the meaning system approach to religion can shed light on the complicated relationship between religion and world change by illuminating the meaning of relevant goals and the means to achieve them.

Inherent Differences across Religious Groups

A second way in which the meaning system approach can contribute to an understanding of the complicated relationship between religion and world change is by exploring whether groups, which endorse different religious meaning systems (e.g., Christianity, Judaism, and Islam), differ inherently from each other in this context. More explicitly, the meaning system approach, by exploring systematically the contents of the beliefs, goals, and actions of different religious groups may be helpful in the challenging effort to construct a meaningful typology of religious groups based on their attitudes toward world change and toward violent or peaceful activism.

In terms of attitudes toward world change, cross-cultural and cross-religious comparisons have indeed yielded several insightful typologies of religious groups based on their openness to social change. Yinger (1965), for example, distinguishes between *church-type* religious groups and *sects*. In order to establish themselves alongside the ruling powers, church-type religious groups are willing to accept the basic pattern of the status quo despite its failure to meet the religious ideal. Sects, on the other hand, choose to maintain their ideals as much as they can within small intimate groups, challenging explicitly or implicitly those aspects of society that contradict their ideal. Lincoln (1985) has distinguished among three basic types of religions based on their attitude toward the status quo: Religions can be "religions of the status quo" (i.e., religions that support the dominant party and the sociopolitical status quo), "religions of resistance" (i.e., religions that define themselves in opposition to the religion of the status quo, defending themselves against the ideological domination of the latter), or "religions of revolution" (i.e., religions that define themselves in opposition to the dominant social party itself, not its religious arm alone, promoting direct action against the dominant party's material control of society). In this context, it is also important to mention the following, somewhat controversial, distinctions. First, the distinction between temporal-oriented religions versus outworldly oriented religions, suggesting that the first type may inspire activism, while the second type tends to inhibit it (Marx, 1967). Second, the distinction between Western religions as encouraging social activism, and Eastern religions as encouraging detachment from the world and passivism (see our earlier discussion on Tibetan Buddhism and Thurman (1998) for criticism on the distinction).

In a similar way, discussions of violent activism versus peaceful activism have suggested that some religious groups tend to be inherently more violent than others. For example, Muslims have sometimes been described as relatively militant (e.g., Huntington, 2003), while groups, which endorse religious systems that include doctrine pacifism, such as Buddhism, have often been viewed as being less prone to conflict (Fox, 2004). In one of the most direct empirical comparisons between Christians, Muslims, and other groups, Fox (2004) found that during the years 1965–2001 Christians were involved in most conflicts on an absolute level. Muslims were involved in most conflicts in proportion to their population size, and the majority of these conflicts were intrareligious rather than interreligious. His results for religious conflicts (e.g., conflicts between two groups, which belong to different religions or between two groups, which belong to different denominations of the same religion) showed that Muslim groups engaged in the most conflicts in both absolute and proportional terms. Fox (2004) was careful in his interpretation of the above results, emphasizing that while they reflected the relationship between religions and conflict during a specific historic period, they did not imply anything about inherent violent tendencies of the religions.

Religions as Complex and Malleable Meaning Systems

As implied above, arguments suggesting inherent differences among religious groups in terms of their wish to change the world and their endorsement of violent or peaceful activism have often been rightfully criticized as overgeneralizations (Fox, 2004). We would like to emphasize that whether the inherent likelihood of certain religious groups to support the status quo or violent or peaceful activism varies or not, historical evidence suggest that each of the major religions, as demonstrated below, has the potential to support both the status quo and opposition to it and to facilitate both violent and peaceful activism (Appleby, 2000; Fox, 2004; Rapoport, 1993).

In discussing the malleability of religions in terms of attitudes toward the status quo, Yinger (1965) proposes that a sect grows out of certain aspects of the teachings of the church, and if it is to survive in the currents of history, it must grow again into a church. One may say that, historically, all major established religions, regardless of how much they may currently support the status quo, have started as small revolutionary movements (Kimball, 2002). Lincoln (1985), in a similar manner, suggests that religions of resistance can transform themselves into religions of revolution, while religions of revolutions can become religions of status quo if they succeed in their struggle, or may fall back into being religions of resistance if they are defeated.

In this context, Catholicism, which historically has often supported the establishment, has also been interpreted as supporting forms of political action in order to affect human liberation from social injustice. Finally, the Muslim belief that the "messianic" Mahdi will return, overturn a disliked social system, and bring justice to earth has been used during certain historical periods, when Shi'i-supported governments came to power, to justify the status quo. During other historical periods this belief fueled Shi'i revolts (Keddie, 1985).

In terms of violent versus peaceful activism the malleability of religious meaning system can be demonstrated in the following historical examples: (a) The same Catholicism, which does not reject the strong pacifism tradition within Christianity, is also responsible for the Crusades and the Inquisition (Fox, 2002), and according to some scholars has facilitated to some extent the Holocaust (Carroll, 2001). (b) Judaism throughout history has usually encouraged peaceful resistance of the often violent repression against the Jews. However, in both modern and ancient times Judaism has inspired some violent activism (Rapoport, 1993; Sprinzak, 1993). (c) Finally, Buddhists in Tibet have, despite a tradition of pacifism, on occasion, violently opposed the Chinese occupation.

The above historical examples raise the question of how can the *same* religion (e.g., Buddhism, Christianity, Islam, or Judaism) support both the goals of status quo and world change, and both violent and peaceful activism as means to achieve them. The meaning system approach to religion attempts to answer this question by emphasizing the complexity of major religious meaning systems that tend to include within themselves a wide variety of messages (e.g., major religious meaning systems can include some messages that encourage support of the status quo and other messages that oppose it; they can also include recommendations for *both* violent *and* peaceful activism as appropriate means to achieve these goals). By emphasizing the malleability of these complicated religious systems (i.e., their ability to accommodate to different situations, and to develop and change over time), the meaning system approach suggests that it is possible to direct both the idiosyncratic religious meaning systems of individuals (e.g., of religious or spiritual leaders) and the collective religious systems of groups toward a variety of goals (e.g., support or challenge of the status quo) or toward peaceful or violent activism by choosing to selectively emphasize certain religious messages over others (Gopin, 2000; Lewis, 2003; Silberman, this issue, 2005b).

The above view of religion as a complex and malleable meaning system that can encourage both the status quo and world change, and can facilitate both violent and peaceful activism as means to achieve these goals has encouraged conceptual and empirical research on the circumstances and the personality variables that are related to whether religious individuals or groups choose to support the status quo or challenge it, and to endorse either peaceful or violent activism. Some of the main findings of this research are demonstrated below:

Context variables: Social, political, economic, and historical. Many contextual factors have been proposed as moderating the relationship between religion and its tendencies to either support the status quo or to challenge it (see Billing & Scott, 1994; Fox, 2002, for reviews). Some of these factors include the level of compatibility between a given theological tradition and the existing social order (Westhues, 1976); oppositional relationship between church and state (Roccas & Schwartz, 1997; Roccas, this issue); the interests of the elites who control the religious institutions (Fox, 2002; Gill, 1998); the secular interests and the class position of the individuals to whom the religious movement appeals or attempts to appeal (Yinger, 1965); whether religious groups see themselves as oppressed minorities in need of protection (Martin, this issue); variation in regime needs for external legitimation (Johnson & Figa, 1988); spatial position in core or peripheral zones of the world system (Budde, 1992; Wuthnow, 1980); and temporal phases (expansion, polarization, and reconstitution) of world system development (Wuthnow, 1980). For example, religious groups tend to change from being a radical challenge to the social structure (i.e., sects), into accepting it (i.e., churches) when their members gain wealth (Yinger, 1965), and the Catholic Church in Latin America generally supports the state unless there are successful competing religious movements in the state, in which case the Church supports the masses in order to avoid losing members (Gill, 1998).

In a similar way, many factors have also been proposed as triggering or magnifying the tendency of religious actors to employ extreme violence (see Appleby, 2000; Stern, 2003, for insightful reviews). Some of these factors include a sense of personal or collective alienation, humiliation, deprivation, and victimization (Stern, 2003); ineffective or inaccessible political institutions that fail to provide basic services, to protect human rights, or to fight extremists (Appleby, 2000; Stern, 2003); claims over territory, demographic shifts; discrimination on the basis of religion, history of devaluation and even demonization of outgroup members (Moghaddan, 2005; Staub, 2004); and encouragement by leaders to displace aggression onto outgroups (Moghaddan, 2005). Poverty may be a risk factor in itself (Appleby, 2000) since terrorists have found cruel ways to prey on, and manipulate the poor and ignorant (Stern, 2003). The communication revolution may magnify religious violence by facilitating the spread of the messages of religious terrorists around the world, and by increasing the sense of personal deprivation (Stern, 2003; Staub, 2004).

A simultaneous exploration of both the conditions that facilitate political activism and those that facilitate violence suggested that religious institutions tend to inhibit peaceful opposition unless there is a sufficient level of perceived threat to the religious institutions or the religion itself, in which case religious

institutions tend to facilitate political opposition among ethno-religious minorities. However, the decision to violently oppose a regime is based mostly on secular factors including the desire for some form of autonomy or independence (Fox,
1999).

Personality variables. Going beyond context variables, one may approach the
question of why do some religious leaders and other individuals choose religious
messages that either support or challenge the status quo or that encourage either
violent or peaceful activism from a perspective of individual differences in personality variables. Decisions of supporting or challenging the status quo by religious
leaders or other individuals may be related to individual differences in views of human nature and of the world as being either malleable or fixed (e.g., Dweck, 1999)
or to personal tendencies toward promotion or prevention (Liberman, Chen-Idson,
Camacho, & Higgins, 1999), which are related to choosing options of change
versus stability across situations.

In the context of choosing violent or peaceful goals or means, attempts to
explain religious violence and terrorism within a personality "defect" model (i.e.,
by searching for personality problems that result from childhood negative experiences) might be helpful in certain cases. However, the appropriateness of this
approach to the study of religious violence as a whole has been criticized (Ruby,
2002, for a review). Instead, the meaning system approach to religious violence
and peace suggests that individual differences in terms of other kinds of personality variables, such as basic beliefs and goals, may impact the choices of religious
leaders and individuals. For example, retributive and forgiveness motivations may
cause individuals to endorse either messages of revenge or messages of forgiveness from within their religious meaning systems (Tsang, McCullough, & Hoyt,
this issue). In addition, individual differences in the ways in which individuals relate to their religious meaning systems may also influence their choices regarding
violence or peace. Relating in a fundamentalist way (i.e., in a way that suggests
closed-mindedness, and the belief that one has access to absolute truth) tends to
be connected to prejudice, discrimination, and violence toward outgroups, while
connecting to religious meaning systems as a quest (i.e., in a doubting, flexible
approach to religious issues) is related to more openness and tolerance toward
others (Hunsberger & Jackson, this issue).

These lines of research imply that both directions of causality are possible in
the context of religion and world change. On one hand, religious meaning systems
may influence whether religious individuals or groups choose world change over
support of the status quo or violence versus peaceful activism. On the other hand,
individual or communal tendencies for change or for violence may influence the
type of religious meaning system that individuals or communities would choose,
or the specific messages regarding world change, violence, and peace within their
meaning system that they would endorse.

Processes through which Religion Influences World Change

The fact that religious meaning systems can facilitate both support for the status quo and opposition to it, raises the question, "What are the processes through which religion facilitates support or opposition to the status quo?" Since processes through which religion can support the status quo have been discussed extensively in the literature (Pargament & Park, 1995; Schwartz & Huismans, 1995; Silberman, 1999, 2005b), we would focus mainly on processes that can facilitate activism.

One process through which religion can facilitate both the status quo and any type of activism is the process of sanctification through which religion can give any belief, goal, or action, as well as any object, a special significance (Pargament, Magyar, & Murray-Swank, this issue; Silberman, this issue). By providing a sacred basis for prevailing norms and social structure, religions can discourage questioning and innovation, and can encourage believers to accept the social order. However, through the process of sanctification religion can also define the goal of world change as sacred evoking strong motivations for either violent or peaceful activism as sanctified means to achieve this goal (Pargament et al., this issue; Silberman, 2004).

In terms of activism, there is general agreement that religious institutions can provide organizational resources for mobilization (see Fox, 1999, for a review) in several ways. For example, religious institutions such as churches, mosques, and temples can facilitate activism by providing convenient meeting places, which might be the safest places under oppressive regimes, and by having extensive access to the media. The meaning system approach to religion (Silberman, this issue) can further illuminate the processes through which religion motivates people to passionately conduct both peaceful and violent activism (see also Silberman, 2005b):

1. Religion as a meaning system may facilitate activism by encouraging a sense of self-efficacy; that is, by suggesting that individuals have the power to change and improve both themselves and the world around them (Silberman, 1999, 2004; Silberman, Higgins, & Dweck, 2000).

2. Religion can also encourage activism by recommending certain values. Two interesting examples for religious values that might facilitate both violent and peaceful activism would be "selflessness" (i.e., nullification in front of God, and a focus on religious goals and objectives, rather than on the self; Silberman, 2004) and "self-sacrifice." Within certain religious meaning systems and under certain circumstances these two values, which may be described by religious meaning systems as means to demonstrate one's faith (Fox, 2002), can guide people to sacrifice other needs and even their lives in religious wars or in acts of homicide (suicide) bombings, while within other religious meaning systems or under other circumstances these values can facilitate selfless acts of love and compassion.

3. Religion can motivate activism by offering a dramatic system of extreme rewards and punishments for people's behaviors. A common contingency in this context is that righteous people would get rewarded for their good deeds, while sinners would get punished. It is hard to compete with the rich and detailed descriptions of both the rewards and punishments that some religious systems offer. Spiritual rewards can include inner happiness and tranquility in this life or beyond, a uniquely powerful experience of closeness to a powerful spiritual force (Pargament, 1997), participation in a utopian redemption, or in the resurrection of the dead (e.g., Miller, 2002). Punishments, on the other hand, may include emotional and physical suffering in this world, rejection by God, or eternity in hell (e.g., Woodward, 2002). While the concept of heaven can be a source of help to those who cope with personal or communal tragedies, both concepts of heaven and hell have been used, sometimes in a cynical manipulative way, by political and terrorist leaders to justify their world views (Miller, 2002). These dramatic promises can, in different conditions, facilitate either support for the status quo or different types of activism (see Rapoport, 1988; Silberman, 1999, for discussions on possible influences of Messianic beliefs).

4. Religion may encourage activism in an indirect way by facilitating the fulfillment of an exceptionally wide range of basic needs beyond the spiritual, such as the search for happiness, optimism, calmness, and decisiveness (Silberman, Higgins, & Dweck, 2001), the search for meaning in the world, positive self-concept and group identity, a search for a shelter from human impulses, a search for community, intimacy, and a social consensus (Pargament, 1997).

Stern's (2003) description of the reported religious and nonreligious motivations of religious terrorists around the world is an excellent example of the many ways in which religious meaning systems can motivate people to intensive violent activism. All the terrorists that were interviewed by her claimed to be motivated by religious and spiritual goals. They emphasized the goals of contributing to the good cause of purifying the world, and of being virtuous by transforming themselves from being spiritually perplexed to focused on action, from being selfish to becoming altruistic. Some mentioned religious goals, such as helping to bring the redemption or the apocalypse and the End of times predicted by Biblical texts. They mentioned heavenly awards, such as pleasing God and getting closer to him, and the sense of spiritual transcendence. Most of them combined spiritual with political goals, such as obtaining political power, imposing religious laws, or expanding their territory, as well as frightening the enemy, damaging the economy, or rousing the troops.

On a more emotional-psychological level, one of the most important motivations seemed to be the simplification of the meaning of life—a life in which good and evil, victims and oppressors, were clearly defined, and martyrdom provided escape from life's dilemmas and difficulties. Other goals on the emotional-psychological level included expression of rage, as well as the achievement of status, glamour, fame; a sense of identity, pride and strength; friendship and community; adventures and fun. Stern adds that some individuals seemed to join religious terrorist groups as a way to cope with their fear of a Godless universe, of chaos, and of loneliness, and to reach a peak experience of transcendence. In her words (p. 282): "To be crystal clear about one's identity, to know that one's group is superior to all others, to make purity one's motto, and purification of the world one's life work—this is kind of a bliss." They also mentioned that the atmosphere at some training camps can be of intense psychological pressure enforced by the torture of those who did not embrace the violent code. On a material level, the terrorists mentioned that terrorist groups often provide cash payments for successful operations or money to "martyr" families, or long-term jobs.

In sum, the meaning-making power of religion can motivate people to intense activism by encouraging a sense of self-efficacy to bring about self-change and world change, through values such as selflessness and self-sacrifice, and by offering both spiritual and nonspiritual rewards and punishments. These processes can facilitate *both* peaceful and violent activism. We next discuss additional processes through which religion can facilitate *either* violent *or* peaceful activism.

Religious meaning systems as facilitators of violent activism. Religion, when internalized as an individual or collective system of meaning, can facilitate violent activism in a variety of ways. First, religions often contain values and ideas that may facilitate prejudice, discrimination, and violence by encouraging the consciousness of belonging to a select and privileged community, and by emphasizing the "otherness" of those who do not follow the tenets of the religion (Appleby, 2000; Martin, this issue; Schwartz & Huismans, 1995; Wellman & Tokuno, 2004). According to Allport (1966), religion includes the following three basic invitations to bigotry: (1) the belief that one's religion teaches absolute and exclusive truth may lead to derogating the teachings of other religions and philosophical formulations as if those teachings are wrong and are a threat to human salvation (Hunsberger & Jackson, this issue; Kimball, 2002); (2) the doctrine of election (e.g., the concepts of God's chosen people or God's country), which may imply the inferiority of others as rejected by God; and (3) theocracy (i.e., the view that a monarch rules by Divine right, that the Church is a legitimate guide for civil government or that the legal code, being divinely ordained, is inviolable on the pain of severe punishment). In addition, some religious teachings seem to explicitly or implicitly tolerate or even encourage prejudice against certain targets such as gay men and lesbians, Jews, or women (Hunsberger & Jackson, this issue).

The second process through which religion can facilitate violence is desecration. Any object, belief, goal, or action that is perceived as sacred can be desecrated by being lost, destroyed, or violated. Since a perception of desecration has unique adverse effects, such as intense negative affect (e.g., feeling distressed, nervous, scared, and upset; Pargament et al., this issue), it may facilitate intensive political or violent activism against those who are believed to have caused the desecration. For example, the Middle East conflict seems to be fueled to a certain extent by a sense of desecration of both Jewish and Muslim Holy sites. A sense of desecration of Saudi Arabia (which is the Muslim Holy Land par excellence), especially of its two holy sites, Mecca and Medina, by the American presence has been mentioned as one of the main sources of Bin Laden's anger toward the United States (Lewis, 2003).

Third, religion as a unique meaning system that can give meaning to every aspect of human life (Silberman, this issue) is often at the core of individual and group identity (Seul, 1999). Accordingly, religious beliefs that seem to threaten one's religious meaning system or other ideological threats to one's religion are often perceived as particularly dangerous attacks on both personal and communal identity. Such perceived threats often provoke violent reactions among the adherents of the challenged religions, who perceive themselves as defending not only their religion but also their most important personal and collective identities (see Fox, 2002, for a review).

Fourth, the rules and standards of behaviors that religions as meaning systems usually provide often result in behavior that is likely to provoke conflicts. This can happen in two ways: First, the prescribed action might be inherently conflictive as in the case of religious calls for "holy wars." Second, the required actions may be perceived as threatening by another group, forcing the members of the second group to defend their beliefs (Fox, 2002). Evangelism, which suggests that there is "either an obligation unfulfilled or spiritual reality unfulfilled as long as the whole world does not profess the tenets of a particular religion" (Gopin, 2000, p. 31), is a good example of the two ways in which religious rules can increase violent conflicts. The idea of evangelism, which requires the effort to change the religious meaning systems of members of outgroups, does not inherently require violence, but when imposed forcefully, it has brought about extreme violence throughout history (e.g., during the time of the Inquisition), and has the potential to do so in the future. Beyond that, evangelism, which is restricted by law in many countries, can provoke a violent response against it. For example, the recent increase (particularly since September 11, 2001) in the activism of Christian missionaries in Islamic countries has been a source of tension. It has been interpreted by some individuals as a threat to the fragile peace among Muslims and Christians in countries like Lebanon, and even as a crusade against Islam on the part of the Bush administration. This missionary activism has coincided with increasing anti-Western militancy in regimes of Islamic-majority countries—militancy, which involved the arrest, imprisonment, or even the murder of some Christian missionaries (Van Biema, 2003).

Fifth, religion can facilitate violence by offering seemingly simple and powerful myths or stories that summarize very complicated situations in a cognitively manageable way within individual or collective systems of meaning. "Such myths are critical means of organizing the world and making sense of one's history, one's origins, and even one's future" (Gopin, 2002, p. 7). Unfortunately, such myths often emphasize the otherness of the nonreligious or of those who hold different religious views in a derogating way. "The facile invocation of religious symbols and stories can exacerbate ethnic tensions and foster a social climate conducive to riots, mob violence, or the random beatings and killings known as hate crimes" (Appleby, 2000, p. 119).

A famous example of a powerful myth is the biblical story of the Abrahamic family—a myth that is part of the lives of hundreds of millions of Jews, Christians, and Muslims. The myth discusses the competition and rivalry between the two sons of Abraham—Isaac, who is described as the key to Jewish lineage, and Ishmael, the key to Arab Islamic lineage, and between their mothers. The sons compete over who is idolatrous and who is authentic, and they compete for the love of their father. "In this metaphor of Abrahamic family, identities are established . . . old wounds are expressed . . . ancient competitions and conflicts are given a quality of cosmic significance"(Gopin, 2002, p. 7). Another famous myth is the portrayal of Jews and Judaism in early Christian writings—an inaccurate myth, which was developed according to some interpretations for political reasons (Carroll, 2001). In that myth, the Jews are portrayed as the killers of Jesus, and the disagreements between Christians and Jews are described dramatically as a cosmic struggle between evil and good, with the Jews defined as evil, as the offspring of Satan. This demonization of the Jews as a symbol of "all evil" has aroused and legitimized hostility toward Jews in the course of Christian history (Carroll, 2001).

Sixth, because of its power to morally justify any goal or action through the process of sanctification, religion can provide an excellent source for the legitimization of the most violent acts within both individual and collective meaning systems (Fox, 1999). It can provide a particularly strong basis for the processes of moral disengagement, such as moral justification, euphemistic labeling, and dehumanization. According to Bandura (2004), individuals, through socialization, adopt moral standards that serve as guides and deterrents for conduct. These internalized moral standards cause individuals to anticipate self-condemnation if they behave in unethical ways, i.e., in ways that are not consistent with their moral standards. When individuals wish to engage in behaviors that are seemingly inconsistent with their moral standards without experiencing a sense of self-condemnation, they endorse psychological mechanisms that allow them to view their unethical behavior as moral. These mechanisms enable them to disengage their moral self-sanctions from their unethical behavior.

The moral disengagement process of moral justification involves the cognitive redefining of a destructive conduct as servicing socially worthy or moral purposes, and, accordingly, as personally and socially acceptable (Bandura, 2004). One example of religious-based moral justification would be the attacks of the al Qaeda organization across the world, which have been described by the organization as part of a holy war, and as consistent with the teaching of spiritual leaders such as Prophet Muhammad and Sheikh Omar Abdel Rahman, and as sanctified by the Ulema or clergy (Bergen, 2002; Silberman, 2003). This idea is expressed in the following description of the self-perception of religious terrorists: "They know they are right, not just politically but morally. They believe God is on their side" (Stern, 2003, p. 282).

Another way in which religious violence is presented as morally justified is by describing it as a response to pressing emergency situations (Appleby, 2000; Selengut, 2003; Stern, 2003). Conditions such as difficult political and economic situations or a sense of threat to religious values or to religious freedom are used by religious individuals and communities to define violence as morally legitimate. In the words of Appleby (2000, p. 88), "Fundamentalists believe themselves to be living in unusual extraordinary times of crisis, danger, or apocalyptic doom: the advent of the Messiah, the Second Coming of Christ, or the return of the Hidden Imam; and so on." The urgency of this special time requires true believers to make exceptions, to depart from the general rule of the tradition (e.g., its preaching for peace), and to subordinate all other laws to the requirements of survival.

Beyond that, as implied above, religion can be successful in the moral disengagement process of euphemistic labeling, which can be seen as based on the psychological idea that people behave more cruelly when assault actions are given a sanitized label than when they are called aggression (Diener, Dineen, Endersen, Beaman, & Fraser, 1975). Religious violence and killing are often redefined through theological reinterpretation as holy wars, as sacred events, or as being fought for God and his honor. These battles are not viewed as violence within the religious meaning systems of those who participate in them. On the contrary, they are viewed as religious battles for justice aimed at making a more peaceful and just world. In their eyes these are battles to educate those who are living in sin, to bring truth and redemption, to inspire truth and faith for which even the fallen enemies will eventually be grateful (Selengut, 2003, p. 20).

Finally, basic beliefs that compose the religious meaning systems of individuals can encourage the process of dehumanization, which is defined as the stripping of individuals from their human qualities by defining them as subhuman or even as satanic or evil (Bandura, 2004; Struch & Schwartz, 1989). Examples include the dehumanization of the Jews in both Christian (Carroll, 2001) and Muslim (Bodansky, 2000) anti-Semitism; the portrayals by some Muslim extremists of the Western civilizations as the "enemies of God" or as the Crusaders, and of the United States and Israel as the "great Satan" and the "small Satan," respectively (Lewis, 2003). Additional examples include the Christian white supremacists' view of Jews and non-whites as "the literal children of the Satan" (Hoffman, 1993), and the dehumanization of Muslims by the Christian Crusaders (Bandura, 2004).

Religious meaning systems as facilitators of peaceful activism. Religious meaning systems, then, can encourage hatred, discrimination, and violence. However, they also seem to have a strong potential for facilitating conflict resolution and peace (Appleby, 2000; Gopin, 2000; Helmick & Petersen, 2001; Silberman, 2005b). First, religious meaning systems (individual or collective) often include values that can facilitate peace (Gopin, 2000, for a review), such as (1) sanctity of life, which is sometimes supported by the religious idea that all humans are created in the image of God (Gopin, 2000; Montville, 2001); (2) selfless love and compassion (Poethig, 2002), including in some systems (e.g., Christianity) the idea that one needs to love or at least care for the enemy (Gopin, 2000); (3) empathy (Gopin, 2000), which can facilitate understanding of the pain and traumas that others, including enemies, are experiencing; (4) forgiveness (Helmick & Petersen, 2001; Tsang et al., this issue); (5) humility (Gopin, 2000), self-examination and self-criticism (Carroll, 2002), which can facilitate apologies and compensation for harm done, therefore facilitating reconciliation between groups; (6) religious discipline; i.e., the religious idea of self-restraint may facilitate restraint in violent situations (Gopin, 2000); (7) the notion of interdependence, that is, the idea that the acts of one individual or nation can affect the whole world (Poethig, 2002); (8) messianism, that is, the vision of a more just society that may, under certain circumstances, encourage yearning for a more peaceful world (Gopin, 2000; Silberman, 1999); (9) the explicit encouragement of nonviolence, and the call for peace and pacifism (which is a critical concept of the inner life in the Eastern traditions of Jainism, Buddhism, and Hinduism) (Gopin, 2000).

Second, religion systems of meaning can include powerful myths in a way that may facilitate peaceful activism. For example, the powerful Abrahamic myth that was discussed above can be reframed as emphasizing the family relations between Jews and Muslims—a family that might be somewhat disturbed, but that is still a family. Reports that religious Jewish and Muslim participants in conflict resolution efforts in the Middle East often refer to each other as cousins may reflect longings for this family unity (Gopin, 2000). When it comes to the myth regarding the relationship between Christianity and Judaism, there have been efforts by the Catholic Church since 1962 to change its hostility toward the Jews, which may eventually lead to a perception of Judaism within the meaning systems of many Catholics as the older sister of Christianity, rather than the rejected religion (Carroll, 2002). Pope John Paul II in some of his actions (e.g., affirming that God "chose" the Jews and asking the Jewish people for forgiveness for their long suffering; Van Biema, 2005) contributed significantly to the process of changing this myth.

Third, religious meaning systems can provide some rules and standards of behavior that may facilitate peaceful relations with outgroup members. For example, biblical Jewish laws instruct the Jewish people to treat the "ger" (non-Jews residents in Israel who abide by basic moral rules) with care and with love, while respecting their different religious beliefs and their needs for unique identities (Gopin, 2000).

Fourth, religions as systems of meaning can increase activism for peace by prescribing special rituals of forgiveness and reconciliation that can be applied in both interpersonal and intergroup contexts (Gopin, 2002). Two examples for such rituals would be the processes of "Sulh" (Arab method of reconciliation), and the Jewish Teshuva (repentance). These processes have the power within religious systems of meaning to reverse harm done in a gradual formal and symbolic process, which may have significant psychological effects (Gopin, 2002).

Concluding Comments

Our article portrays religion as a double-edged sword that can both encourage and discourage the goal of world change, and can facilitate both violent and peaceful activism as means to achieve this goal. Using the meaning system approach to illuminate the complicated relationship between religion and world change, the article suggests that the goal of world change and the means to achieve it may be interpreted differently within different religious meaning systems, and emphasizes the view of religions as complex systems of meaning that tend to include within them a wide variety of seemingly contradictory messages regarding world change, and the appropriate means to achieve it. The article suggests that religious leaders and believers have some flexibility in choosing certain religious messages over others; for example, whether to prefer messages supporting change versus status quo, violent or peaceful activism (see Hunsberger & Jackson, this issue; Martin, this issue; Silberman, this issue; Tsang et al., this issue). The view of individual and collective religious meaning systems as complex and malleable may implicitly underlie recent academic and nonacademic discussions about the continuous struggle between hardliners and moderates for the soul of Islam; i.e., over the future of the faith and its relationship with the West (e.g., Benard, 2004; Lewis, 2003; Powell, 2004). This view suggests that it is extremely important to realize *both* the potential of religious meaning systems to be directed toward a variety of goals and toward more peaceful directions, *and* the tendency of religious systems to resist change (Fox, 2002; Silberman, this issue). This potential resistance suggests that intensive efforts on both national and international levels would be needed in order to motivate violent religious leaders and communities and religious terrorists to redirect their religious meaning systems by choosing more peaceful goals and means within their religious systems. Psychologists who combine knowledge of conflict resolution theories (Deutsch & Coleman, 2000), priming accessibility techniques, (Higgins, 1996) and motivated cognition techniques (Kruglanski, 1996) with knowledge about religion as a complex meaning system that can develop and change and about the decision-making processes of religious terrorists (Silberman, 2003, 2005b; this issue) could contribute significantly to such efforts.

Religious violence and terrorism have been described by leading experts within the academic world and beyond as particularly destructive and dangerous to modern civilization and the entire world (e.g., Ganor, 2005; Hoffman, 1993; Kimball, 2002). The fact that this millennium has started with religions demonstrating their destructive potential in facilitating conflicts and terrorism across the world (e.g., Juergensmeyer, 2003; Silberman, this issue) is not going to make it a unique millennium. Hopefully, through the collaborative efforts of researchers, political and religious leaders and communities, this millennium will become a special and memorable one by revealing the unique potential of religions to facilitate conflict resolution and world peace.

References

Allport, G. W. (1966). The religious context of prejudice. *Journal for the Scientific Study of Religion, 5*, 447–457.

Appleby, R. S. (2000). *The ambivalence of the sacred: Religion, violence and reconciliation.* Lahman, MD: Rowman & Littlefield.

Bandura, A. (2004). The role of selective moral disengagement in terrorism and counterterrorism. In F. M. Moghaddam & A. J. Marsella (Eds.), *Understanding terrorism: Psychological roots, consequences, and interventions* (pp. 121–150). Washington, DC: American Psychological Association.

Benard, C. (2004). Five pillars of democracy: How the West can promote an Islamic reformation. *RAND Review, 8*(1), 10–13.

Berger, P. L. (1969). *The sacred canopy.* New York: Anchor Books: Doubleday.

Bergen, P. L. (2002). *Holy war inc.: Inside the secret world of Osama Bin Laden.* New York: A Touchstone Book published by Simon & Shuster.

Billings, D. B., & Scott, S. L. (1994). Religion and political legitimation. *Annual Review of Sociology, 20*, 173–202.

Bodansky, Y. (2000). *Islamic anti-Semitism as a political instrument.* Tel Aviv, Israel: Tammuz Publishers.

Budde, M. L. (1992). *The two churches: Catholicism and capitalism in the world-system.* Durham, NC: Duke University Press.

Carroll, J. (2001). *Constantine's sword: The Church and the Jews—A history.* Boston and New York: Houghton Mifflin Company.

Carroll, J. (2002). *After Constantine's sword: Past, present, and future of Christian-Jewish relations.* Presentation at the Jewish Theological Seminary, March 19, New York.

Deutsch, M., & Coleman, P. T. (Eds.). (2000). *The handbook of conflict resolution: Theory and practice* (pp. 21–40). San Francisco: Jossey-Bass.

Diener, E., Dineen, J., Endersen, K., Beaman, A. L., & Fraser, S. C. (1975). Effects of altered responsibility, cognitive set, and modeling on physical aggression and deindividuation. *Journal of Personality and Social Psychology, 31*, 328–337.

Durkheim, E. (1954/1912). *The elementary forms of religious life* (Translated by J. W. Swain). Glencoe, IL: The Free Press.

Dweck, C. S. (1999). *Self theories: Their role in motivation, personality and development.* Philadelphia: Psychology Press.

Einsenstadt, S. N. (2002). *Fundamentalism and modernity.* Jerusalem, Israel: Ministery of Defense.

Evans, B. F. (1979). Campaign for human development: Church involvement in social change. *Review of Religious Research, 20*, 262–278.

Fox, J. (1999). Do religious institutions support violence or status quo? *Studies in Conflict and Terrorism, 22*(2), 119–139.

Fox, J. (2002). *Ethnoreligious conflict in the late twentieth century*. Lahman, MD: Lexington Books.

Fox, J. (2004). Are some religions more conflict-prone than others? *Jewish Political Studies Review, 16*, 1–2.

Ganor, B. (2005). *The counter-terrorism puzzle: A guide for decision makers*. New Brunswick & London: Transaction Publishers.

Geertz, C. (1973). *The interpretation of culture*. New York: Basic Books.

Gill, A. (1998). *Rendering unto Caesar: The Catholic Church and the state in Latin America*. Chicago: University of Chicago Press.

Glock, C. Y. (1973). *Religion in sociological perspective: Essays in the empirical study of religion*. Belmont, CA: Wadsworth.

Gopin, M. (2000). *Between Eden and Armageddon: The future of world religions, violence, and peace-making*. Oxford, UK: Oxford University Press.

Gopin, M. (2002). *Holy war, holy peace*. New York: Oxford University Press.

Helmick, R. G., & Petersen, R. L. (Eds.). (2001). *Forgiveness and reconciliation: Religion, public policy and conflict transformation*. Philadelphia: Templeton Foundation Press.

Heschel, A. J. (1975). *The wisdom of Heschel*. New York: Farrar, Strauss & Giroux.

Higgins, E. T. (1996). Knowledge activation: Accessibility, applicability, and salience. In E. T. Higgins & A. W. Kruglanski (Eds.), *Social psychology: Handbook of basic principles* (pp. 133–168). New York: Guilford Press.

Hoffman, B. (1993). *Holy terror: The implications of terrorism motivated by a religious imperative* (RAND Research Paper P-7834). Santa Monica, CA: RAND.

Hoffman, B. (1998). *Inside terrorism*. New York: Columbia University Press.

Hunsberger, B., & Jackson, L. M. (this issue). Religion, meaning, and prejudice. *Journal of Social Issues*.

Huntington, S. P. (2003). *The clash of civilizations and the remaking of the world*. New York: Simon & Schuster.

James, W. (1982/1902). *The varieties of religious experience*. New York: Penguin Books.

Johnson, H., & Figa, J. (1988). The church and political opposition. *Journal of the Scientific Study of Religion, 27*(1), 32–47.

Juergensmeyer, M. (2003). *Terror in the mind of God: The global rise of religious violence*. Berkeley: University of California Press.

Keddie, N. R. (1985). Shi'ism and revolution. In B. Lincoln (Ed.), *Religion, rebellion and revolution* (pp. 157–182). London: Macmillan.

Kimball, C. (2002). *When religion becomes evil*. San Francisco: HarperCollins.

King, M. L. (1958). *Stride toward freedom: The Montgomery story*. San Francisco: Harper and Row.

Kruglanski, A. W. (1996). Motivated social cognition: Principles of the interface. In E. T. Higgins & A. W. Kruglanski (Eds.), *Social psychology: Handbook of basic principles* (pp. 493–520). New York: Guilford Press.

Lewis, B. (2003). *The crisis of Islam: Holy war and unholy terror*. New York: The Modern Library.

Liberman, N., Chen Idson, L., Camacho, C., & Higgins, E. T. (1999). Promotion and prevention choices between stability and change. *Journal of Personality and Social Psychology, 77*(6), 1135–1145.

Lincoln, B. (Ed.). (1985). *Religion, rebellion, revolution: An interdisciplinary and cross-cultural collection of essays*. New York: St. Martin's Press.

Machiavelli, N. (1940). *The prince and the discourses*. Book 1. New York: McGraw-Hill.

Martin, J. P. (this issue). The three monotheistic world religions and international human rights. *Journal of Social Issues*.

Marty, M. E., & Appleby, R. S. (Eds.). (1991–1995). *The fundamentalism project* (Vols. 1–5). Chicago: The University of Chicago Press.

Marx, G. T. (1967). Religion: Opiate or inspiration of civil rights militancy among Negroes? *American Sociological Review, 32*, 64–72.

Marx, K. (1848). *Selected writings in sociology and social philosophy*. Edited by T. B. Bottomore & M. Rubel (Eds., 1964). Baltimore, MD: Penguin.

Mayer, A. E. (1993). The fundamentalist impact on law, politics, and constitutions in Iran, Pakistan, and the Sudan. In M. E. Marty & R. S. Appleby (Eds.), *Fundamentalisms and the state: Remaking politics, economics and militance* (pp. 110–151). Chicago: University of Chicago Press.

Miller, L. (2002). Why we need heaven. *Newsweek,* August 12 , 45–51.

Moghaddam, F. M. (2005). The staircase to terrorism: A psychological exploration. *American Psychologist, 60*(2), 161–169.

Montville, J. V. (2002). Religion and peace making. In R. G. Helmick & R. L. Peterson (Eds.), *Forgiveness and reconciliation: Religion, public policy and conflict transformation* (p. 7–116). Philadelphia: Templeton Foundation Press.

Nasr, S. H. (2003). *Islam: Religion, history and civilization.* San Francisco: HarperCollins.

Pargament, K. I. (1997). *The psychology of religion and coping: Theory, research, practice.* New York: Guilford Press.

Pargament, K. I., Magyar, G. M., & Murray-Swank, N. (this issue). The sacred and the search for significance: Religion as a unique process. *Journal of Social Issues.*

Pargament, K. I., & Park, C. L. (1995). Merely a defense? The variety of religious means and ends. *Journal of Social Issues, 51*(2), 13–32.

Poethig, K. (2002). Moveable peace: Engaging the transnational in Cambodia's Dhammayietra. *Journal for the Scientific Study of Religion, 41*(1), 19–28.

Powell, B. (2004, September 13). Struggle for the soul of Islam. *Time,* 46–64.

Rapoport, D. C. (1988). Messianic sanctions for terror. *Comparative Politics, 20*(2), 195–213.

Rapoport, D. C. (1993). Comparing fundamentalist movements and groups. In M. E. Marty & R. S. Appleby (Eds.), *Fundamentalisms and the state: Remaking politics, economics and militance* (pp. 489–561). Chicago: University of Chicago Press.

Religious leaders meet on terror. (2001, December, 19). Retrieved on April 19, 2004 from http:// www.cnn.com/2001/WORLD/europe/12/19/interfaith.conference/index.html.

Roccas, S. (this issue). Religion and value systems. *Journal of Social Issues.*

Roccas, S., & Schwartz, S. H. (1997). Church-state relations and the association of religiosity with values: A study of Catholics in six countries. *Cross-Cultural Research, 31*(4), 356–375.

Ruby, C. L. (2002). Are terrorists mentally deranged? *Analyses of Social Issues and Public Policy, 2*(1), 15–26.

Schwartz, S. H., & Huismans, S. (1995). Value priorities and religiosity in four Western religions. *Social Psychology Quarterly, 58,* 88–107.

Seul, J. R. (1999). "Ours is the way of God": Religion, identity and intergroup conflict. *Journal of Peace Research, 36*(3), 553–569.

Selengut, C. (2003). *Sacred fury: Understanding religious violence.* Walnut Creek, CA: Altamira Press.

Shakdiel, L., & Shalvi, A. (Eds.). (1998). *Tikkun Olam.* Jerusalem, Israel: The Shachter Institute for the Study of Judaism. (In Hebrew).

Silberman, I. (1999). *Religiosity as a call for world change: Contradiction in terms or messianism?* Unpublished doctoral dissertation, Columbia University.

Silberman, I. (2003). Spiritual role modeling: The teaching of meaning systems. *The International Journal for the Psychology of Religion, 13*(3), 175–196.

Silberman, I. (2004). Religion as a meaning system: Implications for pastoral care and guidance. In D. Herl & M. L. Berman (Eds.), *Building bridges over troubled waters: Enhancing pastoral care and guidance* (pp. 51–67). Ohio: Wyndham Hall Press.

Silberman, I. (this issue). Religion as a meaning system: Implications for the new millennium. *Journal of Social Issues.*

Silberman, I. (2005a). Religion as a meaning-system: Implications for individual and societal well-being. *Psychology of Religion Newsletter: American Psychological Association Division, 36, 30*(2), 1–9.

Silberman, I. (2005b). Religious violence, terrorism and peace: A meaning system analysis. In R. F. Paloutzian & C. Park (Eds.), *Handbook of the psychology of religion and spirituality* (pp. 529–549). New York: Guilford Press.

Silberman, I., Higgins, E. T., & Dweck, C. S. (2000). *The relation between religiosity and openness to change.* Paper presented at the 108th Annual Convention of the American Psychological Association, Washington, DC.

Silberman, I., Higgins, E. T., & Dweck, C. S. (2001). *Religion and well-being: World beliefs as mediators.* Paper presented at the 109th Annual Convention of the American Psychological Association, San Francisco, CA.

Smith, C. (1996). Correcting a curious neglect, or bringing religion back in. In C. Smith (Ed.), *Disruptive religion: The force of faith in social movement activism* (pp. 1–25). New York and London: Routledge.

Spilka, B., & Bridges, R. A. (1992). Religious perspectives on prevention: The role of theology. In K. I. Pargament, K. I. Maton, & R. E. Hess (Eds.), *Religion and prevention in mental health: Research, vision, and action* (pp. 19–36). New York: Haworth Press.

Sprinzak, E. (1993). Three models of religious violence: The case of Jewish fundamentalism in Israel. In M. E. Marty & R. S. Appleby (Eds.), *Fundamentalism and the state* (pp. 462–490). Chicago: University of Chicago Press.

Staub, E. (2004). Understanding and responding to group violence: Genocide, mass killing and terror-ism. In F. M. Moghaddam & A. J. Marsella (Eds.), *Understanding terrorism: Psychological roots, consequences, and interventions* (pp. 151–168). Washington, DC: American Psycholog-ical Association.

Stern, J. (2003). *Terror in the name of God: Why religious militants kill.* New York: HarperCollins.

Struch, N., & Schwartz, S. H. (1989). Intergroup aggression: Its predictors and distinctness from in-group bias. *Journal of Personality and Social Psychology, 56*(3), 364–373.

The Dalai Lama. (1999). *Ethics for the new millennium.* New York: Riverhead Books.

Thurman, R. (1998). *Inner revolution: Life, liberty, and the pursuit of real happiness.* New York: Riverhead Books.

Tsang, J., McCullough, M.E., & Hoyt, W. T. (this issue). Psychometric and rationalization accounts of the religion-forgiveness discrepancy. *Journal of Social Issues.*

Van Biema, D. (2003, June 30). Missionaries under cover. *Time, 36*–44.

Van Biema, D. (2005, April 11). A defender of the faith. *Time, 34*–42.

Walzer, M. (1982). *The revolution of the Saints: A study in the origin of radical politics.* Cambridge and London: Harvard University Press.

Wellman, J. K., & Tokuno, K. (2004). Is religious violence inevitable? *Journal for the Scientific Study of Religion, 43*(3), 291–296.

Wertheimer, J. (1993). *A people divided: Judaism in contemporary America.* Hanover and London: Brandeis University Press.

Westhues, K. (1976). The church in opposition. *Sociological Analysis, 37*(4), 299–314.

Woodward, K. L. (2002). Why we need hell, too. *Newsweek,* August 12, 52.

World religions converge at U.N. conference. (2000, August 29). Retrieved April 7, 2004, from http://www.cnn.com/2000/ASIANOW/east/08/28/peace.summit./index.html.

Wuthnow. (1980). World order and religious movements. In A. Bergesen (Ed.), *Studies of the modern world system* (pp. 57–75). New York: New York Academics.

Yinger, J. M. (1965). *Religion, society and the individual.* New York: Macmillan.

ISRAELA SILBERMAN received her PhD (with distinction) in social-personality psychology in 1999 from Columbia University where she is currently Associate Research Scientist. Dr. Silberman has written extensively on the relations between religion as a meaning system and individual and societal well-being, particularly in the context of recent world events. She got numerous grants and awards including the Richard Christie Award, and awards from the Columbia University Center for the Study of Science and Religion, the Memorial Foundation for Jewish Culture, and the American Psychological Association.

E. TORY HIGGINS is the Stanley Schachter Professor of Psychology and Professor of Business at Columbia University where he received his PhD in 1973. He has received the Donald T. Campbell Award For Outstanding Contributions to Social Psychology, the Thomas M. Ostrom Award For Outstanding Contributions to Social Cognition, the American Psychological Society's William James Fellow Award For Distinguished Achievements in Psychological Science, the American Psychological Association's Distinguished Scientific Contribution Award, and the Society of Experimental Social Psychology's Distinguished Scientist Award.

CAROL S. DWECK is the Lewis and Virginia Eaton Professor of Psychology at Stanford University. Dr. Dweck, a leading researcher in motivation, personality, and developmental psychology, received her PhD from Yale University in 1972. Her recent books include *Motivation and Self-Regulation Across the Life Span* (with Jutta Heckhausen), *Self-Theories: Their Role in Motivation, Personality, and Development* (winner of the book of the year award from the World Education Fellowship), and *The Handbook of Competence and Motivation* (with Andrew Elliot). She is a member of the American Academy of Arts and Sciences.

Journal of Social Issues, Vol. 61, No. 4, 2005, pp. 785–805

Psychometric and Rationalization Accounts of the Religion-Forgiveness Discrepancy

Jo-Ann Tsang*
Baylor University

Michael E. McCullough
University of Miami

William T. Hoyt
University of Wisconsin

World events and psychological research often fail to support a relationship between religion and forgiveness. We suggest that the gap between general religious support of forgiveness and actual forgiveness by religious individuals (the religion-forgiveness discrepancy) described by McCullough and Worthington (1999) may be partly due to methodological shortcomings. We present three studies with 452 undergraduate participants to illustrate how psychometric weaknesses can obscure the relationship between religiousness and transgression-specific forgiveness. We also propose a rationalization explanation that describes how religion might justify unforgiveness. We present a pilot study of 38 undergraduate participants that demonstrates correlations between retributive and compassionate religious beliefs, and transgression-specific forgiveness. We discuss future research directions addressing the religion-forgiveness discrepancy on psychometric and theoretical levels.

Although many different world views can serve as meaning systems, religion is unique in its ability to provide a transcendent reality with concomitant moral standards, making it a potentially exceptional structure for guiding people's

---

*Correspondence concerning this article should be addressed to Jo-Ann Tsang at Baylor University, Department of Psychology and Neuroscience, One Bear Place 97334, Waco, TX 76798-7334 [e-mail: JoAnn_Tsang@Baylor.edu].

This article was supported in part through the generosity of the John Templeton Foundation, Radnor, PA.

interpretation of and interaction in the world. One value that seems to be encouraged by many world religions is forgiveness (e.g., Rye et al., 2000). Because the major world religions place a high importance on forgiveness, it comes as no surprise that highly religious individuals report valuing forgiveness more and seeing themselves as generally more forgiving than less religious individuals (see McCullough & Worthington, 1999, for a review).

Despite religious prescriptions of forgiveness and compassion (Ayoub, 1997; Dorff, 1998; Witvliet, 2001), a look at the world around us demonstrates that people often have difficulty forgiving, despite their religious backgrounds. For example, the conflict in the Middle East between Israel, a Jewish state, and the Palestinian people, who are predominantly Muslim, continues to escalate (e.g., Rouhana & Bar-Tal, 1998), and discord in Northern Ireland between Irish Catholics and Protestants still remains (e.g., O'Donoghue & O'Donoghue, 1981; Stringer, Cornish, & Denver, 2000). Following the 2001 terrorist attacks in the United States and with ongoing terror attacks against U.S. soldiers in Iraq and other locations abroad, many Americans have begun to grapple more intensely with issues such as forgiveness, compassion, and vengeance (e.g., Higgins, 2001; Rice, 2001/2002), and the relationship of these concepts to religion. It may be relatively easy to endorse religious teachings on forgiveness in the abstract, but when, for example, one's life is transformed by a terrorist attack, forgiveness may be harder to implement.

Psychological research also has suggested that religiousness has little or no effect on actual forgiveness for specific transgressions (e.g., McCullough & Worthington, 1999). We call this gap between the general religious doctrine on forgiveness and the actual forgiveness by religious people of specific transgressions the *religion-forgiveness discrepancy.*

In the present article, we review the ways in which religion as a meaning system might influence forgiveness, and outline the corresponding empirical evidence. We then present two explanations to account for the apparent religion-forgiveness discrepancy. First, we address measurement issues that may obscure a positive relationship between religiousness and forgiveness. To clarify these measurement problems, we present data from three studies illustrating the importance of using aggregate measures and reducing recall biases in order to uncover the relationship between religiousness and forgiveness. Second, we propose a rationalization explanation of the religion-forgiveness discrepancy. The rationalization explanation posits that religions can provide people with multiple, often competing, meaning systems that individuals can use selectively to rationalize preexisting motives antithetical to forgiveness. We also describe a preliminary study testing the rationalization hypothesis. Finally, we suggest that addressing the religion-forgiveness discrepancy on both psychometric and theoretical levels should aid researchers in further elucidating the complex relationship between religion and forgiveness.

Forgiveness in the Context of Religious Meaning Systems

As a meaning system, religion would be expected to influence individuals' beliefs, emotions, actions, and goals (Silberman, this issue). These components of the religious meaning system are relevant to understanding how religion might influence forgiveness. For instance, the major world religions prescribe *beliefs* regarding the value of kindness and forgiveness (e.g., McCullough & Worthington, 1999; Rye et al., 2000). Religion can sanctify the act of forgiveness and present adherents with a world view that allows individuals to interpret events and relationships in ways that facilitate forgiveness (Pargament & Rye, 1998). Religions also encourage *emotions* such as compassion and empathy (e.g., Enright, Eastin, Golden, Sarinopoulos, & Freedman, 1992), which may foster forgiveness (McCullough, Worthington, & Rachal, 1997). Forgiving *actions* are modeled in many religious scriptures (Pargament & Rye, 1998), and forgiveness is often integrated into religious ritual—for instance, Catholic individuals are supposed to experience forgiveness from God during confession (e.g., Borobio, 1986). These components of belief, emotion, and action may combine to create *goals* of forgiveness by increasing individuals' motivation to act in a more forgiving manner.

Evidence of these forgiveness-promoting structures can be identified in the major world religions (McCullough & Worthington, 1999; Rye et al., 2000). Judaism defines forgiveness as the removal of a violation, which enables the transgressor to become a candidate for renewed relationship with the offended person (Dorff, 1998). According to Jewish scripture and tradition, God commands that people forgive their transgressors, and followers of Judaism are encouraged to forgive because of the belief that God has forgiven them (Dorff, 1998; Enright et al., 1992). Yet, forgiveness is not required under all circumstances. The offended individual is obligated to forgive only if the transgressor has gone through the process of *teshuvah*, or "return," which requires the expression of remorse and compensation to the victim, as well as a commitment from the transgressor to refrain from repeating the offense. Reconciliation (i.e., the actual restoration of the broken relationship) is not a necessary part of the forgiveness process (Rye et al., 2000).

As in Judaism, Christianity considers forgiveness to be foundational to its doctrine (e.g., Witvliet, 2001). In the Christian religion, God and Christ serve as role models of forgiveness (Marty, 1998). According to some scholars, forgiveness, in the form of having compassion for a transgressor and releasing him/her from the offense, does not necessarily require reconciliation (Rye et al., 2000; cf. Marty, 1998). Also similar to Judaism, Christian believers are encouraged to forgive because God forgave them (Enright et al., 1992). However, unlike Judaism, forgiveness is not conditional upon the transgressor's repentance (Rye et al., 2000).

Forgiveness is also of great importance in Islam (Ayoub, 1997); in fact, one of Allah's appellations is *Al-Ghafoor*, the Forgiving One (Rye et al., 2000). Both Allah and his messenger, Mohammed, are the role models of forgiveness within Islam. Islam places importance on individual forgiveness so that one can receive forgiveness from Allah for one's own sins (Ayoub, 1997), and can have happiness in the present life (Rye et al., 2000).

The Buddhist emphasis on forbearance and compassion is also relevant to forgiveness (Enright et al., 1992). Forbearance within the Buddhist tradition is both the endurance of transgression, and the relinquishing of resentment toward the transgressor. Forbearance is contrasted with forgiveness, which usually incorporates relinquishing, but not endurance (Rye et al., 2000). Forbearance along with compassion is embedded within the larger focus in Buddhism on the amelioration of suffering (Higgins, 2001). Compassion is used to ease the suffering of others, while forbearance functions to prevent further suffering (Rye et al., 2000). Forbearance and compassion are possible within the Buddhist meaning system by focusing believers' awareness on the interconnectedness of all things. There is not an "enemy" to be forgiven; the victim and the transgressor are united rather than separate entities (Higgins, 2001). Buddhism also embraces the concept of *karma*, according to which good actions are rewarded with good, and evil actions with evil. In the context of *karma*, holding on to one's resentment after a transgression will bring resentment from others toward the self in the future (Rye et al., 2000).

Forgiveness is one of the concepts necessary to follow the path of *dharma*, or righteousness, in the Hindu religion (Klostermaier, 1994). As with Buddhism, Hinduism emphasizes a version of *karma*, which would state that lack of forgiveness in this life will be repaid with negative outcomes in a subsequent life (Rye et al., 2000). Forgiveness in the Hindu religion can be defined as the absence of anger or agitation in the face of a transgression (Temoshok & Chandra, 2000). Though some Hindu traditions are nontheistic (Rye et al., 2000), versions of Hinduism that do incorporate belief in a supreme being or beings also provide examples of divine forgiveness for believers to follow (Zaehner, 1962). The Hindu religion asserts that all people have the power to forgive, because each person has divinity within his or her being (Saraswati, 1995).

The centrality of forgiveness in these major world religions suggests that they could serve as meaning systems that facilitate forgiving behaviors and attitudes toward transgressors—systems that shift the goals of their followers from revenge to the repairing of relationships.

Psychological Research on Forgiveness and Religion

In comparison with the rich theological history of forgiveness, the psychological study of forgiveness has emerged only recently (for reviews, see Enright & Coyle, 1998; McCullough, 2001). A number of definitions of forgiveness have arisen to accompany this recent surge in research. For example, Enright, Gassin, and Wu (1992) defined forgiveness as "the overcoming of negative affect and judgment toward the offender, not by denying ourselves to such affect and judgment, but by endeavoring to view the offender with compassion, benevolence, and love…" (p. 101). Exline and Baumeister (2000) defined forgiveness as the "cancellation of a debt" by "the person who has been hurt or wronged" (p. 133). Common to the various definitions is the idea of forgiveness as prosocial motivational change: The offended individual feels less negatively toward the transgressor, and/or begins to feel more benevolent motivations toward that person (McCullough, Fincham, & Tsang, 2003). We therefore define forgiveness as transgression-related motivational change toward one's transgressor, with revenge- and avoidance-related motivations subsiding and being replaced with restored motivations toward benevolence (McCullough et al., 1997).

McCullough and Worthington (1999) reviewed the research on the relationship between religiousness and forgiveness. They demonstrated that forgiveness can be measured on a dispositional level by presenting individuals with self-report items about the value they place on forgiveness and perceptions of how forgiving they actually are. Forgiveness can also be measured at the level of the transgression by assessing the extent to which individuals forgive specific transgressions that have occurred to them. The distinction between dispositional and transgression-specific measures of forgiveness, they argued, could be important for understanding the relationship between religion and forgiveness.

Religion and Dispositional Measures of Forgiveness

Research has shown a positive relationship between religiousness and valuing forgiveness. Religious variables such as frequency of church attendance, self-rated religiousness, intrinsic religious orientation, importance of religion, feeling close to God, and measures of personal prayer, have been positively linked to people's self-reported values, attitudes, and behaviors regarding forgiveness (Edwards et al., 2002; Poloma & Gallup, 1991; Rokeach, 1973). Additionally, when asked how a Christian should live, Christian students ranked "forgiving" second only to "loving" as an ideal Christian value (Shoemaker & Bolt, 1977). These findings suggest that religious individuals place a high value on forgiveness.

Similarly, religiousness seems to be related to moral reasoning about forgiveness. Enright, Santos, and Al-Mabuk (1989) examined the factors that affected individuals' maturity in reasoning about forgiveness. These researchers first gave children, adolescents, and adults two dilemmas from Rest's (1979) Defining Issues Test, and then interviewed these individuals on their thoughts about forgiveness in the context of these dilemmas. Participants' responses were later rated using a six-stage developmental model of reasoning about forgiveness, similar to Kohlberg's (1976) six-stage model of justice reasoning. Participants also completed a questionnaire about their religious beliefs. Enright et al. (1989) found that individuals with stronger religious beliefs tended to reason in a more sophisticated way about forgiveness than those individuals with weaker religious beliefs.

Religiousness is also related to people's self-reported tendencies to forgive. For example, Gorsuch and Hao (1993) found that individuals high in personal religiousness saw themselves as both more motivated to forgive and working harder to forgive others, when compared to individuals lower in personal religiousness. Mauger, Saxon, Hamill, and Pannell (1996) found that a forgiving disposition was related to the use of spiritual coping resources in both clinical and nonclinical samples. These studies suggest that highly religious people tend to report themselves as being especially forgiving.

Religion and Transgression-Specific Measures of Forgiveness

In contrast, studies using *transgression-specific* measures of forgiveness have found few associations between religiousness and forgiveness (McCullough & Worthington, 1999). Transgression-specific measures of forgiveness assess an individual's forgiveness of an offender for a specific transgression. Subkoviak et al. (1995) reported a weak correlation ($r = .09$) between self-reported religiousness and a measure of transgression-specific forgiveness. Similarly, Rackley (1993) found no significant relationship between religiousness and self-reported forgiveness of one's spouse for a specific transgression.

We therefore see an inconsistency in the existing research on forgiveness: Religious people report themselves to be more forgiving in the abstract, but not more forgiving of specific interpersonal transgressions. The existence of this religion-forgiveness discrepancy is especially disturbing because religious doctrines purport to encourage compassion and forgiveness. Though religion may cause its adherents to report that they value forgiveness more, this would be of limited social value unless religious individuals also behaved in a more forgiving manner in specific transgression situations.

We offer two distinct accounts for the religion-forgiveness discrepancy: a psychometric explanation, and a rationalization explanation. The psychometric account posits that the religion-forgiveness discrepancy is an artifact reflecting measurement shortcomings, whereas the rationalization explanation presupposes a real discrepancy between religious doctrine and religious individuals' actual motivations and behaviors in the context of forgiveness.

Accounting for the Discrepancy: Psychometric Issues

It is important to begin by addressing any psychometric shortcomings that previous studies on religion and forgiveness may have had. Measurement issues are fundamental because failures to measure a phenomenon properly undermine subsequent theoretical explanations for that phenomenon.

A measurement explanation for the forgiveness-religion discrepancy was first presented by McCullough and Worthington (1999). First, they mentioned that differences in the aggregation and specificity of measures assessing religion and forgiveness might mask a relationship between religiousness and forgiveness. Single samples of behavior may be influenced by many factors, both dispositional and situational, which can mask the influence of any one particular dispositional variable such as religiousness. However, when behaviors are aggregated across situations, theoretically expected correlations between dispositions and relevant behaviors are more likely to emerge (Epstein, 1983). McCullough and Hoyt (2002) reported that people's self-reports of how much they have forgiven a specific transgressor contain fairly little dispositional variance. Between 22% and 36% of the variance in such reports is due to personality, with the remainder attributable to nondispositional sources, such as the nature of the transgression. As a result, several self-reports of forgiveness for specific transgressions should be aggregated to increase the likelihood of obtaining theoretically expected correlations with individual traits such as religiousness.

Second, McCullough and Worthington (1999) pointed out that methods used to assess transgression-related forgiveness might introduce recall or encoding biases, again obscuring the potential relationship between religiousness and forgiveness. Transgression-specific forgiveness is usually measured by having participants freely recall a past transgression, and then complete a questionnaire about the transgression event. These free recall procedures may introduce error. If we assume that forgiven offenses are more difficult to recall than unforgiven offenses, then a more forgiving individual might have a difficult time recalling a transgression during a forgiveness study. In contrast, a less forgiving individual would more easily recall a salient transgression. Yet, both individuals may end up recalling situations that have been forgiven to approximately equal extents, making it seem like they are equally forgiving people, when, in fact, they are not. Errors such as these might attenuate the extent to which participants' reports of their forgiveness for specific transgressions might correlate with other variables, including religiousness. If, for instance, the more forgiving individual in the above example was also more religious, recall bias would make it seem as if the religious individual and the nonreligious individual were equally skilled at forgiving, even if they were not.

In summary, a psychometric explanation for the religion-forgiveness discrepancy claims that the null relationship between religiousness and forgiveness in transgression-specific studies is in part due to a lack of aggregation in measures of reported behaviors, as well as the presence of encoding and recall biases. These measurement weaknesses may obscure a relationship between religion and transgression-specific forgiveness.

Assessing Psychometric Explanations for the Discrepancy

To address these psychometric accounts for the religion-forgiveness discrepancy, we present the results of three studies in which we examined the associations between religiousness and transgression-specific measures of forgiveness. In each sample, participants completed McCullough et al.'s (1998) Transgression-Related Interpersonal Motivations (TRIM) Inventory and at least one self-report measure of religiousness. The TRIM Inventory consists of 12 items that measure the two negative interpersonal motivations that McCullough et al. posited to underlie forgiveness: (a) *Avoidance* ("I am trying to keep as much distance between us as possible"); and (b) *Revenge* ("I want to see him/her hurt and miserable"). Lower scores on these two motivations indicate more forgiveness. In addition, participants completed at least one multi-item measure of religiousness. These three data sets allowed us to address the extent to which the religion-forgiveness relationship might be distorted by the methodological shortcomings described above.

Sample 1: Religiousness and Forgiveness in a Free-Recall Procedure

Sample 1 consisted of 224 introductory psychology students at a medium-sized Southeastern university who self-identified as Christians (McCullough & Worthington, 1995). Approximately 62% of the participants were women, and the majority of them were White/Caucasian (68%).

Participants were instructed to think of someone whom they had had trouble forgiving at some point in the past. With that specific person in mind, they completed the *Revenge* ($\alpha = .90$) and *Avoidance* ($\alpha = .90$) subscales of the TRIM Inventory (McCullough et al., 1998). To measure religiousness, participants were given the Shepherd Scale ($\alpha = .96$) (Bassett et al., 1981). These items measure traditional (i.e., conservative) Christian beliefs and self-reports of behaviors that are considered to reflect a strong commitment to the Christian message.

We expected religiousness to be positively related to forgiveness. On the other hand, if McCullough and Worthington (1999) were correct about the possible role of measurement error created by differences in how participants select and recall transgressions for the study, then the present unrestrictive measure of forgiveness would obscure any relationship between religiousness and forgiveness.

Results. The Shepherd Scale of religiousness was unrelated to participants' self-reported avoidance motivation, $r(193) = -.02$, n.s., and revenge motivation, $r(200) = -.04$, n.s. These results would suggest that religiousness is not related to forgiveness for specific transgressions—a conclusion also drawn by Rackley (1993) and Subkoviak et al. (1995) from studies involving similar research designs.

Sample 2: A More Restrictive Recall Procedure

In a second data set, we used a more restrictive recall paradigm that induced all participants to utilize similar psychological processes for recalling transgressions. We predicted that, using this restrictive recall procedure, we would uncover positive relationships between religion and forgiveness.

Participants were 91 introductory psychology students at a medium-sized Southern university (36 males and 55 females). To restrict the offenses that participants might recall, we recruited only individuals who reported having received a serious interpersonal transgression within 2 months prior to the study (for details, see McCullough, Bellah, Kilpatrick, & Johnson, 2001). With their specific transgressor in mind, participants completed the TRIM Inventory (Avoidance subscale $\alpha = .91$, Revenge subscale $\alpha = .92$). They also completed Allport and Ross's (1967) 9-item measure of intrinsic religiousness ($\alpha = .93$). About 2 months later, 60 participants completed the TRIM Inventory a second time. We created residualized change scores to reflect the change in avoidance and revenge motivations between the first and second assessments. Decreases in either avoidance or revenge would be indicative of forgiveness (e.g., McCullough et al., 2003)

Results. Intrinsic religiousness was not significantly associated with Time 1 avoidance, $r(90) = -.05$, n.s., Time 2 avoidance, $r(60) = -.08$, n.s., or residualized change in avoidance, $r(60) = -.01$, n.s. However, intrinsic religiousness was significantly correlated with Time 1 revenge, $r(90) = -.22$, $p < .05$, Time 2 revenge, $r(60) = -.33$, $p < .05$, and (marginally) negatively related to residualized change in revenge, $r(60) = -.22$, $p < .10$. Using this more restrictive recall procedure, intrinsic religiousness was related to initial revenge motivation and change in revenge motivation over time. This suggests that intrinsic religiousness is not only related to increased forgiveness (i.e., lowered revenge motivation), but that intrinsic religiousness may have a positive causal effect on forgiveness over time.

Sample 3: A More Restrictive Recall Procedure With Aggregation

In a third data set, we examined whether aggregating self-reports of forgiveness for several transgressions into a single measure of real-life forgiveness behavior would also uncover a higher religiousness-forgiveness relationship. Participants were 137 undergraduate students at a public Midwestern university (gender was not recorded in this study). On three different occasions, they were instructed to complete the TRIM inventory in response to two actual transgressions caused by peers who were related to the respondent in one of three ways: a romantic partner, a same-sex friend, or an opposite-sex friend. For each of these relationship types, participants reported (a) the worst thing that such a relationship partner ever did to them; and (b) a time that they were seriously hurt by such a partner. This restrictive recall procedure was used to eliminate individual differences in recall bias (i.e., the tendency for some people to recall more negative transgressions than others) by focusing people on specific relationships and types of transgressions within those relationships. Participants provided a total of six estimates of their avoidance ($\alpha = .76$) and revenge ($\alpha = .86$) motivations in response to these six real-life transgressions (for details, see McCullough & Hoyt, 2002). The resulting forgiveness estimates involved both highly restrictive recall procedures and aggregation of forgiveness reports, both of which should increase the likelihood of uncovering substantial religiousness-forgiveness relationships.

Participants also completed Worthington et al.'s (2003) Religious Commitment Inventory-10 (RCI-10) on each occasion. The RCI-10 contains two subscales. *Interpersonal* religious commitment consists of four items assessing public or communal manifestations of religious commitment ($\alpha = .96$), and *intrapersonal* religious commitment involves six items assessing private manifestations of religious commitment ($\alpha = .97$). We combined the three measures of interpersonal religious commitment and the three measures of intrapersonal religious commitment that were collected on three different occasions to reduce occasion-specific error (Schmidt & Hunter, 1996).

Results. The range of correlations between the composite measure of interpersonal religious commitment and the six measures of avoidance motivation was $r = (-.21, -.09)$ with a mean correlation of $r = -.15$. We created unit weighted aggregates of the six measures of avoidance and revenge. The aggregated avoidance measure was significantly correlated with interpersonal religious commitment, $r = -.20, p < .05$. The range of correlations between the composite measure of interpersonal religious commitment and the six measures of revenge motivation was $r = (-.19, -.04)$, with a mean correlation of $r = -.11$. The correlation between the aggregated measure of revenge motivation and interpersonal religious commitment was $r = -.14, p < .10$.

The range of correlations between the composite measure of intrapersonal religious commitment and the six various measures of avoidance motivation was $r = (-.24, -.10)$, with a mean correlation of $r = -.17$. When we aggregated the six measures of avoidance motivation, the correlation of this six-transgression composite was significantly correlated with intrapersonal religious commitment at $r = -.21, p < .05$. The range of correlations between the composite measure of intrapersonal religious commitment and the six measures of revenge motivation was $r = (-.27, -.05)$, with a mean correlation of $r = -.17$. The correlation of the six-transgression composite of revenge motivation with intrapersonal religious commitment was r is $-.22, p < .01$. Aggregating people's avoidance and revenge motivations across several transgressions led to appreciable increases in the size of the typical correlation between measures of religiousness and forgiveness, suggesting that religiously committed people do report being slightly more forgiving of specific transgressions than their less religious counterparts.

Conclusion from the Three Data Sets

These analyses suggest that McCullough and Worthington (1999) may have been correct regarding the psychometric shortcomings of previous studies of the relationship between religiousness and forgiveness for specific transgressions. When respondents are free to select any transgression from their past (as in Sample 1), their self-reports of forgiveness are nearly orthogonal to measures of religiousness commitment (i.e., rs range from $-.02$ to $-.04$). When participants are constrained in the types of transgressions they can recall (as in Sample 2), correlations between religiousness and self-reported forgiveness (namely, with motivations to seek revenge) increase considerably. Finally, when self-reports of forgiveness are both based on transgressions that are recalled under restrictive procedures and aggregated across multiple transgressions (as in Sample 3), it appears that the relationships between religiousness and transgression-specific forgiveness are on the order of $r = |0.20|$. We conclude that one explanation for the religion-forgiveness discrepancy is the failure of researchers to use measures that assess the phenomenon properly. Based on this demonstration, we would recommend that researchers attend to psychometric issues such as restrictive recall and aggregation when studying the effects of religiousness (or any other dispositional variable) on forgiveness.

Other Dynamics at Work? A Rationalization Model of Religion and Forgiveness

Though these psychometric issues are an important first step in addressing the religion-forgiveness discrepancy, we doubt that measurement error is the entire story. Though improved methodology seems to establish a positive relationship between religion and self-reported forgiveness for specific transgressions, this relationship is small in magnitude (Cohen, 1988). In our studies, religion accounted for only about 4% of the variance in self-reported forgiveness, even when using restrictive recall and aggregated measures. Since compassion and forgiveness are foundational to so many world religions (e.g., Rye et al., 2000), one would expect the relationship between religiousness and forgiveness to be stronger.

Furthermore, the multitude of stubborn, bloody religious conflicts around the world speak to a different relationship between religion and forgiveness. In many places, individuals who consider themselves to be devout followers of their religions actively work to maintain centuries-old stances of bitterness and hate toward their enemies. The long-standing conflicts between Palestinians and Israelis (e.g., Bar-Tal, 1990; Rouhana & Bar-Tal, 1998), Irish Catholics and Protestants (e.g., O'Donoghue & O'Donoghue, 1981), and the Azerbaijanis and Armenians (e.g., Fraser, Hipel, Jaworsky, & Zuljan, 1990) are just a few examples of religion's failed influence on compassion and forgiveness.

In these, as well as other, more mundane cases, rather than promoting forgiveness, religion appears to fuel resentment and revenge. The rationalization explanation for the religion-forgiveness discrepancy suggests that the discrepancy may occur because religion as a meaning system may be abstract enough to provide people with justification for both vengeful and forgiving behaviors. Religious individuals who are highly motivated *not* to forgive might use religion to rationalize their unforgiving actions, just as religious individuals who are motivated to forgive can find ample justification for forgiveness. This could account for circumstances in which religion does not promote forgiveness, and it might also explain why the empirical relationship between religion and forgiveness is not as strongly positive as religious doctrines would prescribe.

More explicitly, the three assumptions underlying the rationalization explanation for the religion-forgiveness discrepancy are the following: First, rather than providing only a single meaning system, religion can present individuals with multiple meaning systems that may be called into service to address different issues in people's lives (Paloutzian & Smith, 1995). Second, behavior (e.g., forgiving behavior) is more proximally determined by whichever motivation is predominant at the time (e.g., forgiveness vs. revenge), and is less directly influenced by moral and religious principles and values (Ajzen & Fishbein, 1977). Third, if a person's more immediate motivation conflicts with one's religious or moral principles, then that individual may choose to rationalize his or her behavior to fit the relevant principles. We call this process *moral rationalization*—the use of different cognitive methods to convince the self and others that one's seemingly unethical actions actually fall within one's valued moral standards (Tsang, 2002). These three assumptions are discussed in further detail in the following sections.

Religion as Multiple Meaning Systems

Many individuals might possess multiple concrete religious schemata, rather than a single global religious schema (Paloutzian & Smith, 1995). Furthermore, we suggest that religion contains both an overarching meaning system, along with multiple meaning systems subsumed under the general doctrine. Some lower-order meaning systems can be viewed as being in opposition with one another. For example, many religions teach that God is infinitely forgiving, but the same religions can also promote belief in the existence of a just world in which God's justice insures that people get what they deserve (Lerner, 1965; Lerner & Simmons, 1966).

Themes of retributive justice coexist with themes of forgiveness in the major world religions. In both Judaism and Christianity, believers are told to take an "eye for an eye, tooth for a tooth." Christianity's New Testament also has many examples of retributive justice, such as "God is just: He will pay back trouble to those who trouble you" (NIV: 2 Thessalonians 1:6). Similarly, in Islam's Koran, it is written, "O ye who believe! the law of equality is prescribed to you in cases of murder: the free for the free, the slave for the slave, the woman for the woman" (2:178). The Buddhist and Hindu ideas of *karma* and *dharma* also contain indirect elements of retributive justice: all of our actions, both good and bad, have consequences for us in this life or the next. Whereas doctrines of compassion in these religions could lead religious individuals toward forgiveness, doctrines of retribution in these same religions might encourage revenge.

Motivational Determinants of Forgiving Behavior

There are a number of ways in which competing meaning systems within religions might affect forgiveness in religious individuals. One possibility is that different meaning systems might have attentional effects on forgiveness. In this case, a believer would interpret a transgression situation within whichever religious meaning system that happened to be most salient at the time. Similarly, religious groups that emphasize one competing meaning system over another would be expected to have doctrine-specific effects on forgiveness. Groups that emphasize compassion would be more likely to encourage forgiveness, and denominations that emphasize retributive justice would be more likely to encourage revenge.

Although this causal relationship from the religious meaning system to forgiveness is quite plausible, the rationalization model suggests that people's proneness to forgive might also influence them to endorse a particular meaning system. For example, religious individuals who support capital punishment as a tool for retribution might justify their opinion on the basis of "eye for an eye, tooth for a tooth." However, individuals who prefer more forgiving alternatives to capital punishment point out that God calls people "to love our enemies and pray for those who persecute us" (Higi, 1997). In this way, people may select different religious meaning systems to justify their desire for revenge or forgiveness.

This selective endorsement of religious meaning systems can be explained within the framework of Kunda's (1990) theory of motivated reasoning. Kunda proposed that the voice of reason is not always cool and objective, but can be swayed by a person's wishes and desires. The theory of motivated reasoning specifies that if individuals are motivated to arrive at a particular conclusion when making a decision, this motivation will bias the cognitive processes used in reasoning. Reason can be used to rationalize an individual's biased motivations, to oneself and to others, under the guise of objectivity. Kunda posited limits to this process, stating that motivated reasoning would only function successfully if the individual could find enough evidence to support his or her biased conclusion. Applying this theory to the context of religion and forgiveness suggests that religious individuals' forgiving versus vengeful motivations may influence the cognitive processes used in accessing relevant aspects of the religious meaning system.

The Phenomenon of Moral Rationalization

Bandura's theory of moral disengagement (e.g., Bandura, 1999) places motivated reasoning within the specific context of moral behavior and motivation. Bandura proposed that people internalize moral standards and self-sanctions through socialization. Internalized self-sanctions cause individuals to anticipate self-condemnation if they violate moral standards, and self-reward if they uphold those standards. Because of these self-sanctions, and the need for people to see themselves as good and moral (e.g., Aronson, 1969; Steele, 1988), people are usually unable to violate their moral standards with impunity. Yet individuals often do desire to engage in behaviors that are contrary to their internalized standards. In order to behave unethically, but still convince themselves of their morality, people inhibit self-sanctions using different methods of moral disengagement. These cognitive mechanisms bias individuals' reasoning, allowing them to conclude that their unethical behavior is actually moral, thus disengaging moral self-sanctions and permitting them to continue violating their moral standards.

Bandura (1999) identified a number of different methods of rationalization that could lead to moral disengagement. Two methods that may be especially relevant in the context of forgiveness and religious meaning systems are moral justification, and the blaming and dehumanization of victims. With moral justification, individuals depict their unethical behavior as serving a valued social or moral purpose. These individuals ironically present themselves as moral agents while they violate moral principles. People can also blame and dehumanize others in order to rationalize immoral behavior. Dehumanization occurs when perpetrators give bestial qualities to victims, effectively diminishing empathic responses to those victims and subduing moral self-sanctions (e.g., Bandura, Underwood, & Fromson, 1975). Perpetrators can also blame individuals for their plight, portraying victims rather than the perpetrators as those who have violated moral standards.

Religious meaning systems may be employed as moral justification for an unforgiving stance. Rather than viewing themselves in violation of the almost universal religious principle of forgiveness and compassion, vengeful individuals can characterize their revenge as serving valued principles of religious justice. For example, proponents of capital punishment can rationalize their unforgiveness by stating that they are serving "God's justice." While these individuals may be violating valued principles of forgiveness, they focus instead on moral justifications of retribution (see Hunsberger & Jackson, this issue). Religious meaning systems can also be used to blame and dehumanize others. This occurs, for example, when people claim that murderers are sinners deserving of the death penalty, allowing individuals to focus on the justice of retribution rather than the value of forgiveness.

Current and Future Research in Forgiveness and Moral Rationalization

Method

As a preliminary test of the rationalization model, we conducted a pilot study to examine whether people's endorsement of different religious meaning systems was related to their forgiveness toward a recent transgressor. We operationalized moral rationalization as an individual's endorsement of whichever religious meaning system matched that individual's current feelings of forgiveness or unforgiveness toward a transgressor. We recruited 38 Christian participants (29 women, 9 men) from psychology classes at a medium-sized Southwestern private university. Ages ranged from 18 to 22 years (M is 19.50, SD is 1.13). Keeping our psychometric explanation in mind, we restricted participants' recall of transgression by only recruiting individuals who had experienced a transgression in the 7 days prior to their enrollment in the study. We measured forgiveness with a revised version of McCullough et al.'s (1998) Transgression-Related Interpersonal Motivations (TRIM) Inventory. Along with the *Revenge* ($\alpha = .85$) and *Avoidance* ($\alpha = .91$) subscales, we measured *Benevolence* with a new scale ($\alpha = .86$) consisting of five positively worded items (e.g., "Despite what he/she did, I want us to have a positive relationship again") used in other research (McCullough et al., 2003). Using these three subscales, forgiveness is conceptualized as decreases in avoidance and revenge motivations, and increases in benevolence motivation (McCullough et al., 2003; Tsang, McCullough, & Fincham, in press).

We measured rationalization using two religiousness scales. First, participants rated their endorsement of different Judeo-Christian beliefs using a scale modified from a section of Glock and Stark's (1966) Dimensions of Religious Commitment Scale. We altered this scale to include a *retributive justice* item ("Eye for an eye, tooth for a tooth, life for a life") as well as a *forgiveness* item ("Forgive as the Lord forgave you"). We hypothesized that individuals who were motivated toward retribution would give higher endorsement to the retributive scripture, whereas individuals more inclined toward forgiveness would give higher endorsement to the forgiving scripture. Secondly, we measured participants' concept of God (Gorsuch, 1968), using *justice* adjectives such as "just" and "fair" ($\alpha = .77$), *forgiveness* adjectives such as "forgiving" and "merciful" ($\alpha = .84$), and *wrath/retribution* adjectives such as "wrathful" and "avenging" ($\alpha = .79$). We hypothesized that vengeful individuals would be more likely to endorse just and wrathful images of God, whereas a forgiving image of God would be more appealing to forgiving individuals.

Results

Individuals who were highly motivated to avoid their transgressors were less likely to endorse the forgiveness scripture "Forgive as the Lord forgave you," $r(38) = -.34$, $p < .04$. Benevolence, on the other hand, was positively related to the personal endorsement of the forgiveness scripture, $r(38) = .37$, $p < .03$, and marginally negatively correlated with endorsement of the retribution scripture "Eye for an eye, tooth for a tooth, life for a life," $r(38) = -.30$, $p < .07$. There were no significant correlations between Revenge and endorsement of scripture.

Looking at individuals' images of God, avoidance motivations were negatively correlated with forgiving images of God, $r(37) = -.38$, $p < .03$, and marginally negatively correlated with justice images of God, $r(36) = -.32$, $p < .07$. Benevolence was marginally positively related to forgiving images of God, $r(37) = .29$, $p < .09$. There were no significant correlations between Revenge and the images of God subscales.

Taken together, the results of this pilot study suggest that some individuals may use religious meaning systems to rationalize their forgiving or unforgiving attitudes. Individuals who reported being less forgiving (more avoidant or less benevolent) were somewhat more likely to endorse retribution-related scripture and less likely to endorse forgiveness-related scripture. Images of God also seemed to be related to forgiveness motivations. Individuals who reported more benevolence were somewhat more likely to report forgiving images of God. Results were more mixed for individuals reporting higher avoidance motivations, who seemed to shy away from justice images of God, but also from forgiving images of God. Because of the correlational nature of this research, it is difficult to conclude the direction of causality. On one hand, a rationalization explanation posits that retributive and forgiveness motivations cause individuals to access different parts of their religious meaning systems. However, it is also possible that differences in people's religious meaning systems influence their propensity to forgive. Future research with larger numbers of participants and controlled experimental manipulations will aid in uncovering the mechanisms of moral rationalization in religion and forgiveness.

Future Rationalization Research

In the above study, we attempted to use multiple measures of religious meaning systems, including endorsement of retribution- and forgiveness-related scripture, and different facets of people's image of God. Another fruitful avenue of research in moral rationalization might be the use of behavioral measures. Because participants are often concerned with self-presentation (Jones & Pittman, 1982) or may not even be aware of their true motivations (Nisbett & Wilson, 1977), the use of behavioral measures to complement self-reports allows investigators to more accurately assess psychological phenomena. This is especially the case when studying concepts like religion and forgiveness, which tend to elicit socially desirable responses. It is possible to employ behavioral measures in assessments of both forgiveness and moral rationalization. Rather than relying on self-reports of forgiveness, psychologists might use research paradigms such as the Prisoner's Dilemma to measure allocation of resources after a laboratory transgression (e.g., Batson & Ahmad, 2001). In addition, religious moral rationalization might be measured using cognitive dissonance's selective exposure design (e.g., Freedman & Sears, 1965), where individuals who are motivated toward vengeance should be more willing to expose themselves to religious information related to retributive justice than forgiveness. Additional research can shed further light on the possibility that conflicting religious meaning systems can be used to rationalize unforgiveness.

A moral rationalization explanation for the religion-forgiveness discrepancy raises an interesting possibility: Individuals are not only molded by religious doctrine, but they themselves also mold the doctrines to fit their desires. Moreover, the rationalization function of forgiveness-relevant meaning systems is not necessarily specific to religion. Any meaning system—whether religious, philosophical, or political—that presents potentially conflicting meaning systems of retributive justice and forgiveness can be used by an individual to rationalize his or her current forgiveness stance. However, because many religious meaning systems strongly promote both forgiveness and retributive justice, they may be especially easy to use as rationalizations. The discrepancy between the religious message of forgiveness, and the lack of increased forgiveness in highly religious individuals may not necessarily be due to a failure of the religious meaning system to promote the value of forgiveness. Instead, the discrepancy could arise as a consequence of the complex messages regarding forgiveness that are inherent in many religious meaning systems, combined with individuals' varied motivations in this context.

Conclusions

Religion can function as a forgiveness-relevant meaning system, potentially affecting people's beliefs, emotions, actions, and goals related to forgiveness. Yet religion's effect on forgiveness may not be unidirectional—while religion's emphasis on universal love and compassion can work to facilitate forgiveness, the competing meaning system of retributive justice makes it possible for individuals to use religion as rationalization for revenge.

We have presented data that support McCullough and Worthington's (1999) assertion that psychometric shortcomings have obscured the relationship between religion and forgiveness. When forgiveness is assessed using restrictive recall procedures and aggregate measures of forgiveness, a small positive relationship between religion and transgression-specific forgiveness emerges. But this may not be the last we hear of the discrepancy between religion and forgiveness.

All of the studies reviewed by McCullough and Worthington (1999), as well as the data presented in this article, relied on self-reports of forgiveness. Research using behavioral measures of forgiveness is needed to rule out the confound of self-presentation.

It is also possible that religion can be used as a rationalization for unforgiving behavior. Instead of religion causing forgiveness, motivations against forgiveness might cause individuals to endorse religious meaning systems that justify unforgiving behavior. This special form of moral rationalization could explain instances where religion does not seem to facilitate forgiveness, and might also help to explain why empirical work thus far has only uncovered a weak positive relationship between religion and forgiveness. Additional research will help uncover the complex relationship between religiousness and forgiveness.

References

Ajzen, I., & Fishbein, M. (1977). Attitude-behavior relations: A theoretical analysis and review of empirical research. *Psychological Bulletin, 84*, 888–918.

Allport, G. W., & Ross, J. M. (1967). Personal religious orientation and prejudice. *Journal of Personality and Social Psychology, 5*, 447–457.

Aronson, E. (1969). The theory of cognitive dissonance: A current perspective. In L. Berkowitz (Ed.), *Advances in experimental social psychology* (Vol. 4, pp. 1–34). New York: Academic Press.

Ayoub, M. (1997). Repentance in the Islamic tradition. In A. Etzioni & D. E. Carney (Eds.), *Repentance: A comparative perspective* (pp. 96–121). New York: Dryden.

Bandura, A. (1999). Moral disengagement in the perpetration of inhumanities. *Personality and Social Psychology Review, 3*, 193–209.

Bandura, A., Underwood, B., & Fromson, M. E. (1975). Disinhibition of aggression through diffusion of responsibility and dehumanization of victims. *Journal of Research in Personality, 9*, 253–269.

Bar-Tal, D. (1990). Causes and consequences of delegitimization: Models of conflict and ethnocentrism. *Journal of Social Issues, 46*, 65–81.

Bassett, R. L., Sadler, R. D., Kobischen, E. E., Skiff, D. M., Merrill, I. J., Atwater, B. J., & Livermore, P. W. (1981). The Shepherd Scale: Separating the sheep from the goats. *Journal of Psychology and Theology, 9*, 335–351.

Batson, C. D., & Ahmad, N. (2001). Empathy-induced altruism in a prisoner's dilemma II: What if the target of empathy has defected? *European Journal of Social Psychology, 31*, 25–36.

Borobio, D. (1986). Sacramental forgiveness of sins. In C. Floristán & C. Duquoc (Eds.), *Concilium* (Vol.184, pp. 95–112). Edinburgh, Scotland: T. & T. Clark Ltd.

Cohen, J. (1988). *Statistical power analysis* (2nd ed.). Hillsdale, NJ: Erlbaum.

Dorff, E. M. (1998). The elements of forgiveness: A Jewish approach. In E. L. Worthington (Ed.), *Dimensions of forgiveness* (pp. 29–55). Philadelphia: Templeton Foundation Press.

Edwards, L. M., Lapp-Rincker, R. H., Magyar-Moe, J. L., Rehfeldt, J. D., Ryder, J. A., Brown, J. C., & Lopez, S. J. (2002). A positive relationship between religious faith and forgiveness: Faith in the absence of data? *Pastoral Psychology, 50*, 147–152.

Enright, R. D., & Coyle, C. (1998). Researching the process model of forgiveness within psychological interventions. In E. L. Worthington (Ed.), *Dimensions of forgiveness* (pp. 139–161). Philadelphia: Templeton Foundation Press.

Enright, R. D., Eastin, D. L., Golden, S., Sarinopoulos, I., & Freedman, S. (1992). Interpersonal forgiveness within the helping professions: An attempt to resolve differences of opinion. *Counseling and Values, 36*, 84–103.

Enright, R. D., Gassin, E. A., & Wu, C. (1992). Forgiveness: A developmental view. *Journal of Moral Development, 21*, 99–114.

Enright, R. D., Santos, M. J., & Al-Mabuk, R. (1989). The adolescent as forgiver. *Journal of Adolescence, 12*, 99–110.

Epstein, S. (1983). Aggregation and beyond: Some issues in the prediction of behavior. *Journal of Personality, 51*, 360–392.

Exline, J. J., & Baumeister, R. F. (2000). Expressing forgiveness and repentance: Benefits and barriers. In M. E. McCullough, K. I. Pargament, & C. E. Thoresen (Eds.), *Forgiveness: Theory, research, and practice* (pp. 133–155). New York: Guilford Press.

Fraser, N. M., Hipel, K. W., Jaworsky, J., & Zuljan, R. (1990). A conflict analysis of the Armenian-Azerbaijani dispute. *Journal of Conflict Resolution, 34*, 652–677.

Freedman, J. L., & Sears, D. O. (1965). Selective exposure. In L. Berkowitz (Ed.), *Advances in experimental social psychology* (Vol. 2, pp. 58–98). New York: Academic Press.

Glock, C., & Stark, R. (1966). *Christian beliefs and anti-Semitism*. New York: Harper & Row.

Gorsuch, R. L. (1968). The conceptualization of God as seen in adjective ratings. *Journal for the Scientific Study of Religion, 7*, 56–64.

Gorsuch, R. L., & Hao, J. Y. (1993). Forgiveness: An exploratory factor analysis and its relationships to religious variables. *Review of Religious Research, 34*, 333–347.

Higgins, R. (2001). Buddhists practice forgiveness: Mindful suffering. *Christian Century, 118*, 9–10.

Higi, W. L. (1997, June). Timothy McVeigh, the death penalty and Catholic teaching. *Archives: A Word from Bishop Higi*. Retrieved from http://www.dioceseoflafayette.org/wordarchives/wordarchives-062297.html.

Hunsberger, B. E., & Jackson, L. M. (this issue). Religion, meaning, and prejudice. *Journal of Social Issues*.

Jones, E. E., & Pittman, T. S. (1982). Toward a general theory of strategic self-presentation. In J. Suls (Ed.), *Psychological perspectives on the self* (pp. 231–262). Hillsdale, NJ: Erlbaum.

Klostermaier, K. K. (1994). *A survey of Hinduism*. Albany, NY: State University of New York Press.

Kohlberg, L. (1976). Moral stages and moralization: The cognitive-developmental approach. In T. Lickona (Ed.), *Moral development and behavior: Theory, research, and social issues* (pp. 31–53). New York: Holt.

Kunda, Z. (1990). The case for motivated reasoning. *Psychological Bulletin, 108*, 480–498.

Lerner, M. J. (1965). Evaluation of performance as a function of performer's reward and attractiveness. *Journal of Personality and Social Psychology, 1*, 355–360.

Lerner, M. J., & Simmons, C. H. (1966). Observer's reaction to the "innocent victim": Compassion or rejection? *Journal of Personality and Social Psychology, 4*, 203–210.

Marty, M. E. (1998). The ethos of Christian forgiveness. In E. L. Worthington, Jr. (Ed.), *Dimensions of forgiveness* (pp. 9–28). Philadelphia: Templeton Foundation Press.

Mauger, P. A., Saxon, A., Hamill, C., & Pannell, M. (1996, March). *The relationship of forgiveness to interpersonal behavior*. Paper presented at the annual convention of the Southeastern Psychological Association, Norfolk, VA.

McCullough, M. E. (2001). Forgiveness: Who does it, and how do they do it? *Current Directions in Psychological Science, 10*, 194–197.

McCullough, M. E., Bellah, C. G., Kilpatrick, S. D., & Johnson, J. L. (2001). Vengefulness: Relationships with forgiveness, rumination, well-being, and the Big Five. *Personality and Social Psychology Bulletin, 27*, 601–610.

McCullough, M. E., Fincham, F. D., & Tsang, J. (2003). Forgiveness, forbearance, and time: The temporal unfolding of transgression-related interpersonal motivations. *Journal of Personality and Social Psychology, 84*, 540–557.

McCullough, M. E., & Hoyt, W. T. (2002). Transgression-related motivational dispositions: Personality substrates of forgiveness and their links to the Big Five. *Personality and Social Psychology Bulletin, 28*, 1556–1573.

McCullough, M. E., Rachal, K. C., Sandage, S. J., Worthington, E. L., Jr., Brown, S. W., & Hight, T. L. (1998). Interpersonal forgiving in close relationships II: Theoretical elaboration and measurement. *Journal of Personality and Social Psychology, 75*, 1586–1603.

McCullough, M. E., & Worthington, E. L., Jr. (1995). Promoting forgiveness: A comparison of two brief psycho-educational interventions with a waiting-list control. *Counseling and Values, 40*, 55–68.

McCullough, M.E., & Worthington, E. L., Jr. (1999). Religion and the forgiving personality. *Journal of Personality, 67*, 1141–1164.

McCullough, M.E., Worthington, E. L., Jr., & Rachal, K. C. (1997). Interpersonal forgiving in close relationships. *Journal of Personality and Social Psychology, 73*, 321–336.

Nisbett, R. E., & Wilson, T. D. (1977). Telling more than we can know: Verbal reports on mental processes. *Psychological Review, 84*, 231–259.

O'Donoghue, J., & O'Donoghue, M. A. (1981). Toward understanding group conflict in Northern Ireland. *International Journal of Group Tensions, 11*, 119–125.

Paloutzian, R. F., & Smith, B. S. (1995). The utility of the religion-as-schema model. *International Journal for the Psychology of Religion, 5*, 17–22.

Pargament, K. I., & Rye, M. S. (1998). Forgiveness as a method of religious coping. In E. L. Worthington, Jr. (Ed.), *Dimensions of forgiveness* (pp. 59–78). Philadelphia: Templeton Foundation Press.

Poloma, M. M., & Gallup, G. H. (1991). *Varieties of prayer*. Philadelphia: Trinity Press International.

Rackley, J. V. (1993). *The relationship of marital satisfaction, forgiveness, and religiosity*. Unpublished doctoral dissertation, Virginia Polytechnic Institute and State University, Blacksburg, VA.

Rest, J. (1979). *Revised manual for the defining issues test*. Unpublished manuscript, University of Minnesota.

Rice, A. (2001/2002). Considering reconciliation amid the horror of a brother's death. *Harvard Divinity Bulletin, 30*, 34.

Rokeach, M. (1973). *The nature of human values*. New York: Free Press.

Rouhana, N. N., & Bar-Tal, D. (1998). Psychological dynamics of intractable ethnonational conflicts: The Israeli-Palestinian case. *American Psychologist, 53*, 761–770.

Rye, M. S., Pargament, K. I., Ali, M. A., Beck, G. L., Dorff, E. N., Hallisey, C., Narayanan, V., & Williams, J. G. (2000). Religious perspectives on forgiveness. In M. E. McCullough, K. I. Pargament, & C. E. Thoresen (Eds.), *Forgiveness: Theory, research, and practice* (pp. 17–40). New York: Guilford Press.

Saraswati, C. (1995). Hindu: Love. In M. Tobias, J. Morrison, & B. Gray (Eds.), *A parliament of souls: In search of global spirituality* (pp. 153–161). San Francisco, CA: KQED.

Schmidt, F. L., & Hunter, J. E. (1996). Measurement error in psychological research: Lessons from 26 research scenarios. *Psychological Methods, 1*, 199–223.

Shoemaker, A., & Bolt, M. (1977). The Rokeach Value Survey and perceived Christian values. *Journal of Psychology and Theology, 5*, 139–142.

Silberman, I. (this issue). Religion as a meaning system: Implications for the new millennium. *Journal of Social Issues*.

Steele, C. M. (1988). The psychology of self-affirmation: Sustaining the integrity of the self. In L. Berkowitz (Ed.), *Advances in experimental social psychology* (Vol. 21, pp. 261–302). New York: Academic Press.

Stringer, M., Cornish, I. M., & Denver, S. (2000). The transition to peace and young people's perceptions of locations in Northern Ireland. *Peace and Conflict: Journal of Peace Psychology, 6*, 57–66.

Subkoviak, M. J., Enright, R. D., Wu, C., Gassin, E. A., Freedman, S., Olson, L. M., & Sarinopoulos, I. (1995). Measuring interpersonal forgiveness in late adolescence and middle adulthood. *Journal of Adolescence, 18*, 641–655.

Temoshok, L. R., & Chandra, P. S. (2000). The meaning of forgiveness in a specific situational and cultural context: Persons living with HIV/AIDS in India. In M. E. McCullough, K. I. Pargament, & C.E. Thoresen (Eds.), *Forgiveness: Theory, research, and practice* (pp. 41–64). New York: Guilford Press.

Tsang, J. (2002). Moral rationalization and the integration of situational factors and psychological processes in immoral behavior. *Review of General Psychology, 6*, 25–50.

Tsang, J., McCullough, M. E., & Fincham, F. D. (in press). The longitudinal association between forgiveness and relationship closeness and commitment. *Journal of Social and Clinical Psychology*.

Witvliet, C. V. O. (2001). Forgiveness and health: Review and reflections on a matter of faith, feelings, and physiology. *Journal of Psychology and Theology, 29*, 212–224.

Worthington, E. L. Jr., Wade, N. G., Hight, T. L., Ripley, J. S., McCullough, M. E., Berry, J. W., Schmitt, M. M., Berry, J. T., Bursley, K. H., & O'Connor, L. (2003). The religious commitment inventory-10: Development, refinement, and validation of a brief scale for research and counseling. *Journal of Counseling Psychology, 50*, 84–96.
Zaehner, R. C. (1962). *Hinduism.* New York: Oxford University Press.

JO-ANN TSANG is Assistant Professor of Psychology at Baylor University. She received the PhD in psychology from the University of Kansas. Her research interests are in the area of social psychology, and include moral rationalization and moral emotion, the psychology of religion, forgiveness, and gratitude.

MICHAEL E. McCULLOUGH is Associate Professor of Psychology at the University of Miami in Coral Gables, Florida. He received the PhD in psychology from Virginia Commonwealth University. His research focuses on religion, spirituality, and the virtues, how these aspects of people's lives unfold, and how they are linked to social behavior, health, and well-being. In his current research he is exploring evolutionary models of forgiveness and revenge. He is also currently studying the development of religiousness over the life course. He has also authored or edited five books, including *Forgiveness: Theory Research and Practice* (Guilford Press, 2000), *Handbook of Religion and Health* (Oxford University Press, 2001), and *The Psychology of Gratitude* (Oxford University Press, 2004).

WILLIAM T. HOYT is Associate Professor in the department of Counseling Psychology at the University of Wisconsin-Madison. He received his PhD in Psychology from Virginia Commonwealth University. Dr. Hoyt's research includes a substantive focus on social interactions, and on social relationships as markers of psychological well-being. His methodological interests center on analytical techniques for studying interpersonal perceptions, including the study of bias in ratings of self and others, and development of impressions ingroup settings.

Journal of Social Issues, Vol. 61, No. 4, 2005, pp. 807–826

Religion, Meaning, and Prejudice

Bruce Hunsberger
Wilfrid Laurier University

Lynne M. Jackson*
King's University College at The University of Western Ontario

Links between religion and prejudice have been interpreted to suggest that religion can both reduce and exacerbate prejudice. Here, the analysis of religion as a meaning system illuminates how religion can affect intergroup attitudes. Traditional psychological perspectives on religion and prejudice are summarized, followed by a discussion of religion and prejudice in cross-cultural and cross-religious contexts, involving varying target groups. Next, we explore possible explanatory mechanisms by proposing how four levels of meaning associated with religion— cognitive, motivational, societal, and intergroup—may both promote and attenuate prejudice. Finally, additional factors that might facilitate the paradoxical coexistence of religious egalitarian intentions with prejudiced attitudes are considered, and we speculate about the potential for religious groups to reduce prejudice within their adherents.

After the terrorist attacks on the World Trade Center in New York City and the Pentagon in Washington, D.C. on September 11, 2001, the world was in turmoil as people tried to understand the enormity and the implications of the events. The role of religion-based prejudice in this context is exemplified in the claimed involvement of extremist religious elements in the attacks, and in the words of the American Christian fundamentalist, Jerry Falwell, who subsequently blamed the American Civil Liberties Union, abortionists, feminists, and gay and lesbian persons for removing God's protection from the United States and therefore allowing the attacks to happen (Saunders, 2001). Religiously based prejudice and conflict are disturbingly evident in the world, as evidenced in almost daily news reports (see, e.g., Juergensmeyer, 2000): Catholics battle Protestants in Northern Ireland,

---

*Correspondence concerning this article should be addressed to Lynne Jackson, Department of Psychology, King's University College at The University of Western Ontario, 266 Epworth Avenue, London, Ontario, Canada N6A 2M3 [e-mail: ljacks4@uwo.ca].

violence continues between Jews and Muslims in the Middle East, Sikh-Hindu-Muslim clashes occur in India. The U.S.-led invasion of Iraq was associated with religious appeals by both presidents Bush and Hussein, and concerns were voiced that this war was just one example of a broader Christian-Muslim conflict. In an effort to understand these conflicts as well as more subtle links between religion and problematic intergroup attitudes, we review work on the relation between religion and prejudice, and discuss possible explanatory mechanisms in the context of the various meanings provided by religion.

The religion and prejudice literature, involving mostly North American studies, has been reviewed a number of times over the past 30 years (e.g., Batson & Burris, 1994; Batson, Schoenrade, & Ventis, 1993; Gorsuch & Aleshire, 1974; Hood, Spilka, Hunsberger, & Gorsuch, 1995; Hunsberger, 1995). Such reviews have typically focused on the relationship between dispositional religious orientation and overt forms of prejudice such as self-reports of negative attitudes toward, or endorsement of, stereotypic perceptions of other groups. This extensive literature is briefly reviewed here, focusing on *how* religion and prejudice are associated. We note limitations of this religious orientation approach and examine relevant studies in several unique contexts (different targets of prejudice; cross-cultural and cross-religious findings). We then consider *why* religion is related to prejudice, and go beyond dispositional analysis by examining the importance of four different levels of meaning in this relationship. Finally, we address the apparent paradox of how religion and prejudice can coexist for some religious people, despite religious teachings of tolerance.

Our analysis of prejudice is informed by multi-component attitude models (e.g., Esses, Haddock, & Zanna, 1993) that articulate how intergroup attitudes have many domains of experience, such as stereotypes, emotional responses to groups, and symbolic beliefs (beliefs that a group threatens or promotes one's values). We consider not only negative intergroup attitudes, but also the social implications of seemingly more benign intergroup attitudes linked to religion, because subjectively positive attitudes can be of problematic implication. For example, affectionate yet paternalistic attitudes toward underprivileged groups often justify and support inequality (Glick & Fiske, 2001; Jackman, 1994). Thus, we use "prejudice" as an umbrella term that encompasses a potentially wide range of problematic intergroup attitudes.

How Religion Is Related to Prejudice

The Historical, North American Perspective

A central teaching of most religions is that we should love our fellow human beings unconditionally (Coward, 1986). It therefore came as a surprise about 50 years ago when social scientific studies began to report that more religious people tended to be more prejudiced than less religious people. For example, a review by Batson et al. (1993) revealed that, in relevant studies published between 1940 and 1990 (most were prior to 1970), 37 of 47 findings showed a positive relationship between religiousness and prejudice, and just 2 studies indicated a negative relationship. How could this be? Religions teach tolerance (Coward, 1986); how could more frequent church attenders be more prejudiced?

Researchers began to suspect that individual differences in personal religious motivation might be relevant to this dilemma, and that simply "being religious" or "going to church" were oversimplified ways of measuring religiousness. Allport and Ross (1967) formalized this concern by distinguishing between intrinsic and extrinsic religious orientation. An intrinsic orientation was considered to be more mature, stemming from an internalized, committed, and sincere faith. The extrinsic orientation was associated with religious immaturity, involving an externalized, consensual, utilitarian orientation to religion. Intrinsic (I) and Extrinsic (E) scales were developed to measure these orientations (Allport & Ross, 1967) and these scales spawned an impressive array of research projects. Importantly for the present article, Allport and Ross argued that intrinsic religiosity was associated with increased tolerance (or decreased prejudice) and extrinsic with just the opposite. Unfortunately, there have been problems with the I and E scales, the conceptualization and study of intrinsic and extrinsic orientations and their possible contamination with social desirability, and research has not always supported the hypothesized links between these orientations and prejudice (see, e.g., Donahue, 1985; Hunsberger, 1995). Altemeyer (1996) bluntly stated that, in addition to their serious psychometric problems, the I and E scales "plainly failed to measure what they were supposed to measure . . . [and] they plainly failed to show what they were supposed to show" (p. 154).

Going beyond the dichotomous distinction of the I/E orientations, Batson and his colleagues proposed the existence of a quest religious orientation (see Batson et al., 1993) that is theoretically associated with tolerance. The quest orientation involves a questioning, doubting, open, and flexible approach to religious issues. Batson has argued that higher scores on a Quest (Q) scale (Batson & Schoenrade, 1991a, 1991b) are associated with "universal compassion" whereas the Intrinsic scale is, at least under some circumstances, associated with intolerance rather than tolerance (e.g., Batson et al., 1993; Batson, Eidelman, Higley, & Russell, 2001; Batson, Floyd, Meyer, & Winner, 1999).

Another religious orientation, religious fundamentalism (RF) focuses on closed-mindedness, the certainty that one's religious beliefs are correct, and the belief that one has access to absolute truth. RF is distinct from "religious orthodoxy," which focuses on the content of the religious beliefs themselves (see Altemeyer & Hunsberger, 1992). Some attempts to operationalize RF have incorporated specifically Christian beliefs or terminology (e.g., "born again"), whereas others have purposely avoided such links with specific religious traditions (e.g., Altemeyer &

Hunsberger, 1992). Numerous studies have linked religious fundamentalism with prejudice, as well as with right-wing authoritarianism (RWA; e.g., Altemeyer & Hunsberger, 1992; Hunsberger, Owusu, & Duck, 1999; Laythe, Finkel, Bringle, & Kirkpatrick, 2002; Laythe, Finkel, & Kirkpatrick, 2001), which has been conceptualized as a composite of three attitudinal clusters—authoritarian submission, authoritarian aggression, and conventionalism (Altemeyer, 1996). Conceptualized as a personality variable, RWA has been consistently intertwined with many kinds of prejudice (e.g., ethnocentrism; Altemeyer, 1996).

Many studies of religion-prejudice links have included one or more of the intrinsic, extrinsic, quest, and fundamentalist religious orientations. However, there is not complete agreement on the relationship of these orientations with intolerance, possibly because of varying targets of prejudice, cross-cultural and cross-religious factors, and so on. The greatest controversy surrounds the I and E scales where findings, as mentioned above, have been particularly problematic. Quest has often been related to reduced prejudice and RF repeatedly predicts greater intolerance. In order to assess the recent relationships of these four religious orientations with prejudice, we examined studies since 1990 involving I, E, Q, or RF measures, and at least one measure of prejudice or endorsement of discrimination toward racial/ethnic groups, gay or lesbian persons, women, Communists, or religious outgroups, or RWA. We therefore included only studies that used at least one of: (a) the original I or E scales (Allport & Ross, 1967), or a variation (e.g., Batson et al.'s, 1993, Means & End scales); (b) Batson & Schoenrade's (1991a, 1991b) Q scale or a similar alternative (e.g., Altemeyer & Hunsberger, 1992); and (c) an RF scale similar to that of Altemeyer and Hunsberger (1992) or McFarland (1989). We wanted these measures to be as "pure" as possible, so we purposely did *not* include measures such as frequency of church attendance, or extent of interest in religion, even though these have sometimes been considered proxies for intrinsic or extrinsic religious orientation.

Usually the prejudice measures in these studies relied on pencil-and-paper self-reports of prejudice. These measures suffer from problems such as unreported or weak psychometric properties, the transparency or bluntness of items, and associated social desirability effects (see, e.g., Spilka, Hunsberger, Gorsuch, & Hood, 2003). There have been attempts to develop more subtle and more valid pencil-and-paper indices of prejudice (e.g., McConahay, 1986; Rudman, Greenwald, Mellott, & Schwartz, 1999), but these measures have seldom been incorporated into investigations of religion and prejudice.

Samples vary from one study to the next, but we included them all: undergraduate and adult samples; truncated samples (e.g., only people who were at least moderately interested in religion; only white heterosexuals; only members of specific religious groups). We considered multiple samples in a single study to represent different findings if the samples were quite different (e.g., Muslims and Christians), but not if they were simply, for example, different Protestant groups. In

Table 1. Relationships between Four Religious Orientations and Measures of Intolerance: A Survey of Studies from 1990 to 2003

| | Religious Orientation Measure | | | | | | | | | | | |
| | Intrinsic | | | Extrinsic | | | Quest | | | Fundamentalism | | |
Type of Intolerance	+	0	−	+	0	−	+	0	−	+	0	−
Racial/ethnic	0	0	4	3	1	0	0	3	2	5	6	0
Gay/lesbian persons	7	1	1	4	2	2	0	2	7	17	0	0
Women	0	1	0	0	1	0	0	1	0	3	0	0
Communists	1	0	0	0	1	0	0	1	0	3	0	0
Religious out groups	1	0	0	1	0	0	0	1	0	3	0	0
Authoritarianism	2	0	0	0	0	2	0	0	4	13	0	0
Total	11	2	5	8	5	4	0	8	13	44	6	0

Note. Sixteen studies, some with multiple samples and/or multiple measures, are included. "+" = positive relationship between religious orientation and intolerance; "0" = no relationship; "−" = negative relationship. See text for additional details.

the end, we included research reported in 16 articles (Altemeyer, 2003; Altemeyer & Hunsberger, 1992; Batson et al., 1999; Duck & Hunsberger, 1999; Fisher, Derison, Polley, Cadman, & Johnston, 1994; Fulton, Gorsuch, & Maynard, 1999; Griffiths, Dixon, Stanley, & Weiland, 2001; Hunsberger, 1996; Hunsberger et al., 1999; Jackson & Esses, 1997; Jackson & Hunsberger, 1999; Kirkpatrick, 1993; Laythe et al., 2001, 2002; Leak & Randall, 1995; Wylie & Forest, 1992). These studies collectively involved 1,532 adults in 8 samples and 4,329 undergraduate students in 17 studies.

The results of our survey are shown in Table 1. If one simply examines the "total box score" for each religious orientation, it would appear that Intrinsic, Extrinsic, and especially Religious Fundamentalism scales are associated with intolerance (remember, the Intrinsic scale is usually thought to be associated with just the opposite—increased tolerance). Quest is generally associated with increased tolerance. However, the reader will note that this simple tabulation of relationships hides important trends for different targets of prejudice.

Targets of Prejudice

From the 1940s through the 1970s, the most frequently studied target of prejudice in relevant investigations was race and/or ethnicity (see Batson & Ventis, 1982). This earlier literature was more likely to find links between the intrinsic orientation and increased tolerance of (usually racial or ethnic) minority groups. For example, Batson and Ventis's (1982) literature review led them to conclude that intrinsics appeared quite consistently less prejudiced than extrinsics. More recently, interest in gay men and lesbians, women, Communists, and religious outgroups such as the nonreligious, as target groups, has increased (see Table 1).

These recent investigations have sometimes generated findings that conflict with the earlier consensus. For example, Herek (1987) found that an intrinsic orientation was positively linked with prejudice against gay men and lesbians, but consistent with previous research, it was negatively linked with racism.

Our review of studies published since 1990 clearly supports the idea that the target of prejudice is important when considering prejudice-religious orientation relationships (see Table 1). The Intrinsic scale was consistently *negatively* related to self-reported racial/ethnic intolerance (4 of 4 studies), but it was *positively* related to intolerance of gay men and lesbians (7/9 studies) and possibly to authoritarianism and to intolerance of Communists and religious outgroups, though there are few relevant studies. The extrinsic orientation was sometimes positively related to racial/ethnic (3/4) and gay/lesbian (4/8) intolerance. Quest showed a weak tendency to be associated with tolerance for racial groups (2/5); a much stronger effect appeared for gay/lesbian persons as targets (7/9). Finally, RF was consistently related to increased prejudice against gay/lesbian persons, women, Communists, and religious outgroups, as well as authoritarianism (39/39 findings in total), but its relationship with racial/ethnic intolerance is less clear-cut (5 positive relationships, 6 nonsignificant findings).

How can one explain the contingency of the prejudice-religious orientation relationship on the target of prejudice? Herek (1987) had previously suggested that the different relationship between I and racism, compared to negative attitudes toward gay men and lesbians, might be attributable to differences in church teachings, and Batson and Burris (1994) argued that it is necessary to differentiate between prejudice that is proscribed by many religions (e.g., racism) and prejudice that is tolerated or even encouraged by some religions (e.g., prejudice against gay men and lesbians). Duck and Hunsberger (1999) have indeed found evidence confirming the tendency for people to report that racial prejudice was proscribed by their religious group, but that gay/lesbian intolerance was nonsproscribed, on average. These tendencies might be culturally and geographically specific; it has been argued, for example, that in South Africa racial prejudice has been religiously nonproscribed (Lafferty, 1990).

The proscription/nonproscription notion also resembles Franco and Maass's (1999) finding that it is important to consider whether or not groups are normatively protected against prejudice (i.e., whether it is unacceptable or acceptable to express negative judgments about specific groups). Their research suggests that more subtle (implicit) measures might be necessary to tap prejudice against normatively protected targets (in their Italian study, Jews), but that more explicit measures of prejudice would be adequate when investigating targets that are not normatively protected against it (in their study, Islamic Fundamentalists). Rudman et al. (1999) similarly found that, in an American sample, an implicit test of prejudice revealed anti-Semitism that was not as apparent in more explicit measures. However, covert prejudice (i.e., based on behavior or behavioral intention, rather than the usual

self-report of attitude) involving targets where prejudice is proscribed has also
been found among the intrinsically religious (see Batson et al., 1993).

Future research needs to further explore the relationships between religious
orientation and prejudice involving other possible targets of prejudice, such as
women, Communists, and religious outgroups such as the *non*religious (Hunter,
2001; Jackson & Hunsberger, 1999), and a more general "religious ethnocentrism"
(Altemeyer, 2003). There has been little if any research involving additional targets such as the elderly and the physically or mentally challenged. Such research
would illuminate the ways in which attitudes toward these targets of prejudice are
differentially related to I, E, Q, and RF, as well as potentially generating possible
explanations for the patterns of relationships.

Cross-Cultural and Cross-Religious Findings

There have been few true cross-cultural and cross-religious studies on religion
and prejudice; those that do exist sometimes involve confounds between culture
and religion. Some investigations are carried out in seldom-studied non-Western
cultures, but they do not involve any *cross*-cultural comparison. Other research
involves measures or samples that are not directly comparable. In spite of such
problems, some studies do at least take us outside of the traditional Judeo-Christian
North American context. For example, research in Bangladesh (Hewstone, Islam,
& Judd, 1993) examined Muslim (majority group) and Hindu (minority group)
evaluations of target groups that varied by religion (Muslim or Hindu) and nationality (Bangladeshi or Indian). Religion and nationality were both found to be
important in predicting outgroup discrimination.

A series of European studies investigated relationships among religious beliefs, authoritarianism, and prejudice, especially anti-Semitism (e.g., Billiet, 1995;
Duriez & Hutsebaut, 2000; Eisenga, Billiet, & Felling, 1999; Eisenga, Felling, &
Peters, 1990; Konig, Eisenga, & Scheepers, 2000). These studies, carried out in
Belgium and the Netherlands, typically showed little or no relationship, but occa-
sionally a significant positive (e.g., Duriez & Hutsebaut, 2000) or negative relationship (e.g., Billiet, 1995) between measures of Christian belief or attendance
and ethnic prejudice. When positive associations appeared, the authors found that
they could usually be attributed to the effects of other variables such as education, age, localism, authoritarianism, and anomie. However, positive relationships
between Christian beliefs and anti-Semitism were more robust and could not be
"explained" by other variables. Unfortunately, these investigations did not include
any of the primary religious orientation measures (I, E, Q, RF), and therefore
were not included in Table 1. Also, the general finding of little or no relationship
between Christian *beliefs* and racial/ethnic intolerance is consistent with some
North American research (e.g., Altemeyer & Hunsberger, 1992; Jacobson, 1998;
Laythe et al., 2001, 2002). As explained in a subsequent section of this article

it may be that, in addition to the content of beliefs, people's relations with their religious group are also linked to prejudice, and these two factors may interact to determine prejudice. Recently, Karpov (2002) found similar, though somewhat complex, links between "theocratic beliefs" (p. 267) and intolerance in Poland and the United States, using unique measures.

Griffin, Gorsuch, and Davis (1987) studied prejudice toward Rastafarians by Seventh Day Adventists on the Caribbean island of St. Croix. Both commitment to the Adventist church and instrinsic orientation were positively associated with an indicator of prejudice (i.e., withholding human rights from Rastafarians). However, church members reported that they perceived the church itself to be relatively prejudiced. Therefore, these results are consistent with the proposal that greater religiousness is associated with prejudice perceived to be nonproscribed (or possibly prescribed) by the church. Among Venezuelan university students who were mostly Roman Catholic, however, Ponton and Gorsuch (1988) found the more typical negative association between the intrinsic orientation and (ethnic) prejudice, and a positive link for the extrinsic orientation; quest was uncorrelated with prejudice. Proscription was not assessed. Murphy-Berman, Berman, Pachauri, and Kumar (1985) reported a "reverse prejudice" (p. 33) in their study of Northern Indian university students' proclivity to discriminate; Hindu participants hypothetically allocated more money to Muslim than to Hindu targets in vignettes. The reasons for this result are unclear; the authors speculated that it could be due to a social desirability effect. In another Hindu/Muslim study, Hassan and Khalique (1987) reported a tendency for their Muslim college students to reveal more prejudice than did Hindus.

It is difficult to make sense of the hodge-podge of studies carried out in various cultures. Measures and samples vary widely, comparison groups are rare, and findings are sometimes contradictory. The results of these investigations are important within their specific context, but comprehensive cross-cultural research is needed, using the same measures and comparable samples across cultures, and controlling for proscriptive status of specific types of prejudice.

There seems to be more consistency for cross-cultural and cross-religious findings involving religious fundamentalism. Hunsberger (1996) found that RF was significantly positively correlated with right-wing authoritarianism and hostile attitudes toward gay men and lesbians (on an Attitudes Toward Homosexuals (ATH) scale) for adult samples from three non-Christian religious groups (Muslims, Hindus, and Jews) in Canada. The strength of the relationships approximated those found in mostly Christian Canadian adult and university student samples (e.g., Altemeyer & Hunsberger, 1992) and American college students (e.g., Laythe et al., 2001). Furthermore, Hunsberger et al. (1999) essentially replicated these (RF-RWA-ATH) relationships in samples of Ghanaian Muslim and Christian university students. Although additional replication is needed in non-Christian and non-Western settings, the intertwining of RF, RWA, and ATH seems quite robust across some different religious groups and cultural settings.

Summary

The conceptualization and development of religious orientation measures has, in spite of problems, advanced our understanding of the relationship between religion and prejudice. Especially when one takes into account the target of prejudice and whether or not a specific prejudice is seen to be proscribed by one's religious group, clear links between religious orientation and prejudice begin to emerge. Nevertheless, attempts to examine these relationships in cross-cultural and cross-religious perspective have often been problematic, and more and better research is needed in this area. Furthermore, the "religious orientation" studies do not adequately address the important question of *why* religion and prejudice are linked.

Why Is Religion Related to Prejudice

Because religion serves many functions—from providing a frame of reference for individuals to interpret reality and set personal goals, to organizing social and political relations between groups (see Silberman, this issue)—it is likely that multiple mechanisms are responsible for the relations between religion and prejudice described previously in this article. In this section, we outline types of meaning that people derive from religious teachings and affiliation, and explore the implications of these types of meaning for intergroup attitudes.

Personal Religious Orientations and Styles of Cognitive Processes as Sources of Meaning

Religions, as epistemologies, provide a frame of reference for understanding and interpreting the world. Thus, the ways in which people think about religious and other issues may have implications for intergroup attitudes. Relatedly, it has been suggested that the fundamentalism and quest religious orientations are linked to particular cognitive styles, as exemplified by complexity of thought. Some findings suggest that more religiously fundamentalist people think differently in terms of complexity of thought about existential issues, compared to less fundamentalist persons (e.g., Hunsberger, Alisat, Pancer, & Pratt, 1996; Hunsberger, Pratt, & Pancer, 1994). Hunsberger et al. (1996) concluded that, "high and low fundamentalists may actually perceive and deal with their own (and others') religious experiences in different ways" (p. 218). They proposed that high fundamentalists tend to think "convergently," thereby being more likely to incorporate information or doubts into their existing religious schema, bolstering the original beliefs. Low fundamentalists, in contrast, seemed more likely to deal with critical religious questions or new information by adapting or changing their religious beliefs. This could have important implications for prejudice if individuals high in fundamentalism think less complexly about a variety of issues (cf. Pancer, Jackson, Hunsberger, Pratt, & Lea, 1995). High fundamentalists might cling to existing stereotypes, for example, but low fundamentalists might be more open to changing their views of others in light of new information. Such speculation awaits empirical test.

In contrast to people high on religious fundamentalism, people high on the quest orientation have been found to engage in complex thought (Batson & Raynor-Prince, 1983) and to be open to varying perspectives (McFarland & Warren, 1992). Thus, relations between quest and tolerance may reflect, in part, a tendency for people high on quest to think complexly both about religion and about people and diversity. Of course, noncognitive variables may also contribute to this relation; Burris, Jackson, Tarpley, and Smith (1996) suggested that the tendency for people high on quest to value an idiosyncratic versus group-based approach to religious, existential, and social issues may lead them to be relatively little influenced by group or social norms, such as those that tolerate prejudice.

The Motivational Meaning of Personal Religious Orientations

Links between religiosity and intergroup attitudes may also reflect implications of the personal goals and motives that are associated with individuals' religiosity. Allport and Ross (1967) contended that the source of the religion–prejudice link lay in a utilitarian approach to religion typified by people high in extrinsic orientation. These individuals were thought to find religion meaningful as a source of social status, and hence they were thought likely to conform to (historically) popular social trends such as prejudice. Furthermore, an intrinsic orientation theoretically predicted reduced prejudice because high intrinsics derived more "mature" devotional meaning from religion, and were likely to accept religious teachings pertaining to "brotherhood," compassion, etc. Apparently, these hypothesized mechanisms have never been directly empirically assessed as mediators of relations between religious orientation and intergroup attitudes. Also, as discussed earlier, although some studies have confirmed the hypothesized relations between I/E orientations and intergroup attitudes, other findings have been nonsupportive or contradictory; thus, the expected relationships have not been broadly substantiated in several decades of research. This and other problems, such as questions about the conceptualization and psychometric properties of the I/E scales, lead us to wonder about the validity of the presumed mechanisms.

Based on their observation that the proscription/nonproscription distinction helped to explain the relation between the intrinsic religious orientation and prejudice (e.g., explicit prejudice against gay men and lesbians, more subtle forms of ethnic bias), Batson and Burris (1994) suggested a potentially important intervening motivational mechanism—the desire to be viewed by self and others as in good standing with one's religion. Prejudice against gay men and lesbians among those high on the intrinsic orientation may reflect conformity to perceived church positions regarding sexuality because such conformity reinforces one's image as a good group member (see also Deconchy, 1984). In contrast, people high in intrinsic religiosity may try, albeit with imperfect success, to reject or hide other forms of prejudice (e.g., ethnic prejudice) also in order to maintain their self-image as good religious group members. Ironically, this tendency may circumvent attainment of the self-awareness required to challenge one's own subtle prejudices. Indeed, Batson, Flink, Schoenrade, Fultz, and Pyke (1986) found that, among White individuals, the intrinsic orientation was associated with avoidance of a Black person in an attributionally ambiguous situation, when such behavior could be readily justified in nonprejudice terms, but not in a situation in which avoidance would clearly reflect prejudice. Thus, counter to the original position of Allport and Ross (1967), a motive external to devout faith per se—the desire for religious group approval—may be relevant to relations between the intrinsic orientation and prejudice (see also Burris & Jackson, 2000).

Religion as a Meaning System for Personal and Societal Values

Religion provides meaning as an important way for people to participate in their societies and derive values from them. This participation can involve legitimization of social structures and traditions by means of explanations and justifications for the social status quo (e.g., "God rewards those who live a good life"). Hence, religiosity may be associated with prejudice if religion justifies existing inequalities. Suggestive of this possibility are data indicating that religiosity is associated with endorsement of a variety of conservative social values. For example, in an analysis of values among participants in four Western religions, greater self-reported religiosity was associated with higher importance placed on conservative value domains (e.g., tradition and conformity), and lower importance placed on openness-to-change values (e.g., self-direction and stimulation; Schwartz & Huismans, 1995; see also Roccas, this issue).

Moreover, a number of values, such as "freedom" and "heritage," that are associated with intrinsic religiosity, at least in the United States (e.g., Burris, Branscombe, & Jackson, 2000), may be particularly interesting in this context. The apparently positive nature of these values can mask and justify prejudice. For example, with respect to the value "freedom," when people assume that the *ideal* of freedom of opportunity is a *reality*, systemic intergroup biases may be overlooked and underprivileged groups may be blamed for their situation (e.g., stereotyped as lazy). Indeed, Hinojosa and Park (2004) showed that in the United States 1996 General Social Survey, Evangelical Protestants were especially likely to view the social disadvantage of African Americans to be a result of lack of motivation rather than systemic dynamics. Such individualism often corresponds to a lack of support for members of underprivileged groups and is viewed as an element of modern or symbolic prejudice (e.g., McConahay, 1986; Sears, 1988; Sears & Henry, 2003).

Although religiosity often seems to be associated with conservative social values arguably related to prejudice, the values that are associated with personal religiosity are probably influenced by the larger social context in which religions exist. Indeed, Burris et al. (2000) reported that although the intrinsic religious orientation was associated with values related to heritage (e.g, freedom, tradition) in the United States, in Canada it was correlated with an emphasis on the nationally emphasized value of multiculturalism. Thus, the social context in which religiosity exists may determine the role religion plays in prejudice, in addition to (or interacting with) the specific content or form of religiosity; religions can uphold legitimizing myths that explain and sustain problems such as inequality (e.g., conservative and heritage values), but may also sometimes promote and sustain traditions intended to support diversity and tolerance (e.g., multiculturalism).

Religion as a Meaning System for Group Identification
and Group Conflict

Religious group identification and related experiences may provide people with a frame of meaning within which they can cultivate a positive sense of self. The need for positive self-esteem may contribute to links between religiosity and some forms of prejudice. Social Identity theory (Tajfel & Turner, 1986) predicts that people can maintain and enhance their self-esteem by means of downward social comparisons with other groups. In a religious context, maintaining a belief that one's religion teaches absolute truth, or is a unique source of morality, may contribute to ingroup preference (and enhance self-esteem), but may also generate prejudice against members of other religions. The desire for a positive social identity may also foster other forms of prejudice, such as prejudice against sexual minorities. For example, some religious persons who oppose same-sex rights may do so in part because they can gain a positive identity through a combination of identification with a group that has some social status due to exclusive access to a valuable resource or tradition (e.g., marriage) and devaluation of those without such access. Compatible with this view are data presented by Veenvliet and Esses (2005); they reported that among individuals higher in religious fundamentalism, opposition to same-sex marriage was due to antipathy toward gay men and lesbians, and not due to values, past experiences, or conformity.

Religion-based intergroup tensions and prejudice toward outgroups are likely to be intensified if members perceive themselves to be in conflict with other religious or nonreligious groups for valued resources (as described by Realistic Group Conflict theory; Sherif, 1966) and these resources give additional meaning to individuals (e.g., political representation, voting power, or economic benefits). Some recent evidence indicates that prejudice against people from different religions may arise from perceived competition on nonreligious dimensions. Jackson (2001) reported that the (often erroneous) perception that immigrants create competition with members of host populations for jobs can create prejudice against these immigrants' religion in particular (see also Esses, Jackson, & Armstrong,

1998). Other findings demonstrate how perceived competition generates and intensifies the open hostility, discrimination, and aggression that sometimes occur between religious groups. For example, Struch and Schwartz (1989) found that, among Secular, Traditional, and Orthodox Jews in Israel, perceived conflict of interests with Ultraorthodox Jews predicted dehumanization of the Ultraorthodox, and endorsement of a variety of antagonistic behaviors toward them.

Our analysis of religion as a meaning system for group identification and group conflict implies that prejudice against outgroup members is particularly likely to occur among people who identify strongly with their religious group because it is these individuals who derive the most meaning from their religious group affiliations. Religious group identification may be critical to especially devout persons, such as those high on intrinsic religiosity, orthodoxy, or fundamentalism who prize acceptance by their religious group (see Burris & Jackson, 2000; Jackson & Hunsberger, 1999). Indeed, it has been argued that the intrinsic orientation reflects religious self-stereotyping and the desire to be viewed by self and other as a good group member (Batson et al., 1993; Burris & Jackson, 2000). For example, the intrinsic orientation has been found to correlate substantially (+.70) with religious group identification (Burris & Jackson, 2000) and with self-reported degree of religiosity (also +.70; Schwartz & Huismans, 1995). In addition, evidence suggests that religious orthodoxy involves deference to the religious group in defining one's thoughts, language, and behavior (Deconchy, 1984). Moreover, religious fundamentalism has been conceptualized by some in terms of the maintenance of religious group boundaries (Hood & Morris, 1985; Hood, Morris, & Watson, 1986), and Altemeyer (2003) demonstrated that people high in fundamentalism experienced a particular emphasis on their religious group identity during childhood.

The Paradoxical Coexistence of Religion and Prejudice: Additional Explanations

We have suggested in this article that religion provides a variety of forms of meaning (a frame of reference for interpreting reality and setting personal goals, and provision of societal values and group interests) that help us to understand why religiousness is sometimes associated with prejudice. Nevertheless, religiosity no doubt is usually experienced by individuals as a vehicle through which one does good, and as such might be expected to mitigate against prejudice. We would suggest that there are at least three explanations for how people are able to uphold egalitarian values and maintain a tolerant self-image while simultaneously holding attitudes or engaging in behaviors that are problematic from the perspective of intergroup relations.

First, the coexistence of religious teachings related to tolerance and prejudice among religious individuals seems to be a contradiction only if prejudice is defined too narrowly, in terms of antipathy. An equation of prejudice with antipathy is simplistic in part because even evaluatively positive attitudes can be construed as a form of prejudice in that they can legitimize the unequal treatment of groups (Glick & Fiske, 1996, 2001; Jackman, 1994). For example, the belief that women are uniquely nurturant and loving may be associated with affection toward women, and yet it might also be seen as justification for restricting women to low status domestic roles (Eagly & Mladinic, 1994). Thus, some seemingly benign attitudes that are taught by some religious traditions—for example, that men and women are "different but equal"—can serve a function of maintaining intergroup inequality because they frame inequality-maintaining beliefs in an affectionate way. The equation of prejudice with antipathy is also misleading because intergroup attitudes can be ambivalent, containing both negative and positive components (e.g., Katz & Hass, 1988). For example, feeling warmth toward gay men and lesbians while viewing their sexuality as a threat to one's vision of morality constitutes ambivalence between affect (positive feelings of warmth) and cognition (negative judgments about same-sex behavior). People may thus discriminate when their negative attitude toward a group is accessed or salient, while maintaining an egalitarian self-image on the basis of the positive feelings toward members of that group.

Second, religious teachings that advocate love, acceptance, and so on are likely insufficient to mitigate against prejudice and discrimination because intergroup responses involve not only explicit (conscious) attitudes and motives that may be shaped by things such as teachings related to tolerance, but also implicit (nonconscious) attitudes or processes that are shaped by less deliberative mechanisms such as emotional conditioning, early experiences, and so on (Rudman, 2004). Certainly, the evidence is clear that implicit biases are often strong (e.g., Rudman, 2004), that people are frequently unaware of the biased nature of their social responses (e.g., Greenwald & Banaji, 1995), and that discrimination can be rationalized in seemingly benign ways (e.g., Gaertner & Dovidio, 1986). Consequently, people may hold an egalitarian self-image based on their explicitly endorsed attitudes (which may be consistent with religious teachings related to tolerance), yet engage in implicit stereotyping and discrimination. In addition, some religious contexts may reinforce implicit bias through nonproscription or encouragement of subtle prejudice (e.g., heterosexism) and/or exposure to social hierarchies in which power holders are consistently members of socially dominant groups.

Third, as with many belief systems, some religious teachings themselves contain, or are perceived to contain, justification for particular negative attitudes. For example, it is sometimes argued that findings of negative attitudes toward gay men and lesbians among more religious individuals do not reflect prejudice, but rather a moral position denouncing same-sex sexuality (e.g., Fulton et al., 1999). Of concern are findings that such moral positions may at times predict discrimination, even of a type that does not have ideological support. For example, Jackson and

Esses (1997) reported that the belief that gay men and lesbians threaten cherished values predicted discrimination against this group in a context unrelated to sexual behavior, namely employment access (see also Batson et al., 1999). Indeed, once marked as a threat to religiously based moral positions, groups may suffer extreme hostility and inhumane treatment—treatment that would be considered immoral within most other systems of meaning. This phenomenon has been observed throughout history when religiously rooted moral positions have been used to justify acts of terrorism, war, and genocide.

Summary and Conclusions

We have examined how several religious orientations (I, E, Q, RF), as dispositional factors, are related to prejudice. Especially for the intrinsic orientation, the target of prejudice and its proscription or nonproscription by one's religious group, are related to degree of self-reported prejudice and some measures of discrimination. We have also suggested that consideration of the many personal and group functions served by religion (provision of knowledge, personal goals, societal values, and group identity and interests) aid in our understanding of religion-prejudice links. In brief, the content of one's religion (e.g., in proscribing or not proscribing specific prejudice), as well as one's connection to the religious meaning systems (e.g., I, E, Q, RF) and the social context may interact in influencing the meanings derived from religion and hence the levels and forms of prejudice. Religious content might influence not only which specific target groups people are prejudiced against (e.g., anti-Semitism may be tolerated or encouraged by certain religions, proscribed by other religions, and not be relevant for still other religions), but also how others are perceived in general (e.g., ingroup versus outgroup, similar or different) and the specific kind of prejudicial attitudes or discriminating behaviors that may be encouraged toward them (see, e.g., Laythe et al., 2001). Furthermore, it is important in considering the religion-prejudice relationship to recognize that prejudice does not necessarily entail antipathy, that people may be unaware of their own prejudice, and that religious teachings may sometimes be seen to justify prejudice. Given these analyses, links between religion and prejudice become more understandable.

It is important to note the following: Religious persons and groups do many helpful, cooperative, and tolerant things in our world; there are surely many non-prejudiced religious persons as well as prejudiced nonreligious persons on this planet; and the frequently reported positive associations between religion and prejudice are often specific to certain definitions of religion or religious orientation, targets of prejudice, and group and cultural contexts. In spite of this, we cannot ignore the religion-prejudice links found in research on this issue. We hope that our ideas might begin to suggest ways, within a religious context, to reduce prejudice by stimulating religious groups to explore subtle, even unconscious prejudice, ways in which religious teachings and religious group membership might seem to justify intolerance, and so on. Confronting such issues head on in religious groups might help some people to stop using religious justifications for prejudice, and to appreciate that ingroup-outgroup perceptions might be generated by religious group membership, and so on. If the points we make in this article are legitimate, we should be able to go beyond "understanding religion and prejudice"—there should also be considerable potential for "religious intervention" research to investigate the possibility of reducing such prejudice.

References

Allport, G. W., & Ross, J. M. (1967). Personal religious orientation and prejudice. *Journal of Personality and Social Psychology, 5*, 432–443.

Altemeyer, B. (1996). *The authoritarian specter*. Cambridge, MA: Harvard University Press.

Altemeyer, B. (2003). Why do religious fundamentalists tend to be prejudiced? *The International Journal for the Psychology of Religion, 13*, 17–28.

Altemeyer, B., & Hunsberger, B. (1992). Authoritarianism, religious fundamentalism, quest, and prejudice. *The International Journal for the Psychology of Religion, 2*, 113–133.

Batson, C. D., & Burris, C. T. (1994). Personal religion: Depressant or stimulant of prejudice and discrimination? In M. P. Zanna & J. M. Olson (Eds.), *The psychology of prejudice: The Ontario symposium* (Vol. 7, pp. 149–169). Hillsdale, NJ: Erlbaum.

Batson, C. D., Eidelman, S. H., Higley, S. L., & Russell, S. A. (2001). "And who is my neighbor?" II: Quest religion as a source of universal compassion. *Journal for the Scientific Study of Religion, 40*, 39–50.

Batson, C. D., Flink, C. H., Schoenrade, P. A., Fultz, J., & Pych, V. (1986). Religious orientation and overt versus covert racial prejudice. *Journal of Personality and Social Psychology, 50*, 175–181.

Batson, C. D., Floyd, R. B., Meyer, J. M., & Winner, A. L. (1999). "And who is my neighbor?": Intrinsic religion as a source of universal compassion. *Journal for the Scientific Study of Religion, 38*, 31–41.

Batson, C. D., & Raynor-Prince, L. (1983). Religious orientation and complexity of thought about existential concerns. *Journal for the Scientific Study of Religion, 22*, 38–50.

Batson, C. D., & Schoenrade, P. A. (1991a). Measuring religion as quest: I. Validity concerns. *Journal for the Scientific Study of Religion, 30*, 416–429.

Batson, C. D., & Schoenrade, P. A. (1991b). Measuring religion as quest: II. Reliability concerns. *Journal for the Scientific Study of Religion, 30*, 430–447.

Batson, C. D., Schoenrade, P., & Ventis, W. L. (1993). *Religion and the individual: A social-psychological perspective*. New York: Oxford University Press.

Batson, C. D., & Ventis, W. L. (1982). *The religious experience: A social-psychological perspective*. New York: Oxford University Press.

Billiet, J. B. (1995). Church involvement, individualism, and ethnic prejudice among Flemish Roman Catholics: New evidence of a moderating effect. *Journal for the Scientific Study of Religion, 34*, 224–233.

Burris, C. T., Branscombe, N. R., & Jackson, L. M. (2000). For God and Country: Religion and the endorsement of national self-stereotypes. *Journal of Cross-Cultural Psychology, 31*, 517–527.

Burris, C. T., & Jackson, L. M. (2000). Social identity and the true believer: Responses to marginalization among the intrinsically religious. *British Journal of Social Psychology, 39*, 257–278.

Burris, C. T., Jackson, L. M., Tarpley, W. R., & Smith, G. J. (1996). Religion as quest: The self-directed pursuit of meaning. *Personality and Social Psychology Bulletin, 22*, 1068–1076.

Coward, H. (1986). Intolerance in the world's religions. *Studies in Religion, 15*, 419–431.

Deconchy, J. P. (1984). Rationality and social control in orthodox systems. In H. Tajfel (Ed.), *The social dimension: European developments in social psychology* (pp. 425–445). New York: Cambridge University Press.

Donahue, M. J. (1985). Intrinsic and extrinsic religiousness: Review and meta-analysis. *Journal of Personality and Social Psychology, 48*, 400–419.

Duck, R. J., & Hunsberger, B. (1999). Religious orientation and prejudice: The role of religious proscription, right-wing authoritarianism and social desirability. *The International Journal for the Psychology of Religion, 9*, 157–179.

Duriez, B., & Hutsebaut, D. (2000). The relation between religion and racism: The role of post-critical beliefs. *Mental Health, Religion & Culture, 3*, 85–102.

Eagly, A. H., & Mladinic, A. (1994). Are people prejudiced against women? Some answers from research on attitudes, gender stereotypes, and judgments of competence. *European Review of Social Psychology, 5*, 1–35.

Eisinga, R., Billiet, J., & Felling, A. (1999). Christian religion and ethnic prejudice in cross-national perspective: A comparative analysis of the Netherlands and Flanders (Belgium). *International Journal of Comparative Sociology, 40*, 375–393.

Eisenga, R., Felling, A., & Peters, J. (1990). Religious belief, church involvement, and ethnocentrism in the Netherlands. *Journal for the Scientific Study of Religion, 29*, 54–75.

Esses, V. M., Haddock, G., & Zanna, M. P. (1993). Values, stereotypes, and emotions as determinants of intergroup attitudes. In D. M. Mackie & D. L. Hamilton (Eds.), *Affect, cognition, and stereotyping: Interactive processes in group perception* (pp. 137–165). San Diego, CA: Academic Press.

Esses, V. M., Jackson, L. M., & Armstrong, T. L. (1998). Intergroup competition and attitudes toward immigrants and immigration: An instrumental model of group conflict. *Journal of Social Issues, 54*, 699–724.

Fisher, R. D., Derison, D., Polley, C. F., Cadman, J., & Johnston, D. (1994). Religiousness, religious orientation, and attitudes towards gays and lesbians. *Journal of Applied Social Psychology, 24*, 614–630.

Franco, F. M., & Maass, A. (1999). Intentional control over prejudice: When the choice of the measure matters. *European Journal of Social Psychology, 29*, 469–477.

Fulton, A. S., Gorsuch, R. L., & Maynard, E. A. (1999). Religious orientation, antihomosexual sentiment, and fundamentalism among Christians. *Journal for the Scientific Study of Religion, 38*, 14–22.

Gaertner, S. L., & Dovidio, J. F. (1986). The aversive form of racism. In J. F. Dovidio & S. L. Gaertner (Eds.), *Prejudice, discrimination, and racism* (pp. 61–89). Orlando, FL: Academic Press.

Glick, P., & Fiske, S. (1996). The ambivalent sexism inventory: Differentiating hostile and benevolent sexism. *Journal of Personality and Social Psychology, 70*, 491–512.

Glick, P., & Fiske, S. T. (2001). An ambivalent alliance: Hostile and benevolent sexism as complementary justifications for gender inequality. *American Psychologist, 56*, 109–118.

Gorsuch, R. L., & Aleshire, D. (1974). Christian faith and ethnic prejudice: A review and interpretation of research. *Journal for the Scientific Study of Religion, 13*, 281–307.

Greenwald, A. G., & Banaji, M. (1995). Implicit social cognition: Attitudes, self-esteem, and stereotypes. *Psychological Review, 102*, 4–27.

Griffin, G. A., Gorsuch, R. L., & Davis, A.-L. (1987). A cross-cultural investigation of religious orientation, social norms, and prejudice. *Journal for the Scientific Study of Religion, 26*, 358–365.

Griffiths, B., Dixon, C., Stanley, G., & Weiland, R. (2001). Religious orientation and attitudes toward homosexuality: A functional analysis. *Australian Journal of Psychology, 53*, 12–17.

Hassan, M. K., & Khalique, A. (1987). A study of prejudice in Hindu and Muslim college students. *Psychologia: An International Journal of Psychology in the Orient, 30*, 80–84.

Herek, G. M. (1987). Religious orientation and prejudice: A comparison of racial and sexual attitudes. *Personality and Social Psychology Bulletin, 13*, 34–44.

Hewstone, M., Islam, M. R., & Judd, C. M. (1993). Models of crossed categorization and intergroup relations. *Journal of Personality and Social Psychology, 64*, 779–793.

Hinojosa, V. J., & Park, J. Z. (2004). Religion and the paradox of racial inequality attitudes. *Journal for the Scientific Study of Religion, 43*, 229–238.

Hood, R. W., Jr., & Morris, R. J. (1985). Boundary maintenance, socio-political views, and presidential preference among high and low fundamentalists. *Review of Religious Research, 27,* 134–145.

Hood, R. W., Jr., Morris, R. J., & Watson, P. J. (1986). Maintenance of religious fundamentalism. *Psychological Reports, 59,* 547–559.

Hood, R. W., Jr., Spilka, B., Hunsberger, B., & Gorsuch, R. L. (1996). *The psychology of religion: An empirical approach* (2nd ed.). New York: Guilford Press.

Hunsberger, B. (1995). Religion and prejudice: The role of religious fundamentalism, quest, and right-wing authoritarianism. *Journal of Social Issues, 51,* 113–129.

Hunsberger, B. (1996). Religious fundamentalism, right-wing authoritarianism, and hostility toward homosexuals in non-Christian groups. *The International Journal for the Psychology of Religion, 6,* 39–49.

Hunsberger, B., Alisat, S., Pancer, S. M., & Pratt, M. (1996). Religious fundamentalism and religious doubts: Content, connections, and complexity of thinking. *The International Journal for the Psychology of Religion, 6,* 201–220.

Hunsberger, B., Owusu, V., & Duck, R. (1999). Religion and prejudice in Ghana and Canada: Religious fundamentalism, right-wing authoritarianism, and attitudes toward homosexuals and women. *The International Journal for the Psychology of Religion, 9,* 181–194.

Hunsberger, B., Pratt, M., & Pancer, S. M. (1994). Religious fundamentalism and integrative complexity of thought: A relationship for existential content only? *Journal for the Scientific Study of Religion, 33,* 335–346.

Hunter, J. A. (2001). Self-esteem and in-group bias among members of a religious social category. *Journal of Social Psychology, 141,* 401–411.

Jackman, M. R. (1994). *The velvet glove: Paternalism and conflict in gender, class, and race relations.* Berkeley, CA: University of California Press.

Jackson, L. M. (2001, May). Problems and promise in religious intergroup relations. In V. Saroglou (Chair), *Pluralism and Identity.* Symposium conducted at the University Catholique de Louvain, Belgium.

Jackson, L. M., & Esses, V. M. (1997). Of scripture and ascription: The relation between religious fundamentalism and intergroup helping. *Personality and Social Psychology Bulletin, 23,* 893–906.

Jackson, L. M., & Hunsberger, B. (1999). An intergroup perspective on religion and prejudice. *Journal for the Scientific Study of Religion, 38,* 509–523.

Jacobson, C. K. (1998). Religiosity and prejudice: An update and denominational analysis. *Review of Religious Research, 39,* 264–272.

Juergensmeyer, M. (2000). *Terror in the mind of God: The global rise of religious violence.* Berkeley, CA: University of California Press.

Karpov, V. (2002). Religiosity and tolerance in the United States and Poland. *Journal for the Scientific Study of Religion, 41,* 267–288.

Katz, I., & Hass, R. G. (1988). Racial ambivalence and American value conflict: Correlational and priming studies of dual cognitive structures. *Journal of Personality and Social Psychology, 55,* 893–905.

Kirkpatrick, L. A. (1993). Fundamentalism, Christian orthodoxy, and intrinsic religious orientation as predictors of discriminatory attitudes. *Journal for the Scientific Study of Religion, 32,* 256–268.

Konig, R., Eisinga, R., & Scheepers, P. (2000). Explaining the relationship between Christian Religion and anti-Semitism in the Netherlands. *Review of Religious Research, 41,* 373–393.

Lafferty, J. (1990). Religion and racism in South Africa: Conflict between faith and culture. *Social Thought, 16,* 36–49.

Laythe, B., Finkel, D. G., Bringle, R. B., & Kirkpatrick, L. A. (2002). Religious fundamentalism as a predictor of prejudice: A two-component model. *Journal for the Scientific Study of Religion, 41,* 623–635.

Laythe, B., Finkel, D., & Kirkpatrick, L. A. (2001). Predicting prejudice from religious fundamentalism and right-wing authoritarianism: A multiple-regression approach. *Journal for the Scientific Study of Religion, 40,* 1–10.

Leak, G. K., & Randall, B. A. (1995). Clarification of the link between right-wing authoritarianism and religiousness: The role of religious maturity. *Journal for the Scientific Study of Religion, 34*, 245–252.

McConahay, J. B. (1986). Modern racism, ambivalence, and the modern racism scale. In J. F. Dovidio & S. M. Gaertner (Eds.), *Prejudice, discrimination, and racism* (pp. 91–124). Orlando: Academic Press.

McFarland, S. (1989). Religious orientations and the targets of discrimination. *Journal for the Scientific Study of Religion, 28*, 324–336.

McFarland, S. G., & Warren, J. C., Jr. (1992). Religious orientations and selective exposure among fundamentalist Christians. *Journal for the Scientific Study of Religion, 31*, 163–174.

Murphy-Berman, V., Berman, J. J., Pachauri, A., & Kumar, P. (1985). Religious attitudes and perceptions of justice. *Psychologia: An International Journal of Psychology in the Orient, 28*, 29–34.

Pancer, S. M., Jackson, L. M., Hunsberger, B., Pratt, M. W., & Lea, J. (1995). Religious orthodoxy and the complexity of thought about religious and nonreligious issues. *Journal of Personality, 63*, 213–232.

Ponton, M. O., & Gorsuch, R. L. (1988). Prejudice and religion revisited: A cross-cultural investigation with a Venezuelan sample. *Journal for the Scientific Study of Religion, 27*, 260–271.

Roccas, S. (this issue). Religion and value systems. *Journal of Social Issues.*

Rudman, L. A. (2004). Social justice in our minds, homes, and society: The nature, causes, and consequences of implicit bias. *Social Justice Research, 17*, 129–142.

Rudman, L. A., Greenwald, A. G., Mellott, D. S., & Schwartz, J. L. K. (1999). Measuring the automatic components of prejudice: Flexibility and generality of the Implicit Association Test. *Social Cognition, 17*, 437–465.

Saunders, D. (2001, September 15). U.S. got what it deserves, Falwell says. *The Globe and Mail* [Toronto], p. A2.

Schwartz, S. H., & Huismans, S. (1995). Value priorities and religiosity in four Western religions. *Social Psychology Quarterly, 58*(2), 88–107.

Sears, D. O. (1988). Symbolic racism. In P. A. Katz & D. A. Taylor (Eds.), *Eliminating racism* (pp. 53–84). New York: Plenum.

Sears, D. O., & Henry, P. J. (2003). The origins of symbolic racism. *Journal of Personality and Social Psychology, 85*, 259–275.

Sherif, M. (1966). *Group conflict and cooperation: Their social psychology.* London: Routledge & Kegan Paul.

Silberman, I. (this issue). Religion as a meaning system: Implications for the new millennium. *Journal of Social Issues.*

Spilka, B., Hood, R. W., Jr., Hunsberger, B., & Gorsuch, R. (2003). *The psychology of religion: An empirical approach* (3rd ed.). New York: Guilford Press.

Struch, N., & Schwartz, S. H. (1989). Intergroup aggression: Its predictors and distinctness from ingroup bias. *Journal of Personality and Social Psychology, 56*, 364–373.

Tajfel, H., & Turner, J. C. (1986). The social identity theory of intergroup behavior. In S. Worchel & W. G. Austin (Eds.), *Psychology of intergroup relations* (pp. 7–24). Chicago: Nelson-Hall.

Veenvliet, S. G., & Esses, V. M. (2005, July). *The role of emotions in the relation between religious fundamentalism and attitudes toward same-sex marriage.* Paper presented at the annual meeting of the European Association of Experimental Social Psychology, Wurzburg, Germany.

Wylie, L., & Forest, J. (1992). Religious fundamentalism, right-wing authoritarianism and prejudice. *Psychological Reports, 71*, 1291–1298.

BRUCE HUNSBERGER was Professor in the Department of Psychology at Wilfrid Laurier University in Waterloo, Ontario, Canada until his untimely death in October of 2003. He earned his PhD in social psychology at the University of Manitoba. He was a leading authority in the psychology of religion, publishing widely in the field, and earning the Gordon Allport award from Division 36 of the American Psychological Association. His research within the psychology of religion focused on prejudice, socialization, attitudes, doubt, and fundamentalism. He also conducted research on life transitions.

LYNNE M. JACKSON is Associate Professor in the Department of Psychology at King's University College at The University of Western Ontario, in London, Ontario, Canada. She earned a PhD in social psychology at the University of Western Ontario. Her research deals with prejudice, discrimination, and the psychology of religion.

Journal of Social Issues, Vol. 61, No. 4, 2005, pp. 827–845

The Three Monotheistic World Religions and International Human Rights

J. Paul Martin*

Columbia University

Judaism, Christianity, and Islam, and the human rights movement lay claim to much of the same moral territory, notably concepts of human dignity, equality, and social justice. In practice there are many tensions. This article argues that common standards are necessary to govern relationships among religions and that international human rights standards best play that role. To achieve greater consensus and mutual understanding, the religious and human rights communities must examine how their meaning systems can and have changed over time, and differ across regions. Recognition of these variations and empirical evidence that religiosity is not necessarily inherently linked to prejudice can enable both the religious and human rights meaning systems to evolve toward greater consensus on common social norms.

The modern human rights movement grew as a means to mobilize international responses to serious crimes of inhumanity that individual states were either unwilling or unable to stop (Donnelly, 1989; Henkin, 1990a; Kolodziej, 2003). The first truly international such action was the antislavery campaign that began early in the 18th century but only achieved its main objectives more than 100 years later (Korey, 1998). Since then the goals of the human rights movement have expanded exponentially and the language of human rights has become a major tool of international diplomacy (Alston, 1992; Henkin, 1990a). Human rights have also become commonplace in popular discourse, although the word often conjures up quite different images and interests in different people's minds (Donnelly, 1989). The international human rights standards encapsulated in the 1948 Universal Declaration of Human Rights (UN General Assembly res. 217A (111), 10 December 1948, henceforth UDHR, in Martin, 2001) have achieved a universal stature as

---

*Correspondence concerning this article should be addressed to J. Paul Martin, Executive Director, Center for the Study of Human Rights, Columbia University, New York 10027 [e-mail: jpm2@columbia.edu].

common criteria of social justice (Henkin, 1990a). This article examines how the human rights meaning system has interacted with the paradigms of social justice promulgated by Judaism, Christianity, and Islam.

The historical relationship between human rights and the world's major religions has been substantial, complex, and fascinating, especially with respect to the dominant monotheistic religions (Bloom, Martin, & Proudfoot, 1996; Hoffman, 2003). The modern formulation of human rights grew under the influence of Western Christianity and Judaism (Henkin, 1998; Nurser, 2003). The idea of universal rights was partly a response to the diversification of ethical values and their explicit separation from religious foundations (i.e., their secularization) that took place in Western Europe during the last 450 years. During that period, social ethics based on a divine revelation and defined by religious authorities were challenged and, in the case of the new secular societies, replaced by nonreligious concepts, such as natural rights and appeals to reason and common values (e.g., Ashcraft, 1996; Locke, 1698). In both the United States and around the world, the resurgence of religious influences in public policy during the last decade, however, are putting into question the secular definition of the common social order (Fox, 2001; Hackett, 2000; Huntington, 1996; Kepel, 1994; Wuthnow, 1992).

After World War II, the drafters of the various international human rights instruments, working under the auspices of the U.N. Economic and Social Council and its Human Rights Commission (Morsink, 1999) chaired by Eleanor Roosevelt, used secular language to rise above the particularities of individual religious and ethical traditions. The word "nature," for example, was preferred to the word God. The drafters postulated a common understanding of "human dignity" as evidence of a universal commitment to the "equal and inalienable rights of all members of the human family." Once approved (Glendon, 2001; Maritain, 1944; Morsink, 2000), tensions again arose between religiously based ethical traditions and definitions of a common/secular morality, typically focusing on religious freedom (Stahnke, 1999; Van der Vyver & Witte, 1996), and on discrimination associated with family law and the role of women (Price, 2002; Van der Vyver & Witte, 1996). The topic of discrimination is a human rights theme that links this article with that of Hunsberger and Jackson (this issue) that reviews the empirical relations between religious meanings and prejudice. While discussing the conceptual dimensions of both the religious and human rights meaning systems, this article notes that the actual impact of religion on human rights depends on many factors, and thus varies across individuals and from community to community (Hunsberger et al., this issue), as well as from one historical period to another.

Religion can be both a source of prejudice and discrimination as well as of reconciliation and healing (Danchin & Cole, 2002; Hunsberger & Jackson, this issue). Such radical bifurcation leads one to conclude that there must be many other factors that influence and mediate the religious elements. These factors may range from different interpretations of holy texts and individual differences in the ways in which people value their religious meaning systems (e.g., in intrinsic, extrinsic, quest, or fundamentalist ways; see Hunsberger et al., this issue) to the political or religious leadership at a given point in time.

This article focuses on the Abrahamic faiths on account of their common characteristics, notably the acceptance of the authoritative nature of their sacred texts, their common monotheism, and their belief in a God that is in contact with and influencing human existence. In these respects all three differ substantially from other world religions such as Buddhism, Confucianism, and Hinduism (Aijmer, 1992; Kepel, 1994; Price, 2002; Wuthnow, 1992). This article proposes that while the human rights framework does not always reconcile the positions taken by the religious and secular groups, so far, only the international human rights regime provides the standards, language, and institutions necessary to enable religiously and culturally diverse societies to deal with common, and especially transnational, social problems. Furthermore, it will argue that the examination of both the human rights and religious meanings systems and their interaction must take into account the impact of their respective political and social contexts showing that just as changes have taken place in the past, so changes in the future could lead to improved relationships among them.

The Human Rights Approach

The goals of the human rights movement are categorically those of "freedom, justice and peace in the world" (UDHR, Preamble, in Martin, 2001, p. 5). The international human rights agreements seek "a common standard of achievement for all people and all nations" (UDHR, Preamble, in Martin, 2001, p. 5). Human rights are designed to define common values and transcend more particular religious and other views of peace and social justice. A second core tenet of the human rights movement holds that "all human beings are born free and equal in dignity and rights" (UDHR #1, Martin, 2001, p. 5). This means the right to nondiscrimination, namely that human rights are the entitlement of every human being "without distinction of any kind, such as race, colour, sex, language, religion, political or other opinion, national or social origin, property, birth or other status" (UDHR #2, Martin, 2001, p. 5). A third core tenet of the human rights paradigm is that rights imply obligations. In the case of international human rights, this obligation falls specifically on the states that have signed the various treaties implementing the UDHR. Thus the human rights system is not just an ethical code or meaning system. The texts of the major treaties such as that of the International Covenant on Civil and Political Rights (UN, Gen. Ass. 2000A (XXI), 16 December 1966, henceforth ICCPR, Martin, 2001) for example, repeat frequently "The States parties undertake to protect and ensure ..." (Martin, 2001, p. 16). The regime possesses legal enforcement mechanisms that, even if there is no international policing system, oblige states to carry out their obligations (Henkin, 1990b). These mechanisms range from international courts, international commissions and committees to NGOs and the media monitoring and seeking to shame governments (Henkin & Hargrove, 1994). This leads to a fourth core tenet of the human rights movement, namely the principle that many of those whose rights are being violated, such as slaves, prisoners in Dachau, or victims in the Rwanda genocide, need the assistance of third parties to end their sufferings (Korey, 1998). International human rights laws and institutions provide a legal and moral base for such advocacy.

Within the international legal system, religion comes into focus primarily in terms of its potential as a basis for discrimination and the right or freedom to practice (Stahnke, 1999). The two major basic legal instruments that address religion are the UDHR itself and the 1966 ICCPR. In their respective articles 18, parallel to articles on the other rights such as assembly, speech etc., both instruments address religion from the perspective of "freedom of." The version in the UDHR reads *Everyone has the right to freedom of thought, conscience and religion; this right includes freedom to change his religion or belief, and freedom, either alone or in community with others and in public or private, to manifest his religion or belief in teaching, practice worship and observance"* (Martin, 2001, p. 7). Religion is identified as a potential source of discrimination in Article 2 of the ICCPR (Martin, 2001, p. 16). This article requires states parties to guarantee that the rights in the Covenant "be exercised without discrimination of any kind as to race, colour, sex, language, religion, political or other opinion, national or social origin, property, birth or status" (Martin, 2001, p. 16). The link between freedom and discrimination is further refined by the U.N. Human Rights Committee in its 1989 General Comment 18(37) (Stahnke & Martin, 1998, p. 88).

Linked with and implicit in the implementation of freedom of religion and belief and nondiscrimination are other human rights formulated in the UDHR, such as the rights to equal protection of the law, to education, to protection from hatred that incites discrimination and violence, to privacy, as well as to freedom of expression, movement, assembly, and association (Dinstein, 1972). Professing a religious meaning system is thus specifically protected by these human rights standards as well. Article 18 of the ICCPR affirms "the right to have or to adopt a religion or belief of his choice," that is to adopt and live by a religious or nonreligious meaning system without any restrictions other than those associated with "the rights and freedoms of others and of meeting the just requirements of morality, public order and the general welfare of a democratic society" (UDHR #29 and ICCPR #18, 3, Martin, 2001, pp. 6 and 20). In contrast to other rights in both documents, freedom of religion and belief is one of only seven rights of such importance that they cannot be derogated, i.e., set aside, even in a time "of public emergency which threatens the life of the whole nation" (ICCPR #4, Martin, 2001, p. 17).

The human rights regime identifies ways in which a religious meaning system might be discriminatory, namely if it violates either the rights and freedoms of others or the just requirements of morality, public order, and civil power. It ascribes enforcement to the civil power (UDHR #29 and Declaration of Religious Freedom #2 and #4 Martin, 2001, pp. 6 and 94). It does not, however, require that the civil power be independent of a particular religious tradition.

A prima facie comparison between the international human rights movement as a meaning system and the three monotheistic religious systems reveals both similarities and differences (Little, Sachedina, & Kelsay, 1996). The systems all extol human values such as empathy and compassion. All enjoy the support of major international constituencies, maintain multiple lines of communication across national boundaries, and have mobilized highly motivated, deeply committed members (e.g., Kepel, 1994). Unlike the human rights system, the three monotheistic religious systems anchor their systems in the vision of a God that promises rewards, typically "salvation," in return for carrying out his will. More than justice and the rights of others, these systems appeal to notions of service, obedience to God, his laws and those designated to interpret them. Unlike the three monotheistic systems that tend to emphasize loyalty to individual religious communities and to distinguish clearly between members and nonmembers, the human rights movement claims that all human beings are equal in dignity and rights.

A critical element for this article is the impact of the religious meanings systems with respect to the definition and treatment of *nonmembers*; that is, whether the latter are defined (a) as nonbelievers, (b) as separated on account of their unorthodox beliefs or practices, or (c) as members, but enjoying a lesser status within the religion for other religion-specific reasons. The second category typically designates members whose actions or beliefs are considered seriously at variance with a given religion's moral or belief standards, many of which reach beyond social relationships and obligations and define private behavior. Religious codes also define social rules *within* their communities and some of these raise challenges on the basis of human rights (Stahnke, 1999). Is, for example, the exclusion of women from the priesthood in the Catholic Church a violation of their human rights? At the moment the world community tends to agree that such issues are outside the purview of human rights law (Stahnke, 1999). Religious practices also figure in the debates on the role of culture versus universality in the definition of human rights (Bloom et al., 1996; Cohn, 1989; Harvard Law, 1999). Deconstructing such definitions and frameworks is an important part of human rights scholarship (Henkin, 1998).

Religions and the Growth of the Human Rights Movement

History shows that Europe's religious communities appealed to human rights and a common human dignity when (a) the religious and other groups were seeking a common goal, such as in the antislavery movement (Jones, 1911; Korey, 1998; Nurser, 2003) and (b) when the religious groups saw themselves as oppressed minorities and in need of protection, as Catholics saw themselves in Northern Ireland or the Jehovah Witnesses and Scientologists in Europe today (Danchin & Cole, 2002). The situation is more complicated when such minorities become a target of proselytizing activity or other forms of militancy (Stahnke, 1999).

The Spanish Inquisition still stands out as an example of systemic persecution and forced proselytization by a religious majority using civil procedures (Huertas et al., 1999; Kamen, 1985; Putnam, 1967). Its roots were deep. Earlier, in the 13th century, for example, even the innovative and influential theologian Thomas Aquinas (1225–1274) held that the civil authorities could tolerate heathens or pagans but not heretics, and that latter ought to be "severed from the world by death" (Aquinas, II, 2, Q.11 Art 8, p. 1226). Beginning in 1478 in the kingdom of Castile and until it was terminated in 1834, the Catholic Church in Spain was authorized by successive Popes to create and maintain the infamous Inquisition. The initial tasks of this judicial body were to ensure religious orthodoxy and to fight heresy, but these expanded to using its powers to eliminate heretics and recruit new members to the Catholic Church. Its procedures included coercive measures that flaunted basic rules of due process and freedom of conscience. Professions of faith, for example, were elicited under torture and threat of execution. The scope of the courts was later expanded to include sorcery, magic, and eventually usury, bigamy, blasphemy, other violations of ecclesiastical law, and even mysticism. Accusations of usury brought Jews within the courts' jurisdiction. Soon Muslims and Jews (before their enforced exile in 1492) in Castile were being coerced to convert under the threat of exile or public execution. To defend the Church against the ideas of the Protestant Reformation in the 16th century, all books published in Spain (and shortly after throughout the Catholic world) had to be approved by the bishops. Their decisions were enforced by the civil authorities. Today Spain, however, has among the most sophisticated provisions for the protection and political representation of religious minorities (Stahnke & Martin, 1998, p. 245).

Ideas about religious freedom in Western Europe grew in reaction to religious and other forms of totalitarianism (Bloom, 1996). Religious minorities within Christianity, a legacy of the fragmentation of Christianity in Western Europe that began with the Reformation in the 16th century, called on civil authorities to permit religious pluralism (Woodhouse, 1951). Just before Luther broke with Rome, he argued for human dignity and individual freedom of belief in his tract entitled *Freedom of a Christian* (Althaus, 1966; Witte, 2003). The 1648 Treaty of Westphalia sought to solve the problem of religious pluralism by adopting the principle that he who rules the land determines the religion of its inhabitants, *cujus regio, ejus religio* (Eyck, 1997, p. 335). Religious dissenters would thus have to move to a state or region where the beliefs of the leaders matched their own. Until this period, tolerance was defined from the perspective of a given religion rather than as an individual right.

Within the Western World, modern arguments for religious tolerance were stimulated by more rational or secular premises such as those enunciated by Locke. He marshaled arguments to support the case that "No private Person has any Right, in any manner, to prejudice another Person in his Civil Enjoyments, because he is of another Church or Religion" (Locke, 1689, p. 31). The care of souls and religious choice, he argued, do not belong to the magistrate. He adds: "The sum of all we drive at is, That every Man may enjoy the same Rights that are granted to others" (Locke, 1689, p. 53). It is the responsibility of the state to protect these rights for all citizens. Locke's principles of tolerance for all were severely tested by his perception of Roman Catholics, whom he portrayed as irreconcilable enemies for any Protestant government, as a conspiracy that "made them ready upon any occasion to seize the government and possess themselves of the estates and fortunes of their fellow subjects" (Ashcraft, 1996, p. 207).

In Europe it still took more than another century for an official formulation of religious tolerance such as that found in the Declaration of the Rights of Man and the Citizen, a code that adopted in August 1789 by the French Constituent Assembly formed in the wake of the French Revolution. The Declaration read: "No person shall be molested for his opinions, even such as are religious, provided that the manifestations of opinion do not disturb the public order established by the law" (retrieved from http://www.magnacartaplus.org/french-rights/html, French National Assembly, 1789). The French Declaration and the U.S. Bill of Rights set the trend by listing rights and using the secular definitions now dominant in Western legal systems. Freedom of religion was one of the four freedoms featured in Franklin D. Roosevelt's epoch-making speech in 1941 (Congressional Record, 1991, p. 87, Pt.1). This assured that religious freedom would later be high on the rights agenda for the then soon-to-be-created United Nations.

Long used to being a dominant religion, the Catholic Church reached its own definition of religious freedom at the Vatican Council II in 1965. The document *Dignitatis Humanae* (Stahnke & Martin, 1998) sought to reconcile the Catholic Church's traditional belief in its being the one, true church with the right of the individual conscience. Individual freedom, it stated, means "that all men are to be immune from coercion on the part of individuals and social groups and of any human power" and that this "is to be recognized in the constitutional law" (Stahnke & Martin, 1998, p. 211). The document also affirms the freedom of the Church to live in accordance with its beliefs, including the right to spread its message. Much of the document is written in inclusive or generic terms, setting principles that should govern all religions. There is little discussion of the rights of other religions as such, other than a vague exhortation to "love and have prudence and patience in his dealings with those who are in error or ignorance with regard to faith" (Stahnke & Martin, 1998, p. 217).

The last three centuries of public debate on religious freedom contributed significantly to the growth of the whole human rights movement (Little et al.,

1996; Tierney, 1996; Tutu, 1996). They showed how a right might be claimed by all human beings and how its enforcement could be an obligation on the civil authority. Moreover, while the concepts of "natural" rights and human dignity clearly had their roots in a vision of nature ordered by a single Supreme Being, the drafters of the 1948 UDHR could distance the concepts of rights and human dignity from their religious roots (Glendon, 2001). The preamble of the 1948 UDHR identifies such other shared motives as membership in a common human family, the common desire for freedom, justice, social progress, friendly relations among nations and peace, the aspirations of all for freedom from fear, barbarous acts and want, and the need for rule of law in order to avoid having to use violence to resist tyranny and oppression. These aspirations coincide closely with those of the religions and map out conditions necessary for the realization of human dignity. The 1981 UN Declaration on the Elimination of All Forms of Intolerance and Discrimination based on Religion or Belief (Stahnke & Martin, 1998, p. 102) further defined the interface between the human rights and religious meaning systems. It recognized the nature and power of individual religious meaning systems and proposed a common framework for their coexistence. The Declaration has yet to be followed by a treaty or convention that would give its principles the force of law.

Religious Critiques of International Human Rights:
The Promotion of Secularism

The religion-inspired critiques of human rights typically reflect a substantial sociological dimension, namely whether the group enjoys a minority or majority position. Religions enjoying social preeminence in a given society tend to ignore or reject the human rights paradigm. Minority or persecuted religions embrace human rights more readily. Theological interpretations can be reinforced in civil law, such as when national constitution of Greece enshrines beliefs of the Orthodox Church. Since the reasons why minority groups might support human rights are more obvious, let us look at the critique of human rights by two religious traditions that enjoy majority status in a number of countries, Christian Orthodoxy and Islam.

In August 2000, the Russian Orthodox Church published a document entitled "Bases of the Social Concept of the Russian Orthodox" (Orthodox Church (2000) retrieved from http://www.russian/orthodox-church.org.ru/sd00e.htm, May 2004, henceforth Concept). This was a major departure from past Church pronouncements in that, rather than focus only on dogma, ecclesiastical law, or liturgy, the document defined the Church's provisions on a number of social problems including human rights and church-state relations. According to an analysis of this document by Naletova (2001), the Orthodox Church portrays the modern secularized world as worshipping self-centered sinful human beings moving toward further estrangement from God. The authors of the Social Concept treat human rights and, particularly, the principle of freedom of conscience, as manifestations of man's fallen nature, signs of cultural anarchy, an absence of proper moral order and degradation of the system of spiritual values. In the Concept's words:

> *Outside God there is only the fallen man, who is rather far from being the ideal of perfection aspired to by Christians and revealed in Christ (Ecce homo). For the Christian sense of justice, the idea of human freedom and rights is bound up with the idea of service. The Christian needs rights so that in exercising them he may first of all fulfill in the best possible way his lofty calling to the "likeness of God. . . ." (Concept IV, p. 7)*

Elsewhere the document juxtaposes human rights defined as secular, and human dignity defined as relationship to God. It accentuates the Western-inspired divisions between secular and sacred, material and spiritual, to value highly the latter of each polarity. The document does admit, however, that the principle of freedom of conscience "has proved to be one of the means of the Church's existence in the nonreligious world, enabling her to enjoy a legal status in the secular state and independence from those in society who believe differently or do not believe at all" (Concept IV, p. 8). True freedom, however, is the discovery of God's nature in man. "Freedom outside the Church is illusory and sinful" (Concept IV, p. 8). In the eyes of the Orthodox Church, human rights are thus not even a supportive, let alone an alternative meaning system. Rather they are secular values that draw believers away from God. Writing on the Greek Orthodox Tradition, Pollis (1993) concludes that individual human rights cannot be derived from Orthodox theology. This vision juxtaposing religious and nonreligious worldviews, as well as believers and others, has serious consequences for the way in which Church members view others, both those outside the community and those within who are seen to diverge from core beliefs.

This Russian Orthodox view of human rights contrasts with the current positions of the other branches of Christianity, at least since 1948. The Secretary General of the National Council of Churches of Christ, Joan Brown Campbell, wrote: "As Christians we can affirm the Declaration (UDHR) as an expression of our understanding that each person is to be valued because each is made in the image of God. We know also that denial of access to the bounty of God's creation is not simply a crime against humanity but it is a violation of God's intention for creation" (National Council of Churches, 1992, p. 4). The Jewish Torah talks more about duties to God and man rather than rights. Most Jewish communities recognize that human rights offer necessary, although not always adequate, protection from discrimination and persecution. Furthermore, in contrast to Christianity and Islam, by eschewing proselytizing Judaism eliminates a source of friction that is detrimental to religious tolerance and peaceful relations.

In spite of the fact that many Islamic states such as Afghanistan, Algeria, Egypt, and Morocco (UNESCO, 2004) have ratified major human rights treaties, as a whole, Islamic religious leaders have not embraced the international consensus on human rights. Their position is illustrated in the wording of the 1990 Cairo Declaration of Human Rights in Islam drafted by the Organization of the Islamic

Conference (Nineteenth Islamic Conference of Foreign Ministers, 5 August 1990, in Martin, 2001, p. 174). The Declaration ends with Article 25, which reads: "The Islamic Shariah is the only source of reference for the explanation of any of the articles in this Declaration" (Martin, 2001, p. 177). Moreover, while the wording of the other articles compares favorably with those of the international treaties, their meanings are explicitly subjected to interpretation in the light of Shariah, the body of Muslim beliefs and laws based on the Qur'an and other authoritative sources (Schacht, 1979). A recent example of this hierarchy within the Islamic system could be seen at a meeting of the UN Committee against Torture, where the Saudi representative argued that the Committee had no jurisdiction over Shariah provisions that allow amputations for theft and floggings and over capital punishment for certain sexual offenses and the consumption of alcohol (*New York Times*, May 19, 2002, Sec 8, p. 44).

Islamic legal texts emphasize communitarianism, that is the supremacy of the Ummah or Islamic community, as opposed to what they see as the individualistic nature of Western civil law and humanistic ethical thinking (Bulliet, 1996). The Cairo Declaration claims a universalist role, "Reaffirming the civilizing and historical role of the Islamic Ummah which God made the best nation that has given mankind a universal well-balanced community ... to guide all humanity which is confused because of competing trends and ideologies and to provide solutions to the chronic problems of this materialistic civilization" (Martin, 2001, p. 174). The Declaration thus defines Islam not only as the preferred system for the world's Muslims and for others living in Muslim countries, but also as *the* universal meaning system and *the* privileged religion.

In the case of religious freedom in particular, the Qur'an offers contrasting texts. The classic texts in favor include: "There is no compulsion in matters of religion" (Qur'an, 2:256, in Pickthall, 2000, p. 49); and " ... if thy Lord willed, all who were in the earth would have believed together. Wouldst thou (Muhammad) compel men until they are believers?" (Qur'an, Jonah, 99, in Pickthall, 2000, p. 159). "Now hath the truth from your Lord come unto you. So whatever is guided, is guided for (the good of) his soul, and whosoever erreth, erreth only against it. And I am not a warder over you" (Qur'an, Jonah, 108, Pickthall, 2000, p. 160). This tolerant tradition is expressed in Article 10 of the Cairo Declaration, which declares "Islam is the religion of unspoiled nature. It is prohibited to exercise any form of compulsion on man or to exploit his poverty or ignorance in order to convert him to another religion or to atheism." On the other hand, other verses in the Qur'an order Muslims to fight unbelievers "and fight them until persecution is no more and religion is for Allah" (Qur'an 2:193, Pickthall, 2000, p. 42; Hoffman, 2003). The Qur'an also warns that God will punish harshly Muslims who renounce their faith (Qur'an 2:217; Pickthall, 2003, p. 44) and Shariah interprets this as a mandate to the state to sentence apostates to death. The laws and practices of Muslim countries allow Muslims to proselytize non-Muslims but not vice versa (Stahnke,

1999). The Cairo Declaration does not incorporate the privileges traditionally accorded to *dhimmis*, people of the book, that is Christians and Jews living in Muslim communities. Though somewhat less than those accorded to Muslims, the privileges were significantly more than those granted to all other nonbelievers (*kafir* or *mushrik*). Recently some contemporary Muslim scholars have called for a more inclusive view of religious freedom but they remain a minority (An Na'im, 2003; Afshari, 1994; Little et al., 1996).

The respective theological critiques of Orthodox Christianity and Islam coincide with voices in those societies contending that human rights are one of the tools of Western imperialism, alongside individualism, consumerism, and materialism. The religious critiques are based on the primacy of the revealed truth and ethics as contained in the Christian Orthodox tradition and in Shariah, respectively. Neither religion advances theological or faith-based arguments that protect the rights or interests of nonmembers. Both traditions portray international human rights as a secular, read antireligious, meaning system designed to weaken their core loyalties, whether religious, nationalistic, or a combination of both.

Human Rights Critiques of Religion: "Otherness" and Discrimination

September 11, 2001 brought home to the world the intensity of religious motivation, when 19 Muslim men killed both themselves and over 3,000 other people, believing that their act merited huge rewards in the next life. To others it was unjustified prejudice that had boiled over into merciless hate. The media have since presented us with all sorts of analyses of the religious dimension. One, for example, argued that we face a religious war and that "there is something inherent in religious monotheism that lends itself to terrorist temptation" (Sullivan, 2001). Recent suicide bombings also appear to illustrate the power of a religious meaning system to motivate people in ways that override all other data, emotions, values, interpretations, and interests, let alone the rights of their innocent victims. The September 11 events were especially dramatic because they involved not only multiple suicides and a vision of martyrdom for the cause, but also the killing of thousands of innocent people, including members of the attackers' own faith. While the actions were extreme and their goals could be construed as political, their moral premises, if not their actual strategies, were rooted in beliefs based on spiritual, transcendental, and unverifiable tenets seen to belong to the core of the religious beliefs of their tradition. The human rights implications arise from the ways in which *others* are defined as enemies without rights, and from the consequences of such discriminatory definitions.

Unfortunately, both recent and ancient history can supply many examples of similar religiously based forms of prejudice, discrimination, and persecution. One of the most long-standing and criticized patterns of religious discrimination, dating from the very birth of Christianity, has been anti-Semitism, which found its roots in the ways in which Christians portrayed the emergence of their faith from Judaism in the first century of the common era. The four Christian Gospels, the main accounts of the life, arrest, trial, and execution of Jesus, emphasize his rejection by the Jewish people of the time. He is portrayed as the stone rejected by the people (interpreted as the Jews of the time), who became the cornerstone (Matthew 21, 34) of the new edifice, the Christian Church. The covenant with God once held by the Jewish people is portrayed as now held by the Christian Church (e.g., Corinthians, 3, 4–11). Such portrayals of Judaism and the Jewish people have provided a basis for later patterns of discrimination and persecution, exemplified dramatically in Nazi Germany (Kung, 1974). Recently, however, many Christian churches have responded to criticisms and reinterpreted the anti-Semitic premises to emphasize not so much the withdrawal of the promise or covenant from the Jewish people but rather the enduring faithfulness of God to the original Jewish covenant as well as to its universalizing in the message of Jesus (Bosch, 1991; Kung, 1974; Carroll, 2001). The important additional point is that this and other shifts in emphasis are evidence of change within a tradition, and thus imply the possibility of future change within the religious meaning systems.

If anti-Semitism is an example of discrimination between two monotheistic traditions, there are also many forms of discrimination within each of the three traditions, some of which encroach on the civil sphere and have been subject to civil scrutiny (Stahnke, 1999). Judaism, Christianity, and Islam, for example, all have within them sizeable communities with beliefs and practices at variance with one another. One has only to think of Orthodox and Reform Judaism, Protestant and Orthodox Christianity, Sunni and Shiite Islam (Goldziher, 1981). Discrimination within a tradition might be caused by accusations of heresy (beliefs not endorsed by the community), and by schism or apostasy (refusal to accept the authority of the community). It might also arise from moral positions, notably with regard to gender roles, family laws, and more recently sexual orientation. In these cases discrimination is based on definitions of otherness associated with biological factors such as the Catholic Church's belief that only men can be ordained to the priestly ministry and the Jewish tradition of accepting the children of a mixed marriage as Jewish, provided the mother is Jewish. Homosexuality is a contemporary issue where the ethical standards of substantial segments within Judaism, Christianity, and Islam are at variance with emerging international human rights standards (Clapham, 1993; Laycock, 1998). In question are the legitimacy of definitions of otherness by the different religious communities and whether the resulting discrimination is a violation of human rights.

In its basic sense, otherness simply states that any two people are not the same person. Typically, however, the factual reality is accompanied by an explicit or implicit definition or construct of the differences involved. The classic grounds of proscribed discrimination formulated in the Universal Declaration of Human Rights, are those of "race, color, sex, language, religion, political or other opinion or social origin, property, birth or other status" (UDHR #2, Martin, 2001, p. 5). In practice the characteristics that individuals ascribe to others often include subtle, expressed or implied, emotional, and attitudinal connotations in addition to the objective criteria (e.g., Aboud & Levi, 1999). The stereotypes or prejudices people construct of "others" can be placed along spectra that range from very negative to very positive (Allport, 1966; Neuberg, 1994; Batson & Burris, 1994). The negative can range from an innocuous view of the other as simply different, to feelings and convictions that define those others as competitors, oppressors, enemies, less than human, even as the devil or evil personified (Carroll, 2001; Struch & Schwartz, 1989). Similarly, the positive part of the spectrum defines others in terms ranging from neutral to seeing others as collaborators, sympathizers, friends, and even lovers (Gopin, 2000). These emotional and attitudinal constructs are often much more important than the more objective criteria of otherness. Strategies to move groups or individuals to more mutually sympathetic points of the spectrum are difficult but quite consonant with religious goals (Hackett, 2000; Shriver, 1995).

In addition to beliefs and practice, the consciousness of belonging to a select and privileged community is central to most religious meaning systems. While this consciousness and its implications vary, religious meaning systems divide human beings into "us" and "them." Distinctions between "us" and "them," however, pose a challenge to the human rights paradigm in that these distinctions provide a basis for discrimination and thus undermine the belief that human rights are truly universal.

Social psychologists have studied the relationship between religiosity and universalism, arguing that the greater the religiosity, the more likely persons and groups are less universalist, that is, less appreciative and accepting of others. Schwartz and Huismans (1995, p. 102) argue that

> ... the particularism of religions, binding their members into exclusionist, solidary groups, reduces the importance attributed to concern for all others, a core aspect of Universalism values. Moreover, the emphasis of Universalism values on using own judgment and on accepting diversity may make it difficult for person guided strongly by Universalism values to develop or maintain a commitment to established religions, because the latter emphasize acceptance of authoritative truth by the whole religious community.

In his examination of the relationship between religion and prejudice, Allport (1966) noted that on average churchgoers tended to harbor more prejudice than did non-churchgoers. But when he distinguished among churchgoers, namely between those for whom religion was the dominant force in their lives and those for whom their religious beliefs were only one of many, he found that prejudice was only higher among the less frequent churchgoers (Allport, 1966). Later, other scholars (Griffin et al., 1987; Hunsberger, 1995; Hunsberger & Jackson, this issue; Struch & Schwartz, 1989) have delineated other patterns and mechanisms through which religion both promotes and attenuates prejudice.

These studies suggest that the degrees of prejudicial discrimination coincide less with a given tradition and reflect more individual social currents and circumstances within traditions and other common social forces. In other words, degrees of prejudice vary as much within each religious tradition as they do between them. This idea was demonstrated in South Africa after the end of apartheid when it was found that "Religious dogmatism and exclusivism have taken a heavy toll on South African society. Adjacent to this exclusivism there has, however, also been universalism, inclusivism and openness within these religions" (Villa-Vicencio, 1996, p. 532; also Price, 2002, on Islam).

Slavery is a classic example of major, although protracted, ethical change on the part of all three religious traditions. After being accepted for many centuries after their respective foundations, today few religious authorities argue that the enslavement of other human beings is consistent with their faith. In other words, all three religions not only changed their moral standards, namely what they believed to be good or bad (Roccas, this issue), but also came to affirm a common ethical position.

Today a group of religious ideas, priorities, and practices that are coming under scrutiny, and as a result being changed, are associated with what is now called "the human rights of women." This is a complex international movement that exploded before and increasingly since the 1995 UN Conference on the Rights of Women in Beijing (Martin & Carson, 1996). At issue is the degree to which cultural and legal traditions treat men and women differently in both principle and practice, whether members or nonmembers. While the patterns of gender discrimination vary from society to society, the net results are shown to be consistently detrimental to women. Discrimination against women in religious law and practice is accompanied by discrimination in the civil sphere, as evidenced by women's share of the labor required to support a family and limited official responses to domestic violence and trafficking.

Distinguishing between cultural adaptations on one hand, and core beliefs and moral standards on the other, is thus not only an interesting field of enquiry for human rights, social science, and religious scholars, it is also a major issue for the religions themselves. Past changes in religious meaning systems and practices outlined above have come about on account of moral rethinking stimulated by wider social scrutiny. Such changes illustrate the thesis advanced by Henkin (1990a, p. 186) that "now religions—at least some religions—increasingly recognize that the idea of human rights is needed to move religions—at least some religions—to reexamine ancient practices that may be less a matter of theological doctrine or other enduring values than relics of the sociology of societies long gone." This rethinking is taking place in such different ways within each religion that it is hard to generalize about its implications for religious meaning systems, even the three monotheistic ones.

Conclusion

Religion is more than just a belief system and a way of construing the multiple elements that make up a given worldview. It is a normative meaning system built upon participation in a clearly defined, exclusive historical community. In contrast, the human rights meaning system minimizes exclusivity to emphasize respect and freedom for different ideas, beliefs, and practices. In order to live together peacefully in the future, each religious tradition must promulgate to its own members a coherent, universalist, and inclusive meaning system that reconciles tolerance of other faiths and nonmembers with the central dictates of its own sacred and transcendental elements (Tillich, 1963). This has proved most difficult for traditions in nonpluralist societies, such as in Islamic and Christian Orthodox countries, where the religions benefit from the support of the civil power and/or are closely associated with national identity. Ultimately, common social ethics require recognition of the benefits of the golden rule that possesses both religious and secular philosophical roots: "treat others as you would like to be treated."

Acceptance of the international human rights regime does not need to be based on a deeply shared worldview, or on common values or premises. The standards are still formulas "in the making" which rely for their legal and moral force on acceptance by the parties. As general principles, they admit diversity in their application from society to society. This is not to say that torture can be acceptable in one society and not in another. Rather, it says that intelligent persons and governments may oppose human rights violations in general but still disagree on their application, such as, for example, whether the death penalty is a violation of the right to life.

Islam is the largest single population segment where expert thinking and popular attitudes are least accepting of the international human rights regime. In this case, the immediate task is neither to ask Islam to conform its meaning systems and practices to those advocated by all others, nor that it should tolerate "all" other beliefs or practices, nor that it should develop its own domestic codes isolated from the rest of the world. Rather, the task is to reexamine the common rules and domestic codes to find ways in which Islam and other religious communities can live together without having to compromise their core beliefs, ethical principles and practices. As indicated above, this process requires sorting out core beliefs and core ethics from changeable elements associated with culture, nationality, and political interest. Particularly important will be the subtle attitudinal accretions and connotations mentioned above that refine more objective definitions of otherness. If slavery was an example of revisionism from the past, the status of women might be one for the present (Hassan, 1996; Cooke & Lawrence, 1996; Cook, 1993).

Scholars are well placed to delineate the cultural and historical variations within each of the traditions, challenging the latter to decide which are and which are not core beliefs and moral standards. Scholars are also well positioned to examine the ways in which societies, and the civil authorities in particular, have dealt with religious diversity. Some parts of the world, such as South Asia, have long traditions of religious diversity during which there were both periods of peaceful coexistence and major strife. What factors made a difference?

Whether monotheistic or not, religious meaning systems enshrine a person's moral convictions with social identity, approval, and support. The interpretation, the power, and the universalism of such meaning systems over both individuals and political systems vary significantly (a) within each tradition, (b) across historical periods, (c) from place to place, and even (d) from person to person. The ways in which religious meaning systems define other human beings, namely whether they are portrayed as hostile, friendly, neutral, or otherwise, also differ substantially. The human rights framework defines a set of common values and norms based, in the words of the UN Charter, on the "dignity and worth of the human person," the need "to practice tolerance and live together in peace with one another as good neighbors" and to encourage "fundamental freedoms for all without distinction as to race, sex, language or religion" (Martin, 2001, p. 1). The important lesson of the histories of all these meanings systems, religious and otherwise, is that none offers a definitive formulation. Each shows evidence of change over time and of substantial diversity among its contemporary formulations. It is possible therefore that the three monotheistic religious systems could eventually subscribe to a broad-enough base of common, civic norms, values, and institutions to enable them live peacefully in the same space.

References

Aboud, F. E., & Levy, S. R. (Eds.). (1999). Reducing racial prejudice, discrimination, and stereotyping: Translating research into programs. *Journal of Social Issues, 55*(4).

Afshari, R. (1994). An essay in Islamic cultural relativism in the discourse of human rights. *Human Rights Quarterly, 16*(2), 235–276.

Aijmer, G. (Ed.). (1992). *A conciliation of powers: The force of religion in society.* Gothenburg: University of Gothenburg Press.

Allport, G. (1966). The religious context of prejudice. *Journal of the Scientific Study of Religion, 5,* 447–457.

Alston, P. (1992). *The United Nations and human rights, a critical appraisal.* Syracuse, NY: Syracuse University Press.

Althaus, P. (1966). *The theology of Martin Luther.* Philadelphia, PA: Fortress Press.

An-Na'im, A. A. (Ed.). (1999). *Proselytization and communal self-determination in Africa.* Maryknoll, NY: Orbis Books.

An-Na'im, A. A. (2003). Synergy and independence of religion, human rights and secularism. In J. Runzo, N. Martin, & A. Sharma (Eds.), *Human rights and responsibilities in world religions* (pp. 27–49). Oxford, UK: Oneworld Publications.

Aquinas, T. (1947). *Summa theologica.* Domenican Province of New York (Eds.), New York: Benziger Brothers.

Ashcraft, R. (1996). Religion and Lockean natural rights. In I. Bloom, J. Martin, & W. Proudfoot (Eds.), *Religious diversity and human rights* (pp. 195–212). New York: Columbia University Press.

Batson, C., & Burris, C. T. (1994). Personal religion: Depressant or stimulant of prejudice and discrimination. In M. P. Zanna & J. M. Olson (Eds.), *The psychology of prejudice* (pp. 149–169). Hillsdale, NJ: Erlbaum.

Bloom, I., Martin, J., & Proudfoot, W. (Eds.). (1996). *Religious diversity and human rights*. New York: Columbia University Press.

Bosch, D. J. (1991). *Transforming mission, paradigm shifts in the theology of mission*. Maryknoll, NY: Orbis.

Bulliet, R. (1996). The individual in Islamic society. In I. Bloom, J. Martin, & W. Proudfoot (Eds.), *Religious diversity and human rights* (pp. 175–191). New York: Columbia University Press.

Carroll, J. (2001). *Constantine's sword, the Church and the Jews*. New York: Houghton Mifflin.

Clapham, A. (1993). *Human rights in the private sphere*. Oxford: Clarendon.

Cohn, H. H. (1989). *Human rights in the Bible and Talmud*. Tel Aviv, Israel: Mod Books.

Cooke, M., & Lawrence, B. B. (1996). Muslim women between human rights and Islamic laws. In I. Bloom, J. Martin, & W. Proudfoot (Eds.), *Religious Diversity and Human Rights* (pp. 313–331). New York: Columbia University Press.

Cook, R. J. (Ed.). (1993). *The human rights of women*. Philadelphia: University of Pennsylvania Press.

Corinthians, Letter of St. Paul, New Testament, *3*, 4–11.

Danchin, P., & Cole, E. (Eds.). (2002). *Protecting the rights of religious minorities in Eastern Europe*. New York: Columbia University Press.

Dinstein, Y. (1972). Freedom of religion and the protection of religious minorities. In Y. Dinstein & M. Tabory (Eds.), *Israel yearbook on human rights* (pp. 145–169). Tel Aviv, Israel: University of Tel Aviv.

Donnelly, J. (1989). *Universal human rights in theory and practice*. Ithaca, NY: Cornell University Press.

Eyck, F. (1997). *Religion and politics in German history*. New York: St. Martin's Press.

Fox, J. (2001). Religion as an overlooked element of international relations. *International Studies Review, 3*(3), 53–73.

French National Assembly. (1789, August 26). The French Declaration of the rights of man and of citizen. Retrieved June 3, 2004, from http://www.magnacartaplus.org/French-rights/1789.html.

Glendon, M. A. (2001). *A world made new, Eleanor Roosevelt and the Universal Declaration of Human Rights*. New York: Random House.

Goldziher, I. (1981). *An introduction to Islamic theology and law*. Princeton, NJ: Princeton University Press.

Gopin, M. (2000). *Between Eden and Armageddon: The future of religion, violence and peacemaking*. New York and Oxford: Oxford University Press.

Griffin, G. A., Gorsuch, R. L., & Davis, A. L. (1987). A cross-cultural investigation of religious orientation, social norms and prejudice. *Journal for the Scientific Study of Religion, 26*(3), 358–365.

Hackett, R. J., Silk, M., & Hoover, D. (2000). *Religious persecution as a U.S. policy issue*. Center for the Study of Religion in Public Life. Hartford, CT: Trinity College.

Harvard Law School Human Rights Program. (1999). *International aspects of the Arab human rights movement*. Cambridge, MA: Harvard University Press.

Hassan, R. (1996). Rights of women within Islamic communities. In J. Van der Vyver & J. Witte (Eds.), *Religious Human Rights in Global Perspective* (Vol. 2, pp. 361–386). Boston: Martinus Nijhoff.

Henkin, L. (1990a). *The age of rights*. New York: Columbia University Press.

Henkin, L. (1990b). *International law, politics, values and functions*. Dordrecht, Netherlands: Martinus Nijhoff.

Henkin, L. (1998). Religion, religions and human rights. *Journal of Religious Ethics, 26*(2), 229–239.

Henkin, L., & Hargrove, J. (Eds.). (1994). *Human rights: An agenda for the next century*. Washington, DC: American Society for International Law.

Hoffman, V. J. (2003). Contending legitimacies: Muslim perspectives. In E. Kolodziej (Ed.), *A force profonde* (pp. 45–68). Philadelphia: University of Pennsylvania Press.

Huertas, P., de Miguel, J., & Sanchez, A. (1999). *La inquisicion tribunal contra los delitos de fe*. Madrid: Libsa.

Hunsberger, B. (1995). Religion and prejudice: The role of religious fundamentalism, quest, and right wing fundamentalism. *Journal of Social Issues, 51*, 113–129.

Hunsberger, B., & Jackson, L. M. (this issue). Religion, meaning, and prejudice. *Journal of Social Issues.*

Huntington, S. T. (1996). *The clash of civilizations and the remaking of world order.* New York: Simon and Schuster.

Jones, R. M. (Ed.). (1911). *The Quakers in the American colonies.* London: Macmillan.

Kamen, H. (1985). *Inquisition and society in Spain.* London: Weidenfeld and Nicolson.

Kepel, G. (1994). *The revenge of God: The resurgence of Islam, Christianity and Judaism in the modern world.* Cambridge, UK: Polity Press.

Kolodziej, E. (Ed.). (2003). *A force profonde.* Philadelphia: University of Pennsylvania Press.

Korey, W. K. (1998). *NGOs and the Universal Declaration of Human Rights.* New York: Palgrave.

Kung, H. (1974). *On being a Christian.* New York: Doubleday.

Laycock, D. (1998). Religious freedom and international human rights in the United States today. *Emory International Law Review, 12*(2), 951–971.

Little, D., Sachedina, A., & Kelsay, J. (1996). Human rights and the world's religions. In I. Bloom, J. P. Martin, & W. L. Proudfoot (Eds.), *Religious diversity and human rights* (pp. 213–239). New York: Columbia University Press.

Locke, J. (1689). *A letter concerning toleration* (J. Tilly, Ed., 1983). Indianapolis, IN: Hackett.

Locke, J. (1698). *Two treatises on government* (P. Laslett, Ed., 1967). Cambridge, UK: Cambridge University Press.

Maritain, J. (1951). *Man and the state.* Chicago: Chicago University Press.

Martin, J. P. (Ed.). (2001). *Twenty five+ human rights documents.* New York: Center for the Study of Human Rights, Columbia University.

Martin, J. P., & Carson, L. (Eds.). (1996). *Women and human rights: The basic documents.* New York: Center for the Study of Human Rights, Columbia University.

Matthew, G., Christian New Testament, *21*, 34.

Morsink, J. (2000). *The Universal Declaration of Human Rights, origins, drafting and intent.* Philadelphia: University of Pennsylvania Press.

Naletova, I. (2001). Symphony reconsidered: The Orthodox Church in Russia on relations with modern society. *Osterreischishes Archiv fur Recht & Religion, 1*(IV), 12–65.

National Council of Churches. (1992). *The word of God and human rights.* New York: American Bible Society.

Neuberg, S. L. (1994). Expectancy-confirmation process in stereotype-tinged social encounters: The moderating role of social goals. In M. P. Zanna & J. M. Olson (Eds.), *The psychology of prejudice: The Ontario Symposium* (Vol. 7, pp. 103–130). Hillsdale, NJ: Erlbaum.

New York Times, available at www.nytimes.com.

Nurser, J. (2003). Human rights: The future for a revisioned "Christendom"? In J. Halama (Ed.), *The idea of human rights: Tradition and presence* (pp. 163–182). Prague, Czechoslovakia: Charles University.

Orthodox Church. (2000). Jubilee Bishops' Council, Bases of the Social. *Concept of the Russian Orthodox Church, August 13–16, 2000.* Retrieved October 1, 2004, from http://www.mospat.ru/chapters/e-counci/2000/

Pickthall, M. M. (Transl.). (2000). *The Glorious Qur'an.* Elmhurst, Queens, NY: Tahrike Tarsile Qur'an.

Pollis, A. (1993). Eastern Orthodoxy and human rights. *Human Rights Quarterly, 15*(2), 339–356.

Price, D. (2002). Islam and human rights: A case of deceptive first appearances. *Journal for the Scientific Study of Religion, 41*(2), 213–225.

Putnam, G. H. (1967). *The censorship of the Church of Rome and its influence upon the production and distribution of literature.* New York: B. Blom.

Roosevelt, F. (1941). Address to Congress, January 6, *Congressional Record*, 87, Pt 1. Retrieved June 3, 2004, from www.ibiblio.org/pha/7-2-188/188-22.

Schacht, J. (1979). *An introduction to Islamic law.* Oxford, UK: Oxford University Press.

Schwartz, S. H., & Huismans, S. (1995). Value priorities and religiosity in four Western religions. *Social Psychology Quarterly, 58*(2), 66–107.

Shriver, Jr., D. W. (1995). *An ethic for enemies, Forgiveness in politics.* New York: Oxford University Press.

Stahnke, T. (1999). Proselytism and the freedom to change religion in international human rights law. *Brigham Young University Law Review, 1*, 251–350.

Stahnke, T., & Martin, J. P. (Eds.). (1998). *Religion and human rights, Basic documents.* New York: Center for the Study of Human Rights, Columbia University.

Sullivan, A. (2001). This is a religious war. *The New York Times Magazine,* October 7, Sec. 8, 44–53.

Struch, N., & Schwartz, S. H. (1989). Intergroup aggression: Its predictors and distinctness from in-group bias. *Journal of Personality and Social Psychology, 56*(3), 364–373.

Tierney, B. C. (1996). Religious rights: An historical perspective. In J. Van der Vyver & J. Witte (Eds.), *Religious human rights in global perspective* (Vols. I & II, pp. 17–45). Boston: Martinus Nijhoff.

Tillich, P. (1963). *Christianity and the encounter of world religions.* New York: Columbia University Press.

Tutu, D. (1996). Religion and human rights. In H. Kung (Ed.), *Yes to a global ethic* (pp. 164–174). New York: Continuum.

UNESCO. (2004). *Human rights major international instruments.* Paris: UNESCO Publications.

Van der Vyver, J., & Witte, J. (Eds.). (1996). *Religious human rights in global perspective* (Vols. I & II). Boston: Martinus Nijhoff.

Villa-Vicenzo, C. (1996). Identity, difference and belonging: Religious and cultural rights. In J. Van der Vyver & J. Witte (Eds.), *Religious human rights in global perspective* (Vol. II, pp. 517–538). Boston: Martinus Nijhoff.

Witte, J. (2001). A Dickensian era of religious rights: An update on religious rights in global perspective. *William and Mary Law Review, 42*(3), 707–770.

Witte, J. (2003). Between sanctity and depravity: Human dignity in protestant perspective. In R. P. Kraynak & G. Tinder (Eds.), *In defense of human dignity: Essays for our times* (pp. 119–137). London/Notre Dame, IN: Notre Dame University Press.

Woodhouse, A. S. P. (Ed.). (1951). *Puritanism and liberty: Being the army debates 1647–1649.* Chicago: University of Chicago Press.

Wuthnow, R. (1992). *Rediscovering the sacred: Perspectives on religion in contemporary society.* Grand Rapids, MI: Eerdmans.

J. PAUL MARTIN, currently the Executive Director of Columbia University's Center for the Study of Human Rights, studied philosophy and theology in Rome during the time of the Vatican Council (1962–1965). After teaching at the university in Lesotho in Southern Africa, he completed a PhD at Columbia, writing a dissertation on the role of Christian missionaries in 19th Century Lesotho. Since 1978 he has been Executive Director of the Columbia Center. His writings have focused on religion and rights as well as on human rights education. He has edited three volumes of human rights documents and co-edited *Religious Diversity and Human Rights,* published by Columbia University Press. His recent articles on include "Human Rights NGOs in Africa, the Emerging Agenda" (with Kury Cobham, *Brown Journal of World Affairs*); "Assessing The Outcome of Proselytization: Missionaries among Moshesh's Sotho in Nineteenth Century Southern Africa" (*Emory International Law Review*); "Religious Proselytization: Historical and Theological Perspectives at the end of the Twentieth Century" (with Harry Winter, in *Proselytization and Communal Self-Determination in Africa,* edited by Abdullahi Ahmed an Na'im) and the chapter on Ethnicity and Racism in *The Columbia History of the 20th Century.*

Journal of Social Issues, Vol. 61, No. 4, 2005, pp. 847–867

Religion as a Meaning System: Policy Implications for the New Millennium

Kenneth I. Maton*
University of Maryland, Baltimore County

Daniel Dodgen
Washington, D.C.

Mariano R. Sto. Domingo
University of Maryland, Baltimore County

David B. Larson
National Institute for Healthcare Research

The development of social policy related to religion has received increasing focus in recent years, yet psychology continues to play a relatively minor role in this important domain. In the current article, religion's positive and negative influences as a meaning system on individual, community, and societal well-being are delineated. The challenges facing psychology in contributing to public policy development in the religious arena are examined, challenges that stem from profound differences in the meaning systems of religion, government, and psychology. These challenges notwithstanding, a number of different pathways in the domains of applied research, community practice, and policy development are delineated through which psychology can help to maximize positive, and minimize negative, outcomes in the religion and social policy arena.

"A Faith-Based Rorschach Test" (Diament, 2001), "Black Religious Leaders Hear Bush's Call" (Allen & Edsall, 2001), and "Bush's faith-based group initiative

*Correspondence concerning this article should be addressed to Kenneth I. Maton, UMBC, Department of Psychology, Baltimore, MD, 21250 [e-mail: maton@umbc.edu].

The first three authors would like to acknowledge the passing away of coauthor, colleague, and collaborator David Larson. A pioneer in research on the intersection of spirituality, health, and mental health, Dave will be greatly missed by all who had the privilege of knowing and working with him.

will meet resistance" (Milbank, 2001). These represent a sampling of titles of news articles and op-ed pieces that appeared in 2001 in the *Washington Post*. The stream of news articles and opinions followed from President George W. Bush's executive order establishing the White House Office of Faith-Based and Community Initiatives (Executive Order No. 13199, 2001), which primarily seeks to eliminate barriers to participation by religious organizations in federal social service programs (Bush, 2001). These news articles as a group reflect passionate, articulate, and widely contrasting reactions to the development of this White House office. As indicated by the strong public reactions to this and related issues, religion clearly remains an extremely important meaning system in our country, one with major implications for individual and societal well-being. Equally clear, as reflected by the wide range of responses to these issues, the nature and perceived role of religion as a meaning system vary tremendously across individuals and social groups, including policy makers (e.g., Dionne & DiIulio, 2000).

A key, guiding assumption of the current article is that religion and social policy are each very complex, multifaceted phenomena with important implications for the common good. The complexity of religion is reflected in the diversity of religious groups, beliefs, experiences, motivations, behaviors, pathways of influence, and forms of organization (e.g., Pargament & Maton, 2000; Wuthnow, 1996). Furthermore, religion can have an influence on various social levels, including the individual, group, community, and societal (Maton & Wells, 1995). In any situation, the nature of religious influence will likely depend on the specific religious component involved, the specific context, and the level of focus. Thus, one major way in which religion has the potential to influence the common good is by providing meaning to individuals, groups, and societies, thereby influencing values, attitudes, affect, and behavior (cf. Silberman, this issue).

Social policy impacts the common good through influencing what citizens can and cannot (legally) do, providing needed resources, and more broadly influencing public values and norms. Policy making, particularly in the legislative arena, is a multistage process that includes agenda setting, policy formulation, implementation, and evaluation, which are connected in an ongoing, iterative manner (cf. Anderson, 1997; Friedman, 1999). The judicial system, through its role in enforcing and interpreting laws and regulations, is an important and often overlooked component of the policy world. For both the legislative and judicial processes, the levels of influence range from the local to the national, with the state level representing an increasingly important domain of policy during the last 15 years (e.g., Matthews, 1999). The current administration's efforts to enhance support for faith-based organizations, for example, encourages the establishment of state-level Offices of Faith-Based and Community Initiatives (Bush, 2001). Following Executive Order 13198 (2001), five major cabinet-level departments (Health and Human Services, Housing and Urban Development, Labor, Justice, and Education) each created a Center for Faith-Based and Community Initiatives. Furthermore, a series of faith-based initiatives have received bipartisan sponsorship in the U.S. Senate, focused in part on removing "unfair barriers" facing faith-based groups in competing for community-based federal funding initiatives (e.g., Charity Aid, Recovery and Empowerment Act of 2002).

The potential interface between religion and policy exists across all domains and levels of the policy process. It is our view that despite its historical neglect, psychology has an important role to play in helping to develop these varied religion-policy interfaces—through research, collaborating with religious and community groups, and working with policy makers.

Public policies and religious influences both share the capacity for producing either great benefit or great harm. In this article the positive potential for linkage between religion and the common good is emphasized. We choose this focus because knowledge about the negative aspects is much more widespread, and because relatively little focus in psychology to date has been placed on the potential for positive linkages between religion and policy (Andrews, 1995). Nonetheless, throughout the article the potential negative influences of religion on the common good are noted as well, for it is extremely important that they be considered carefully in the worlds of both research and action.

In the first section of this article the nature of religion as a meaning system is explored, with special focus on the potential for influence at the individual, group, community, and cultural/societal levels of analysis. In the second section, the challenges of contributing to public policy development in the religious arena for psychology are examined—challenges that stem in part from profound differences between and among the meaning systems of religion, government, and psychology. The challenges notwithstanding, in the final section of the article a number of different pathways through which psychology can help to maximize positive, and minimize negative, outcomes in the religion and social policy area are examined. It should be noted that, given space and knowledge limitations, the article's policy focus is limited to the United States—the nature of the challenges and policy implications drawn might differ significantly in societies with fundamentally different structural, functional, and historical interrelationships between church and state.

Religion as Meaning System: The Potential for Influence at Individual, Group, Community, and Cultural/Societal Levels of Analysis

Religion as a meaning system evinces positive potential for social policy at all levels of analysis. For the individual, two important pathways through which individual well-being can be enhanced are prevention and healing (cf. Maton & Wells, 1995). Religion contributes to prevention in multiple ways, including provision of protective factors such as meaning in life, religious coping skills, and social and spiritual support systems, which often serve to enhance resilience in the face of major life stressors (e.g., Pargament, Magyar, & Murray-Swank, this issue; Park, this issue), and through normative individual and community proscriptions and prescriptions concerning lifestyle choices, healthy behaviors, and purposeful understanding and goals, which contribute directly to health and well-being (cf. Pargament, Maton, & Hess, 1992; Winett et al., 1999). Religion contributes to healing, as well, through multiple mechanisms, including intrapsychological transformations in life goals, meaning, personal spirituality, and self-value and self-acceptance, and concurrent social, instrumental, and spiritual support from pastoral counselors, fellow believers, and spiritually based self-help (12-step) groups, among others (e.g., George, Larson, Koenig, & McCullough, 2000; Maton & Wells, 1995). As cited in various articles in this volume, many studies have linked aspects of religiosity and/or religious involvement to positive indices of health, longevity, behavior, and psychological well-being (cf. Johnson, Li, Larson, & McCullough, 2000; McCullough, Hoyt, Larson, Koenig, & Thoresen, 2000).

In addition to potential positive influences of religion for the individual, there are potential negative influences of religion as a meaning system as well. Beliefs, motivations, emotions, and behaviors of individuals can be powerfully influenced in problematic directions by various facets of religion. For instance, specific facets and styles of religion as a meaning system have been linked to negative psychological outcomes (Pargament et al., this issue; Park, this issue) and to prejudice (Hunsberger & Jackson, this issue). In the case of the September 11, 2001 terrorist attacks in New York and Washington, D.C., the individuals responsible for the hijacking of four airplanes, the subsequent destruction of the World Trade Center's twin towers, and the resulting deaths of thousands of people, held religious views that promoted acts of violence against other individuals and nations (e.g., Ethics & Public Policy Center, 2002).

At the group level of analysis, the meaning system of religion can greatly enhance the resilience and empowerment of varied groups in society, perhaps especially those facing oppression and discrimination, and those with limited economic and political resources. For example, the historical resilience of African Americans has been attributed by many analysts, in part, to the faith provided by religion, and to the solidarity and support provided by the Black Church in a larger, hostile society (e.g., Moore, 1991). Beyond serving as a source of coping and a basis of group cohesion, religion also has the potential to serve as a resource contributing to group empowerment for social groups lacking in power (cf. Maton & Wells, 1995), providing a basis for shared economic resources, social networks, and social action (e.g., Moore, 1991; Silberman, Higgins, & Dweck, this issue). Thus, religion as a meaning system has served to mobilize social and political activism in service of ethnic minority and lower-income groups, at community, state, and national levels (e.g., Industrial Areas Foundation, 1990; Speer, Hughey, Gensheimer, & Adams-Leavitt, 1995; Yarnold, 1991).

At the same time, religion as an institution and as a meaning system can be seen as a barrier to group empowerment (Roccas, this issue; Schwartz & Huismans, 1995). For example, certain religious beliefs can lead social groups to withdraw from the larger society, and/or focus on individual salvation with little emphasis on changing oppressive social conditions and policies (cf. Pargament & Maton, 2000). Furthermore, certain religious ideologies and structures have historically oppressed, rather than empowered, social groups such as women, gays and lesbians, and ethnic minorities (e.g., Clark, Brown, & Hochstein, 1989). For example, after September 11, conservative Christian leaders Jerry Falwell and Pat Robertson blamed the terrorist attacks in part on American tolerance for gay rights, abortion, and feminism (Harris, 2001).

At the community level of analysis, religion has the potential to contribute to community capacity building—the capability of key community institutions, such as schools, social services, families, neighborhood groups, and government, to accomplish effectively their institutional roles. Faith-based organizations, and the meaning system provided by religion more generally, have often contributed to such efforts via the ongoing mobilization of volunteers and financial resources, the provision of social service programs, and through access to hard-to-reach ethnic minority and lower-income populations. For example, congregations are often important players in coalitions formed to address community wide problems, in the development of mentoring and volunteer programs for schools and troubled youth, and in generating substantial financial contributions, which are channeled to a wide spectrum of social programs (cf. Kloos & Moore, 2000; Maton & Sto. Domingo, in press; Maton, Sto. Domingo, & King, 2005; Pargament & Maton, 2000; Queen, 1997; articles in current issue). And, in the specific case of our most troubled urban and lower-income communities, religious groups often represent one of the few viable community institutions located in poor areas, capable of providing access and services to local citizens (cf. Hale & Bennett, 2000).

The positive potential of religion at the community level notwithstanding, religious institutions and practices can also be important contributors to community problems. For example, religious differences can contribute to distrust, prejudice, and intergroup discord, rather than community capacity (cf. Hunsberger & Jackson, this issue). Such problems can be even more problematic when religious differences are associated with differences in socioeconomic status and, in related fashion, to differential access to political and economic power.

Finally, at the cultural/societal level of analysis, the values promoted by religion, at their best, can challenge an excessive cultural focus on materialism, self-absorption, and narrow individual, group, and national interests (e.g, Bellah, Madsen, Sullivan, Swidler, & Tipton, 1985; Kloos & Moore, 2000; Maton, 2000). Religion's meaning systems also have the potential to affirm a greater cultural focus on empowering those who lack status and power in society, and promoting a sense of common cause, which transcends group-based and societal-based boundaries (e.g., Maton, 2001; Pargament & Maton, 2000; articles in this issue).

On the other hand, at the cultural and societal levels, religion and religious beliefs have often led to systematic oppression (e.g., Martin, this issue), and to conflict and war (e.g., Gopin, 2000; Silberman, Higgins, & Dweck, this issue). Indeed, over the centuries, national and international tragedies have often had religious discord or ideology as an underlying cause, rather than as a preventive or ameliorative resource (cf. Carter, 2000). The September 11 terrorist attacks, the dramatic escalation of the conflict in the Middle East in early 2002, and the religio-political conflict in India and Pakistan all provide recent examples of this sad reality (cf. Ethics & Public Policy Center, 2002).

Those open to greater linkages between policy and religion believe, as the current authors do, that the potential for positive benefits of such linkages outweigh the potential for negative outcomes (e.g., Dionne & DiIulio, 2000). Clearly, this remains an empirical question. Beyond this overarching concern, there are a number of intrinsic challenges to effective work at the religion, social policy, and psychology interface, to which we next turn.

Religion, Social Policy, and Psychology: The Challenges

There are a number of challenges facing the development of social policies intended to capitalize upon religion as a resource, and for psychology's constructive participation in the process. One major challenge is the constitutional separation of church and state. A second is the major difference in meaning systems between religion and policy, and of each from the meaning system and culture of psychology. Finally, there is the challenge provided by the tremendous diversity and complexity of religion. Below we briefly touch upon these challenges.

Separation of Church and State

The explicit, legal separation of church and state, as indicated in the First Amendment of the Constitution, is meant at least in part to ensure that government does not directly encourage (or discourage) specific religious activities or beliefs. Public policies cannot be developed whose goals are to promote religion *per se*. For instance, in the case of governmental funding of social services provided by faith-based organizations, the Supreme Court in *Lemon* v. *Kurtzman* (1971) and *Bowen* v. *Kendrick* (1988) laid down several key tests: (a) Funding agencies cannot limit their services to people affiliated with any particular religious denomination; (b) Services provided under an act cannot be religious in character; (c) There can be no substantial risk that aid to a religious institution results in religious indoctrination; (d) Religious institutions must not be the sole or primary beneficiaries of legislation; and (e) Any arguable effect of advancing religion must be "incidental and remote." A number of court decisions (e.g., *Santa Fe Independent School District* v. *Doe*, 2000; *Mitchell* v. *Helms*, 2000) have further elaborated the relationship between government and religion and have attempted to safeguard the antiestablishment of religion clause of the First Amendment, without undermining the religion free-exercise clause.

Various policy proposals at state and federal levels, ranging from public funding of vouchers for parents to send their children to religious schools to President Bush's proposal to fund faith-based social services, have been assailed as breaching the constitutionally defined separation of church and state (Rogers, 2000). Interestingly, critics of President Bush's initiative hail from both ends of the political spectrum. Those on the left emphasize that federal funding of religious groups to provide social services represents the use of public dollars, directly or indirectly, for religious programming, religious discrimination (e.g., hiring of staff, relevance of services), and religious proselytizing. Those on the right emphasize that the religious integrity of faith-based groups will be jeopardized as the result of accepting federal monies and accompanying conditions, and are also concerned about the funding of non-Christian and fringe religious groups (Milbank, 2001).

Clearly, the interface of religion and policy raises major issues and "red flags" to multiple sectors of society. Nevertheless, countless faith-based organizations have, over the years, received various categories of funding from the government, and worked in partnership with governmental entities in a variety of social problem areas (Centers for Disease Control & Prevention, 1999; Glenn, 2000). For instance, an audit of federal programs by the Centers for Faith-Based and Community Initiatives in five federal departments revealed that in order to deliver social services, some faith-based and community-based service groups gain funding either through federal discretionary funds or through gaining a share of federal formula grants used by state and local governments (The White House, 2001). Psychologists who desire to work at the interface of religion and social policy will need to have some understanding of the meaning, and operational realities, of the separation of church and state.

Differences across Meaning Systems and Cultures

In addition to important First Amendment concerns, fundamental differences in the meaning systems and cultures of religion, policy, and scientific psychology challenge the potential for positive interface and collaboration. Table 1 depicts ways in which the meaning systems of religion, policy, and psychology differ, in terms of knowledge system, view of people, basic orientation, guiding norms and objectives, valued attributes, milieu of influence, source of values, time perspective, decision-making process, and distinctive bases of knowledge (see also Richards & Bergin, 1997; Solarz, 2000). For example, religion's knowledge system

Table 1. The Meaning Systems of Religion, Policy, and Psychology

Meaning System Component	Religion	Policy	Scientific Psychology
Knowledge system	Transcendent	Pragmatic	Testable (falsifiable)
View of people	Spiritual/moral agents free will, holistic	Economic, rational, categorical	Psychological/behavioral, Deterministic, deficits-based
Basic orientation	Serve/please the divine	Serve/please constituents	Serve the discipline/please peers
Guiding norms and objectives	Seek and/or obey, holiness/righteousness, Benevolence/altruism	Act/decide, compromise	Understand/explain, getting published/sharing knowledge, experimenting
Valued attributes	Knowledge of scriptures, discernment	Power/influence, inside information	Research knowledge, research skills
Milieu of influence	Religious institutions	Legal system/government	Academia
Source of values	Religious scriptures	Legal and policy writings	Principles of scientific conduct
Time perspective	Eternal, medium-term, short-term	Short-term	Medium-term, long-term
Decision-making process	Authority structure	Majority vote, adversarial	Peer review
Distinctive bases of knowledge	Received tradition, spiritual experience	Common sense, intuition, opinion surveys	Experimental findings, what can be observed & measured

is transcendent, policy makers' pragmatic ("whatever works"), and psychology's testable (falsifiable). Concerning views of people, religion tends to view people in spiritual/moral, free will and holistic terms, policy in economic, rational and categorical terms, and scientific psychology in psychological/behavioral, deterministic, and deficit-based terms. The differences across meaning systems depicted in Table 1 underscore primary difficulties that will affect collaboration and interactions involving religion, government, and psychology.

Table 1 paints with quite broad strokes components of the meaning systems and cultures of the three sectors, and emphasizes psychology as a research discipline. Of course, there is tremendous diversity and variation within each sector on each component (see below). Nonetheless, the table should serve to underscore the reality that psychologists entering the spheres of religion and social policy will face challenges related to differences and discontinuities in basic assumptions, language, communication, and worldviews.

The Diversity and Complexity of Religion

The United States is now home to over 20 major religious families of the world, including Buddhists, Roman Catholics, Presbyterians, Muslims, Southern

Baptists, Hindus, Seventh-Day Adventists, Sikhs, Pentecostals, Jews, Episcopalians, Mormons, Evangelicals, Eastern Orthodox, and Lutherans (Bedell, 1997; Richards & Bergin, 2000). Each of these, and belief subgroups within each, will vary tremendously on the general meaning system components presented in Table 1, with critically important implications for the world of action. Furthermore, policy makers and psychologists vary greatly in their religious beliefs and views, and members of all three sectors vary tremendously in their political views.

In addition to a great diversity in fundamental tenets of belief, religion is a very complex social phenomenon, with multiple agendas in operation, multiple potential pathways of interface with government, and multiple levels of influence on individual and community well-being (cf. Pargament & Maton, 2000). Concerning multiple agendas, for example, a faith-based organization may simultaneously be committed to local community efforts to help the poor, to dramatically expanding their financial base, and to supporting their national denomination in opposing birth control related education in the schools. A second faith-based organization may simultaneously be committed to proselytizing nonbelievers, supporting health promotion programs in the community, and providing substantial donations to relieve world hunger. As a result, partnerships with any given religious group need to be entered into with a full awareness both of areas of common cause and of potential difference. Before deciding to partner with a faith-based organization, any concerns about specific aspects of its mission or practice in each case will need to be outweighed by the perceived benefits of partnership.

The multiplicity of pathways through which religion influences, and is influenced by, the world of policy is a related source of complexity. On the one hand, religion can be seen as a special interest group, with vested interests in a variety of controversial public issues (McCarthy, 1996). Examples include public support of religious schools, abortion, creationalist science curricula, and the legality of marriage among gays and lesbians. On the other hand, religion can be viewed as a community-based partner and resource for helping government serve the public good (Cnaan & Yancey, 2000; DiIulio, 2000). Thus, as described in the first section of the article, faith-based organizations can be sites for prevention programs, sources of volunteers and financial resources for community-based programs, and advocates for fighting poverty. Additionally, given its potential for causing harm, religion is a social institution with which the government at times needs to intervene, as is the case with extreme activities by cults (Walker, 1995), refusals to provide medical treatment (particularly for children) based on religious doctrine (Muramoto, 1998), polygamous marital practices (Booth, 2001), and child sexual molestation by clergy (cf. by Catholic priests).

Further complicating these matters is the fact that value-based conflicts may take different forms, or have different meanings, at different levels of analysis. For instance, funding of religion-based programs may be viewed as acceptable at the individual level of analysis if these programs can be shown to be an option available to individuals, and to have a transforming effect on those who may not be reached through traditional, secular approaches. On the other hand, support for faith-based programs may be problematic at the organizational level, where the funding is viewed as supporting, directly or indirectly, a religious group's institutional practices such as proselytization, or intolerance of religious, racial, or sexual orientation differences.

Given the diverse and complex nature of religion, the challenges for constructive policy development in general, and for psychology's positive contribution to the process in particular, are great. A sophisticated, differentiated understanding by psychologists is needed to be effective in this important, emerging arena. Any simple, general characterization of religious individuals, groups, or institutions used across the board to guide research, practice, policy development, or policy advocacy will likely prove problematic, and in the end, counterproductive.

The Development of Policy that Builds upon the Positive Potential of Religion: Psychology's Role

Given the above challenges, along with the differences in meaning systems depicted in Table 1, it is likely that developing successful interfaces between religion and policy will not be possible to achieve in some areas, especially those involving clear issues of separation of church and state, or where psychology's values are in clear conflict with religion on a given issue. However, there is a middle ground where faith-based progressive reform efforts involving government and religion should be considered, without neglecting consideration of the potential for harm or the constitutional separation of church and state (cf. Working Group on Human Needs and Faith-based and Community Initiatives, 2002). What psychology uniquely offers to this work is its foundation as an empirically based discipline that brings the scientific method to the study of social issues. It also brings to bear experience in working with individuals, groups, and communities, and in public interest advocacy. These three major assets are involved, to varying extents, in the pathways of involvement for psychology that are briefly reviewed below.

Enhanced Research Focus on Faith-Based Approaches to Social Problems

Sound research is necessary to more objectively inform policy makers about the strengths and weaknesses of various faith-based approaches to social and community problems. One important focus for such a research is program and policy evaluation. Such evaluation research, ideally, would encompass current social programs developed by faith-based organizations (e.g., Teen Challenge, Prison Fellowship; see Johnson, Tompkins, & Webb, 2002), those developed by professionals and implemented in faith-based settings (e.g., health promotion and disease prevention initiatives; social outreach programs administered by organizations such as Jewish Family Service or Catholic Charities), programs outside of the realm of formal religion but which include a spiritual basis (e.g., 12-step programs), and governmental policy initiatives (e.g., 1997 Charitable Choice legislation).

Ideally, evaluation research should not be limited to delineating the extent of program or policy impact, but also the relative importance of various dimensions of the religious programs (e.g., spiritual versus behavioral), the pathways of influence (including religious versus nonreligious mechanisms), the valence of outcomes (both positive and negative), implementation, the linkage to extant psychological theory and constructs, and the ecological context within which the program or policy operates.

Take, for example, the State Children's Health Insurance Program (CHIP), passed by Congress in 1997. CHIP is a federal program that provided $24 billion to the states to give health insurance benefits to uninsured children at up to twice the poverty level (Balanced Budget Act of 1997). Until 1999, families were not enrolling in the program and states seemed unable to develop strategies for getting them to participate. In 1999, as partnerships with community-based organizations (CBOs), including churches and other faith-based organizations were developed, many families began to enroll (Places of Worship, 2001). Evaluation research is needed to examine the factors that contributed to the success of faith-based organizations in enrolling families in CHIP, and to compare these efforts to previously unsuccessful approaches by CBOs and/or other continuing efforts of state agencies. Furthermore, the mechanisms by which faith-based organizations facilitated enrollment of people in the program, including the role of psychological theory in areas such as communication, interpersonal influence, and help-seeking, would inform future program and policy development.

Beyond program evaluation per se, research is needed to examine further the naturally occurring conditions, dimensions, and mechanisms linking religion or spirituality to important positive (e.g., health, community building, social justice) and negative (e.g., prejudice, discrimination, oppression, conflict) outcomes. The previous articles in this volume review what is known in a number of these areas, and indicate the many needs for future research on religion as a meaning system. Based on the results of systematic, strategic research efforts in these areas, important new programmatic interventions and policy directions can be developed over time.

Both evaluation and applied research should ideally examine processes and outcomes at multiple levels of analysis. When government interfaces with religion, examination of the impacts on program recipients, their families, faith-based volunteers, religious settings, other service providers, and larger community norms and capacity are all important. As indicated above, the positive and negative potential of religion exists across individual, community, and societal levels of analysis. To make a difference, research needs to understand potential impacts and mechanisms at these different levels, and as research gains in sophistication, across levels.

At the policy level, enhanced research funding priorities are needed within national research institutes (e.g., National Institutes of Health) and state research agencies. Psychology has an important role to play in summarizing research to date and engaging in efforts, ideally in collaboration with allied groups, to inform policy makers and research institute leaders of the importance of additional research efforts. Individual psychologists can contribute to the process by informing their elected officials of their work in this area. They need also to encourage private foundations and religious nonprofit groups to make evaluation of faith-based programs a priority, and to allocate sufficient resources for such evaluation efforts. Clearly, to make a difference, increased numbers of psychologists are needed to take part in research and in research funding development efforts in the areas outlined above, ideally in collaboration with other disciplines, including religion.

*Work Directly with Government and Religion to Enhance
the Positive Impact of Programs and Policies*

Psychologists have important skills and expertise that can be utilized to enhance individual and community well-being at the interface of religion and policy. In terms of program development, our knowledge of prevention theory and practice, for example, can usefully inform the development of religion-based efforts and initiatives. In terms of enhancing community capacity, psychologists with expertise and experience in various community-based areas, including education, mental health, health, and social problems, can similarly make valuable contributions. At the level of governmental policy, our research knowledge and practical experience in various high priority social problem areas should prove a critical resource informing the development of viable religion-government policies.

Wolff's (2001) work in the area of community capacity building represents an example of the contribution of psychology in this domain. Wolff is a community psychologist whose community-based organization helps to implement the Healthy Communities program in Massachusetts. He works with local communities throughout the state, facilitating the development of community coalitions to address locally defined health and social problems. Faith-based organizations and religious leaders are important players in the coalitions, working together with government, human services, education, and citizen groups and leaders. For example, in one African American community the coalition dispersed mini-grants to faith-based organizations to support summer violence prevention activities; in another community, a homelessness prevention program was developed in partnership with the coalition. Using skills of community organization, community development, and team building, Wolff helps bring religion, government, and community together with the goal of enhancing community capacity.

There are multiple sources of evidence that faith-based organizations will increasingly be asked to serve as partners with government and human services to enhance individual and community well-being, particularly for those most vulnerable for whom government programs have not been found to be effective. For example, the Centers for Disease Control and Prevention (CDC) has had a growing history of engagement with faith-based organizations in its public health outreach work (Centers for Disease Control & Prevention, 1999). Thus, in the effort to reduce the burden of HIV infection and AIDS cases within African American communities, the CDC made available over $1.2 million to support comprehensive HIV/AIDS education and prevention programs within African American faith, religious and spiritual communities in three categories: community-based HIV prevention services, capacity building assistance, and curriculum development and training (CDC Program Announcement 99096). Funded projects in this and other CDC high priority disease areas encompass partnerships with national, regional, and local faith-based organizations.

Since the passage of federal welfare reform legislation in 1996 that supported this kind of collaboration, a number of states have developed contracts and collaborations with faith-based organizations to provide supportive services for individuals and families transitioning from welfare dependency, including job training, mentoring, mental health, transportation, life skills training, and other services (Sherman, 2000). And, with the support of President Bush's Office of Faith-Based and Community Initiatives, increasing numbers of states will likely develop an array of projects and programs in partnership with faith-based organizations.

Ideally, psychologists will provide consultation to faith-based organizations and spiritually based programs, help establish standards for service providers, provide leadership in program development, and contribute to broader community capacity building and social policy development (cf. Melton, 2000). In each of these and related areas, adherence within the requirements of the Constitution and of the Supreme Court is needed. And, as noted earlier, research will have a critical role to play in determining such adherence, and more broadly in examining effectiveness and ineffectiveness, and both anticipated and unanticipated outcomes.

Policy Advocacy and Culture Challenge

Involvement in advocacy efforts, whether at the community, state, or national level is another important way psychology can contribute to the public welfare in this area. One value that psychology shares with many religious groups, and one supported by extensive empirical research, is the urgency of improving conditions for those living in poverty, and those facing injustice, discrimination, and oppression. Armed with research findings, we can join forces with like-minded groups, including faith-based ones, to advocate for social programs and enhanced resources for the poor and oppressed. Examples of the latter include living wage legislation, tax laws that discourage charitable giving, and laws that support immigrants and refugees. Individual psychologists, their state associations, and the American Psychological Association at the national level all have a role to play in such efforts. Ideally, psychologists will work with like-minded faith-based and community groups, and help communicate relevant research to policy makers in a way that usefully informs the debate and ensuing policy decisions.

In addition, individual psychologists can take part in social action efforts, in partnership with religion and other community-based groups, to influence directly the policy agenda and policy formulation. Organizing efforts in many high poverty urban areas have involved mobilization of faith-based organizations to push for more services and resources for citizens and neighborhoods (e.g., Industrial Areas Foundation, 1990). At the community level, psychologists have worked with community organizing groups such as the Pacific Institute for Community Organization (PICO; cf. Speer et al., 1995), bringing to bear community expertise, interpersonal skills, and research knowledge. Nationally, psychologists can join forces with emerging movements on issues related to poverty and oppression, many of which involve a diversity of religious and nonprofit advocacy groups (Hale & Bennet, 2000).

Beyond policy advocacy and social action, psychology can join with like-minded voices in religion to challenge problematic cultural values and norms, such as excessive consumerism, self-absorption, and blaming the victim. Only if such overarching components of mainstream culture are challenged and changed, over time, is it likely that our public discourse and policies will be sufficiently altered in a way to mobilize the human and financial resources necessary to make a fundamental difference in the lives of the poor (cf. Bellah et al., 1985; Maton, 2000).

Our training as psychologists did little to prepare most of us for policy advocacy, social action, or culture challenge involvement, given the differences in meaning systems (Table 1), particularly when it comes to collaborating with the religious sector. However, in the area of religion and social policy, as in other areas of social policy, it may be that involvement in advocacy, social action, and culture challenge has the greatest potential for making a difference in the lives of those most at risk, including the oppressed in our society.

Minimizing the Negative Impact of Religion

Just as psychologists have a responsibility to promote policies and programs that enhance human welfare, they also have a responsibility to discourage policies and programs that may impede human welfare. The potential for religion to cause harm, as revealed throughout the course of history, is great. Psychologists, through the research, practice, and advocacy pathways noted above, have a special responsibility to work to minimize these potential negative effects.

In terms of research, special attention must be paid to the anticipated and unanticipated outcomes, negative as well as positive, of faith-based programs and policies. In terms of community practice, psychologists need to help ensure that appropriate safeguards are included in programs and policies to ensure an absence of religious discrimination or proselytization, and to ensure that services meet an appropriate standard of care. In terms of social advocacy, organized psychology must remain a voice for social justice, and one that bears witness to the negative influences of existing policies and programs in the religious domain.

In such work, the implications of psychological expertise and research may be counter to the wishes of certain religious groups. An example can be found in the 1996 reauthorization of the Child Abuse Prevention and Treatment Act (CAPTA). CAPTA is the law that establishes much of the federal role in child protection, including definitions for abuse and neglect, support for prevention and treatment of abuse, and creation of the federal Office on Child Abuse and Neglect. CAPTA contains a provision stating that the law cannot be construed to mean that parents or legal guardians must provide medical treatment to their children, against personal religious beliefs (Child Abuse Prevention and Treatment Act Amendments of 1996). This provision was the source of much controversy when it was added in 1996, and it remains controversial to this date. However, much of the controversy has played out in a vacuum. Psychologists are uniquely qualified to address questions about the impact of such legislation: To what extent are parents purposely withholding medical attention from their children for religious reasons? Are there ways families can be persuaded to give needed medical attention to their children without offending their religious sensibilities? The judicial system, which must ultimately decide whether to over-rule parents in such cases, merits special attention in this example. Psychologists can assist judges by providing them information about child development and child maltreatment and helping them develop appropriate decision making procedures. Finally, psychological research on child abuse and neglect can be used to make the case, when this exemption needs to be overridden for the good of the child.

Clearly, value judgments will play a role in controversial social issues involving policy and religion, and we must proceed cautiously and respectfully when we oppose governmental policies or religious practices that, in our view, are a definite force for harm. In a clash of meaning systems, there likely will be many areas of ambiguity and thus many potential tensions, and many potential difficulties in dialogue and communication. To the extent possible, empirical evidence, and collaboration with allied groups and disciplines, including faith-based ones, will help to ensure that our efforts to minimize harm are well-guided, and maximally effective.

September 11 and Beyond: A Case Example

No event in recent years has impacted America as broadly as did the hijacking of four planes and the subsequent attack on the Pentagon and the New York World Trade Center on September 11, 2001 (Ethics & Public Policy Center, 2002; Haynes, 2003). The aftermath of these events increased attention to the possible negative impact of religion and to the interface of religion and policy. This attention was focused in areas where psychology is uniquely positioned to contribute. Through past research, for example, psychology was able to inform the debate regarding the prevention of hate crimes and the promotion of tolerance toward Muslims, who were frequent targets of hate immediately after the attack (DeAngelis, 2001). Further research is needed, however, to develop strategies that religious communities can use to promote tolerance toward each other, as well as in their interactions with secular communities, and to decrease both religious and secular discrimination.

In addition, psychological research on ethno–political conflict, group dynamics, and personality development can help policy makers examine and perhaps challenge facets of foreign and domestic policy that may inadvertently promote intense, religiously grounded acts of terrorism against the United States or other countries (e.g., policies that maintain wealth inequality or disempower local people). Psychologists can address these issues in a way that is sensitive to both religious and political realities. Such research could be a key factor in articulating theory and formulating policy to minimize the negative impacts of religious extremism and the factors that nurture them. Finally, in many communities, religious groups developed projects to promote healing and recovery in highly impacted communities. Psychologists can serve as resources in the development and evaluation of such initiatives.

Conclusion: Meaning Systems and the New Millennium

Psychology's meaning system traditionally has attached relatively little significance to religion. As we move forward in this new millennium, it behooves our field to attach greater significance to the role of religion in individual and community life. The psychological, behavioral, and social processes through which religion exerts its influence as a meaning system have been usefully portrayed in this volume. The articles as a whole speak to the resilience of religion as a meaning system over time and place, and to both the positive (as a resource for prevention, group empowerment, community capacity building, culture challenge, and healing) and negative (as a contributor to conflict, prejudice, and oppression) potentials of religion.

As is abundantly clear from the newspaper headlines on many days, the policy sector represents one important domain where both the positive and negative potential of the religious sector will be considered, debated, and negotiated. The challenges facing psychology's work in the area of religion and policy are many, including the lack of collaborative history, the separation of church and state, the discontinuities in meaning systems between religion, policy, and psychology, and the diversity and complexity of religion. To face these challenges effectively there is a great need for psychologists to become knowledgeable about and culturally competent in the areas of religion and policy. It is our hope that the current article will contribute to an enhanced and productive engagement of psychological research, practice, and advocacy in this important arena.

References

Allen, M., & Edsall, T. B. (2001, March 20). Black religious leaders hear Bush's call: Self-avowed 'white-guy Republican' urges clerical push for 'faith-based' program. *Washington Post*, p. A06.

Anderson, J. E. (1997). *Public policymaking: An introduction* (Third Ed.). Boston: Houghton Mifflin.

Andrews, J. (1995, Summer). Religion's challenge to psychology. *Public Interest, 120,* 79–88.

Balanced Budget Act of 1997. (1997). Pub. L. No. 105–33, SS 4901, 111 Stat. 552.

Bedell, K. B. (1997). *Yearbook of American and Canadian Churches.* Nashville, TN: Abingdon.

Bellah, R. N., Madsen, R., Sullivan, W. M., Swidler, A., & Tipton, S. M. (1985). *Habits of the heart: Individualism and commitment in American life.* Berkeley: University of California Press.

Booth, W. (2001, May 20). Polygamist is found guilty of bigamy: Utah traveling salesman flaunted his lifestyle with 5 wives, 29 children. *Washington Post,* p. A02.

Bowen v. Kendrick, 487 U.S. 589, 610 (1988).

Bush, G. (2001). Rallying the armies of compassion. Retrieved March 15, 2002, from www.whitehouse.gov.

Carter, S. L. (2000). *God's name in vain: The wrongs and rights of religion in politics.* New York: Basic Books.

Centers for Disease Control and Prevention. (1999). *Engaging faith communities as partners in improving community health: Highlights from a CDC/AATSDR forum.* CDC: Public Health Practice Program Office.

Charity Aid, Recovery and Empowerment Act of 2002. (2002). Retrieved on May 13, 2002, from www.deathandtaxes.com/s1924.htm.

Child Abuse Prevention and Treatment Act Amendments of 1996. (1996). Pub. L. No. 104-235, SS 115, 110 Stat. 3079.

Clark, J. M., Brown, J. C., & Hochstein, L. M. (1989). Institutional religion and gay/lesbian oppression. *Marriage & Family Review, 14,* 265–284.

Cnaan, R., & Yancey, G. I. (2000). Our hidden safety net. In E. J. Dionne, Jr. & J. J. DiIulio, Jr. (Eds.), *What's God got to do with the American experiment?* (pp. 153–159). Washington, DC: Brookings Institution Press.

DeAngelis, T. (2001, November). Understanding and preventing hate crimes. *APA Monitor on Psychology,* 60–63.

Diament, N. J. (2001, March 20). A faith-based Rorschach test. *Washington Post,* p. A27.

DiIulio, J. J., Jr. (2000). Supporting Black churches: Faith, outreach, and the inner-city poor. In E. J. Dionne, Jr. & J. J. DiIulio, Jr. (Eds.), *What's God got to do with the American experiment?* (pp. 121–127). Washington, DC: Brookings Institution Press.

Dionne, E. J., Jr., & DiIulio, J. J., Jr. (Eds.). (2000). *What's God got to do with the American experiment?* Washington, DC: Brookings Institution Press.

Ethics & Public Policy Center. (2002). *Religion, culture, and international conflict after September 11: A conversation with Samuel P. Huntington.* Center Conversations, Number 14, 1-16. Retrieved June 18, 2003, from http://www.eppc.org/publications/pubID.1537/pub_detail.asp

Executive Order No. 13198. (2001). 66 *Federal Register,* 8495–8498.

Executive Order No. 13199. (2001). 66 *Federal Register,* 8499–8500.

Friedman, R. M. (1999). *A conceptual framework for developing and implementing effective policy in children's mental health.* University of South Florida: Research and Training Center for Children's Mental Health.

George, L. K., Larson, D. B., Koenig, H. G., & McCullough, M. E. (2000). Spirituality and health: What we know, what we need to know. *Journal of Social and Clinical Psychology, 19,* 102–116.

Glenn, C. L. (2000). *The ambiguous embrace: Government and faith-based schools and social agencies.* Princeton, NJ: Princeton University Press.

Gopin, M. (2000). *Between Eden and Armageddon: The future of religions, violence and peace making.* New York: Oxford University Press.

Hale, W. D., & Bennett, R. G. (2000). *Building healthy communities through medical-religious partnerships.* Baltimore: Johns Hopkins University Press.

Haynes, J. (2003). Religion and politics: What is the impact of September 11? *Contemporary Politics, 9,* 7–15.

Harris, J. F. (2001, September 14). God gave U.S. 'what we deserve,' Falwell says. *Washington Post,* p. C-03.

Hunsberger, B., & Jackson, L. M. (this issue). Religion, meaning, and prejudice. *Journal of Social Issues.*

Industrial Areas Foundation. (1990). *The first 50 years.* New York: Franklin Square.

Johnson, B. R., Li, S. D., Larson, D. B., & McCullough, M. (2000). A systematic review of the religiosity and delinquency literature. *Journal of Contemporary Criminal Justice, 16,* 32–52.

Johnson, B. R., Tompkins, R. B., & Webb, D. (2002). *Objective hope: Assessing the effectiveness of faith-based organizations. A review of the literature.* Retrieved on June 12, 2003, from http://www.manhattan-institute.org/crrucs_objective_hope.pdf.

Kloos, B., & Moore, T. (Eds.). (2000). Spirituality, religion and community psychology (Part I) [Special Issue]. *Journal of Community Psychology, 28,* 115–236.

Lemon v. Kurtzman, 403 U.S. 602, 91 S. Ct. 2105, 20 L. Ed.2d 745 (1971).

Martin, J. P. (this issue). The three monotheistic world religions and international human rights. *Journal of Social Issues.*

Matthews, M. A. (1999). The impact of federal and state laws on children exposed to domestic violence. *Future of Children, 9,* 50–66.

Maton, K. I. (2000). Making a difference: The social ecology of social transformation. *American Journal of Community Psychology, 28,* 25–57.

Maton, K. I. (2001). Spirituality, religion, and community psychology: Historical perspective, positive potential, and challenges. *Journal of Community Psychology, 29,* 599–613.

Maton, K. I., & Sto. Domingo, M. R. (in press). Mobilizing adults for positive youth development: Lessons from religious congregations. In G. Clary & J. Rhodes (Eds.), *Mobilizing adults for positive youth development.* Springer: Search Institute Series on Developmentally Attentive Community and Society.

Maton, K. I., Sto. Domingo, M. R., & King, J. (2005). Faith-based organizations. In D. L. DuBois & M. J. Karcher (Eds.), *Handbook of youth mentoring* (pp. 255–289). Thousand Oaks, CA: Sage.

Maton, K. I., & Wells, E. A. (1995). Religion as a community resource for well-being: Prevention, healing, and empowerment pathways. *Journal of Social Issues, 51,* 177–193.

McCarthy, M. M. (1996). People of faith as political activists in public schools. *Education & Urban Society, 28,* 308–322.

McCullough, M. E., Hoyt, W. T., Larson, D. B., Koenig, H. G., & Thoresen, C. (2000). Religious involvement and mortality: A meta-analytic review. *Health Psychology, 19,* 211–222.

Melton, G. B. (2000, October 30). *Introductory remarks: Symposium on faith-based organizations and community development.* Author: Clemson University Institute on Family & Neighborhood Life.

Milbank, D. (2001, January 27). Bush's faith-based group initiative will meet resistance. *Washington Post,* p. A10.

Mitchell v. Helms, 120 S. Ct. 2530 (2000).

Moore, T. (1991). The African American Church: A source for empowerment, mutual help, and social change. *Prevention in Human Services, 10,* 147–168.

Muramoto, O. (1998). Bioethics of the refusal of blood by Jehovah's Witnesses: Part I. Should bioethical deliberation consider dissidents' views? *Journal of Medical Ethics, 24,* 223–230.

Pargament, K. I., Magyar, G. M., & Murray-Swank, N. (this issue). The sacred and the search for significance: Religion as a unique process. *Journal of Social Issues.*

Pargament, K. I., & Maton, K. I. (2000). Religion in American life: A community psychology perspective. In J. Rappaport & E. Seidman (Eds.), *Handbook of community psychology* (pp. 495–522). New York: Kluwer Academic/Plenum Publishers.

Pargament, K. I., Maton, K. I., & Hess, R. E. (Eds.). (1992). *Religion and prevention in mental health: Research, vision and action.* Binghamton, NY: Haworth Press.

Park, C. L. (this issue). Religion as a meaning-making framework in coping with life stress. *Journal of Social Issues.*

Places of worship provide trusted voice for outreach. (2001, Winter). *Sign them up! A Quarterly Newsletter about the Children's Health Insurance Program,* 1–2.

Queen, E. L., II. (1997). Seeing ourselves in others: Changing civic roles for religious organizations. *Wingspread Journal, 19,* 10–12.

Richards, P. S., & Bergin, A. E. (1997). *A spiritual strategy for counseling and psychotherapy.* Washington, DC: American Psychological Association.

Richards, P. S., & Bergin, A. E. (2000). Toward religious and spiritual competency for mental health professionals. In P. S. Richards & A. E. Bergin (Eds.), *Handbook of psychotherapy and religious diversity* (pp. 3–26). Washington, DC: American Psychological Association.

Roccas, S. (this issue). Religion and value systems. *Journal of Social Issues.*

Rogers, M. (2000). The wrong way to do right: A challenge to charitable choice. In E. J. Dionne, Jr. & J. J. DiIulio, Jr. (Eds.), *What's God got to do with the American experiment?* (pp. 138–145). Washington, DC: Brookings Institution Press.

Santa Fe Independent School District v. Doe, 120 S, Ct. 2266 (2000).

Schwartz, S. H., & Huismans, S. (1995). Value priorities and religiosity in four Western religions. *Social Psychology Quarterly, 58,* 88–107.

Sherman, A. (2000). *The growing impact of charitable choice.* Annapolis, MD: The Center for Public Justice.

Silberman, I. (this issue). Religion as a meaning system: Implications for the new millennium. *Journal of Social Issues.*

Silberman, I., Higgins, E. T., & Dweck, C. S. (this issue). Religion and world change: Violence and terrorism versus peace. *Journal of Social Issues.*

Solarz, A. (2000). Investing in children, families, and communities: Challenges for an interdivisional public policy collaboration. *American Journal of Community Psychology, 29,* 1–18.

Speer, P. W., Hughey, J., Gensheimer, L. K., & Adams-Leavitt, W. (1995). Organizing for power: A comparative case study. *Journal of Community Psychology, 23,* 57–73.

Walker, S. (1995, August 2). Reno stands by Waco decision. *Christian Science Monitor,* p. 3.

The White House. (2001). *Unlevel playing field: Barriers to participation by faith-based and community organizations in federal social service programs.* Retrieved on April 1, 2002, from http://www.whitehouse.gov.

Winett, R. A., Anderson, E. S., Whiteley, J. A., Wojckik, J. R., Rovniak, L. S., Graves, K. D., et al. (1999). Church-based health behavior programs: Using social cognitive theory to formulate interventions for at-risk populations. *Applied & Preventive Psychology, 8,* 129–142.

Wolff, T. (2001). A practitioner's guide to successful coalitions. *American Journal of Community Psychology, 29,* 173–191.

Working Group on Human Needs and Faith-based and Community Initiatives. (2002) *Common ground: 29 recommendations of the working group on human needs and faith-based and community initiatives.* Retrieved on April 12, 2002, from http://www.working-group.org.

Wuthnow, R. (1996). Restructuring of American religion: Further evidence. *Sociological Inquiry, 66,* 303–329.

Yarnold, B. W. (Ed.). (1991). *The role of religious organizations in social movements.* New York: Praeger.

KENNETH I. MATON, PhD is a community psychologist and Director of the Community-Social Program in Human Services Psychology at University of Maryland Baltimore County. His research has focused on various aspects of the community psychology of religion. He co-authored with Kenneth I. Pargament the *Handbook of Community Psychology* chapter, "Religion in American life: A community psychology perspective." Earlier, he co-edited with Kenneth I. Pargament and Robert E. Hess the volume, *Religion and Prevention in Mental Health: Research, Vision and Action.* He is past president of the Society for Community Research and Action, the Community Psychology Division of the American Psychological Association, and is on the editorial board of the SPSSI electronic journal, *Analysis of Social Issues and Public Policy (ASAP).*

DANIEL DODGEN, PhD is the Emergency Management Coordinator for the Substance Abuse and Mental Health Services Administration in the U.S. Department of Health and Human Services. Previously, he was Special Assistant to the CEO of the American Psychological Association (APA), Co-Director of the APA Congressional Fellowship Program and Senior Legislative and Federal Affairs Officer in APA's Public Policy Office. Prior to joining APA, Dr. Dodgen was a Congressional Fellow with the U.S. House of Representatives. Before coming to Washington, D.C., he practiced at Didi Hirsch Community Mental Health Center in Los Angeles. He received his PhD in Clinical Psychology at the University of Houston and bachelor's degrees in Spanish and Psychology from the University of Southern California, where he graduated Phi Beta Kappa.

MARIANO R. STO. DOMINGO, MA is currently a student in Human Services Psychology PhD Program in Community–Social Psychology at the University of Maryland Baltimore County. He earned his masters degrees in International Relations and Social Psychology from the International University of Japan and University of the Philippines, respectively. He was also an exchange student at the Johns Hopkins University's School of Advance International Studies in Washington, D.C. He is past vice president of the Pambansang Samahan sa Sikolohiyang Pilipino (National Association for Philippine Psychology).

The late DAVID B. LARSON, MD was the President and Chief Executive Officer of the International Center for the Integration of Health and Spirituality (ICIHS), a research institute he founded after leaving a position at the National Institutes of Health. A recognized leader in the study of health and spirituality, he had nearly 300 publications on this and related topics. Dr. Larson obtained his medical degree from Temple University and completed his psychiatry residency, chief residency in psychiatry, and geriatric fellowship training at Duke University Medical Center.

During an epidemiology fellowship from the National Institutes of Health, he earned a Master of Science in Public Health (M.S.P.H.) in epidemiology from the School of Public Health at the University of North Carolina. At the time of his death, Dave served as adjunct professor of psychiatry and the behavioral sciences at both Duke University Medical Center and Northwestern University Medical School. He was a fellow of the American Psychiatric Association (F.A.P.A.), and the Southern Psychiatric Association.

STATEMENT OF OWNERSHIP, MANAGEMENT, AND CIRCULATION
(Required by 39 U.S.C. 3685)

1. Publication Title	2. Publication No.	3. Filing Date
Journal of Social Issues	001-652	9/1/2005

4. Issue Frequency	5. No. of Issues Published Annually	6. Annual Subscription Price
Quarterly	4	$ 78.00 Individual $ 536.00 Institutional

7. Complete Mailing Address Of Known Office of Publication *(Street, City, County, State, and ZIP+4)*
   (Not Printer)

Blackwell Publishing Inc, 350 Main Street, Malden, MA 02148

8. Complete Mailing Address of Headquarters or General Business Office of Publisher *(Not Printer)*

Blackwell Publishing Inc, 350 Main Street, Malden, MA 02148

9. Full Names and Complete Mailing Addresses of Publisher, Editor, and Managing Editor *(Do Not Leave Blank)*

Publisher *(Name and Complete Mailing Address)*
Blackwell Publishing Inc
350 Main Street
Malden MA 02148

Editor *(Name and Complete Mailing Address)*
Irene Hanson Frieze
Prof Of Psychology & Women's Studies
405 Langley Hall
University of Pittsburgh
Pittsburgh PA 15260

Managing Editor *(Name and Complete Mailing Address)*

10. Owner *(If owned by a corporation, its name and address must be stated and also immediately thereafter the names and addresses of stockholders owning or holding 1 percent or more of the total amount of stock. If not owned by a corporation, the names and addresses of individual owners must be given. If owned by a partnership or other unincorporated firm, its name and address as well as that of each individual must be given. If the publication is published by a nonprofit organization, its name and address must be stated.) (Do not leave blank.)*

Full Name and Address
The Society for the Psychological Study of Social Issues
1901 Pennsylvania NW Ste 901
Washington DC 20006

**11. Known Bondholders, Mortgagees, and Other Security Holders Owning or Holding
1 Percent or More of the Total Amount of Bonds, Mortgages, or Other Securities. If
none, check here. __X__ None
Full Name and Complete Mailing Address**

12. Tax status (*For completion by nonprofit organizations authorized to mail at special rates*). Check one. The purpose, function, and nonprofit status of this organization and the exempt status for federal income tax purposes. *(Check one)*   N/A

_____Has not Changed During Preceding 12 Months

_____Has Changed During Preceding 12 Months

(If changed, publisher must submit explanation of change with this statement)

13. Publication Name	14. Issue Date for Circulation Data Below
Journal of Social Issues	V61:3 2005

15. Extent and Nature Of Circulation		Average No. Copies Each Issue During Preceding 12 Months	Actual No. Copies Of Single Issue Published Nearest to Filing Date
a. Total No. Copies *(Net Press Run)*		5222	5155
b. Paid and/or Requested Circulation	(1)Paid/Requested Outside-County Mail Subscriptions Stated on Form 3541. (*Included advertiser's proof and exchange copies*).	3300	3148
	(2) Paid In-County Subscriptions Stated on Form 3541 (*Include adversiter's proof and exchange Copies*)	0	0
	(3)Sales Through Dealers and Carriers, Street Vendors, Counter Sales, and Other Non-USPS Paid Distributuion	806	787
	(4) Other Classes Mailed Through the USPS	0	0
c. Total Paid and/or Requested Circulation [Sum of 15b. (1), (2), (3) and (4)		4106	3935
d. Free Distribution by Mail (Samples, compiment ary,and other free)	(1) Outside-County as Stated on Form 3541	63	62
	(2) In-County as Stated on Form 3541	0	0
	(3) Other Classes Mailed Through the USPS	0	0
e. Free Distribution Outside the Mail (Carriers or Other Means)		474	457
f. Total Free Distribution *(Sum of 15d and 15e)*		537	519
g. Total Distribution *(Sum of 15c and 15f)*		4643	4454
h. Copies Not Distributed		579	701
i. Total *(Sum of 15g, and h)*		5222	5155
j. Percent Paid and/or Requ j. Percent Paid and/or Requested Circulation *(15c/15gx100)*		88%	88%

16. This Statement of Ownership will be printed in the December 2005 issue of this publication.

______Check here if not required to publish.

17. Signature and Title of Editor, Publisher, Business Manager, or Owner   Date

Barbara Sasso, Customer Service Manager, Blackwell Publishing Inc   9/1/2005

I certify that all information furnished on this form is true and complete. I understand that anyone who furnishes false or misleading information on this form or who omits material or information requested on the form may be subject to criminal sanctions (*including fines and imprisonment*) and/or civil sanctions (*including multiple damages and civil penalties*).*Failure to file or publish a statement of ownership may lead to suspension of second-class. authorization.*

PS Form 3526 October 1999 (Facsimile)

ISSN: 0361-6843

PSYCHOLOGY OF WOMEN QUARTERLY

Editor: JAYNE E. STAKE

PSYCHOLOGY OF WOMEN QUARTERLY (PWQ) is a feminist journal that publishes primarily qualitative and quantitative research with substantive and theoretical merit, along with critical reviews, theoretical articles, and invited book reviews related to the psychology of women and gender. Topics include career choice and training; management and performance variables; education; lifespan role development and change; physical and mental health and well-being; physical, sexual, and psychological abuse; violence and harassment; prejudice and discrimination; psychobiological factors; sex-related comparisons; sexuality, sexual orientation and heterosexism; social and cognitive processes; and therapeutic processes.

PUBLISHED ON BEHALF OF THE *SOCIETY OF THE PSYCHOLOGY OF WOMEN,* DIVISION 35 OF THE *AMERICAN PSYCHOLOGICAL ASSOCIATION*

For further details on the society and membership, please visit their website at

www.apa.org/about/division/div35.html

PSYCHOLOGY OF WOMEN QUARTERLY IS ONLINE AT BLACKWELL SYNERGY! WWW.BLACKWELL-SYNERGY.COM

Sign up to receive Blackwell Synergy free e-mail alerts with complete **PSYCHOLOGY OF WOMEN QUARTERLY** tables of contents and quick links to article abstracts from the most current issue. Simply go to www.blackwell-synergy.com, select the journal from the list of journals, and click on *"Sign-up"* for FREE email table of contents alerts.

Blackwell Publishing

Call **1-800-835-6770** *(toll free in N. America)* or: +1 781-388-8206 (US Office); +44 1865 778315 (UK office)
subscrip@bos.blackwellpublishing.com
www.blackwellpublishing.com

View a **FREE** Online Sample Issue
www.blackwellpublishing.com/pwq

Printed and bound by CPI Group (UK) Ltd, Croydon, CR0 4YY

07/07/2026

14916222-0002